D0856528

Southern Living® Growing Vegetables & Herbs

with Recipes for the Fresh Harvest

by the Garden and Landscape Staff
Southern Living® **Magazine**

John Alex Floyd, Jr.	Senior Horticulturist
Lois B. Trigg	Garden Editor
Linda C. Askey	Associate Garden Editor
Vicki Ingham	Assistant Garden Book Editor
Bill McDougald	Associate Garden Design Editor
Van Chaplin	Senior Garden Photographer
Sylvia Martin	Garden Photographer
Mary Gray Hunter	Garden Photographer
Yukie McLean	Illustrator

SOM TY LIBRARY
BRIDG R, N. J. 08807

Cover photo: The kitchen garden of William B. and Mary Lib McGehee, Talladega, Alabama; design by Garden Designs, Birmingham, Alabama.

Credits, pages 1-4. Spring garden at Old Salem, North Carolina; an early morning harvest from the summer garden at Mount Vernon, Virginia; the growing summer garden of Mr. and Mrs. George Gambrill, Birmingham, Alabama; a fall garden at Old Salem, North Carolina.

Copyright© 1984 by Oxmoor House, Inc.
Book Division of Southern Progress Corporation
P.O. Box 2463, Birmingham, Alabama 35201

All rights reserved. No part of this book may be reproduced in any form or by any means without the prior written permission of the Publisher, excepting brief quotes in connection with reviews written specifically for inclusion in a magazine or newspaper.

Southern Living® is a federally registered trademark of Southern Living, Inc., Birmingham, Alabama.

Library of Congress Catalog Number: 83-60426
ISBN: 0-8487-0542-4
Manufactured in the United States of America

Southern Living® _Growing Vegetables and Herbs_

Editor: Karen Phillips Irons
Design: David Morrison, Steve Logan
Editorial Assistants: Patty E. Howdon,
   Cecilia Robinson

With special assistance from the Foods Staff of *Southern Living*® magazine.

Jean Wickstrom Liles	Foods Editor
Margaret Chason	Associate Foods Editor
Lynn Lloyd	Test Kitchens Director
Charles Walton	Senior Foods Photographer
Beverly Morrow	Photo Stylist (Foods)

Special assistance was also provided by The Herb Volunteers of the North Carolina Botanical Gardens, Chapel Hill, North Carolina.

Contents

8407825

Preface

I enjoy gardening, as does the entire staff of editors and photographers whose work you see in this book. In fact, many of the photographs were taken in our gardens. For the text, we called on experts across the South, as well as on our own practical and technical knowledge.

For our recipes, we turned to the *Southern Living®* Foods Staff. Associate Foods Editor Margaret Chason was in charge of recipe development, under the direction of Jean Wickstrom Liles, our Foods Editor. Lynn Lloyd, our test kitchens director, made sure all the recipes passed the inspection of the test kitchens staff.

For information on growing herbs in the South, we relied heavily on the experience and work of members of the Herb Volunteers of the North Carolina Botanical Gardens. These workers, who helped not only with the general herb information but also with the recipes, include Mercer Hubbard, Chairman of Herb Volunteers; Beverly Connor McSwain, Curator of the Herb Garden; Katherine Bream, Coordinator of the Culinary Garden; Martha Schofield, Coordinator of Recipes; and volunteers Betty Bell, Alice Dorman, Louisa Douglass, Eleanor George, Wayne Goodall, Margaret Gretz, Fran Hollister, Gladys Lindley, Mayapriya Long, Anders Lunde, Clara Murray, M. K. Ramm, Irma Stein, Bernice Stone, Molly and Bill Williams, and June Wilson.

Other *Southern Living®* staff who helped either with visuals or with text include Susan D. Breeden, Beth Maynor, Linda Schneider Sapp, Frederica Georgia, Louise Mimbs, and Rebecca Sconyers. Others whose valuable assistance we wish to acknowledge include David Baggett, Tupperware staff horticulturist; Dean Bond, Extension horticulturist, Auburn University; Dr. David Bradshaw, associate professor of ornamental horticulture, Clemson University; Dr. Milo Burnham, Extension horticulturist, Mississippi State University; Dr. James Cannon, Extension specialist in horticulture, Louisiana State University; Dr. Oyette Chambliss, professor of vegetable crops, Auburn University; Wilton Cook, Extension horticulturist, Clemson University; Dr. Sam Cotner, Extension horticulturist, Texas A & M University; Dr. Gary Elmstrom, Center Director, Agricultural Research Center, Leesburg, Florida; Linda Harris, horticulturist, Burpee Seed Company; Herb Society of Nashville, a unit of the Herb Society of America; Madalene Hill, Hilltop Herb Farm, Cleveland, Texas; Dr. Bryson James, consulting horticulturist, McMinnville, Tennessee; Gary Litzinger, horticulturist, Tupcraft Company; Dr. W. L. Ogle, professor of horticulture, Clemson University; Marsha Presnell-Jeanette, Mordecai House, Raleigh, North Carolina; Marion Redd, Greenway Nursery, Charlotte, North Carolina; Dr. Ron Robbins, professor of horticulture, Clemson University Coastal Experiment Station; Dr. W. T. Scudder, professor of horticulture, Agricultural Research and Education Center, Sanford, Florida; Jim Stephens, Extension vegetable specialist, University of Florida; Dr. Homer Swingle, professor emeritus of horticulture, University of Tennessee; and Jim Wilson, Savory Farms, Donalds, South Carolina, and formerly of All America Selections.

John Alex Floyd, Jr.
October, 1983

Introduction

Publishing a new book on growing vegetables and herbs in the South continues a long tradition in our company. It started over two decades ago with *The Progressive Farmer's® Garden Book for the South*. In that book, Clarence Poe, then president of the company, promoted some rules that are as useful for today's gardeners as they were for the largely rural audience he addressed. They are:

1. Be lazy enough—not too lazy. By this, we mean be smart enough to do all necessary work, but lazy enough not to do unnecessary work. For example, we recommend more mulching and less hoeing. Mulching with leaves, straw, sawdust, or compost should be practiced much more than it is now. Mulching saves labor, conserves moisture, and keeps down weeds. With fertilizer and plenty of organic matter added to the soil, you will produce more vegetables with less work. You can also get the most from your garden with vegetables like asparagus, which you can plant once in a lifetime, and those like okra, which keep bearing right on until frost.

2. Grow an abundance of vegetables for a healthy diet. Fresh vegetables are full of vitamins. As an example, here are eighteen such vegetables:

a) For vitamins A and C: leafy and yellow vegetables such as turnip and mustard greens, collards, kale, broccoli, spinach, and cantaloupes.

b) For more vitamin A: sweet potatoes, carrots, pumpkins, winter-type squash, and Swiss chard.

c) For more vitamin C: tomatoes, peppers, cabbage, Chinese cabbage, cauliflower, and kohlrabi.

Many other vegetables that provide these and other vitamins could be added to the list.

And do not forget canning and freezing for off-season or year-round use. This should be more than a matter of merely preserving "surplus" produce. Plan and plant the garden to provide enough for this purpose. With food preservation, you can enjoy garden vegetables year-round, even when you cannot get fresh vegetables.

3. Make gardening an adventure by constantly trying out new vegetables and herbs, new selections, and new methods of cooking. Experimenting with innovative ways of cooking and serving vegetables can add variety and please everybody's taste.

4. Have the garden near the house—and make it attractive. The nearer it is, the fewer steps you have to take, and the more likely you are to make 100 percent use of all vegetables and herbs. And make the garden so attractive that you will enjoy having it near the house—so carefully laid off, so neatly kept, and so bordered with flowers, shrubbery, or hedge that it will be a real addition to the landscape.

5. Get the youngest members of your family interested. Let them have a few rows of their own for which they are responsible. To help ensure their success, start them with easily grown, fast-maturing vegetables such as radishes and squash. And include treats such as watermelons and cantaloupes.

Regardless of your level of gardening expertise, you should find it easy to use *Growing Vegetables and Herbs—with Recipes for the Fresh Harvest*. If you are a beginning gardener, we suggest you take the time to read the first ten sections before you turn a spadeful of soil. If you are an advanced gardener, use these sections for reference and new ideas.

In the section on individual vegetables, we present the most popular Southern vegetables as well as some that may be new challenges for experienced gardeners. The beginner will find basic information on growing each vegetable, as well as tips to help ensure success. If you have already mastered growing tomatoes, sweet corn, and eggplant, try your hand at growing leeks, rhubarb, salsify, or celery.

For quick and easy reference, the "At A Glance" for each vegetable is a handy source of information. And as a bonus, we have included a collection of recipes, each carefully tested by our *Southern Living*® test kitchens staff. Our aim here is not to provide a cookbook for meal planning; rather, we wish to suggest some excellent new dishes that emphasize the fresh flavor of the vegetables.

The section on culinary herbs combines the practical knowledge of our staff with the wealth of information supplied to us by the Herb Volunteers of the North Carolina Botanical Gardens. This information is presented in the same format as the vegetables, with new recipes that have been carefully tested. Our mild climate presents a unique set of conditions for growing herbs, and reliable information has been hard to find; so for both present and future Southern herb gardeners, this section should be a valuable guide, providing concise growing information specifically geared to our region. And we hope that the suggestions for use will encourage you to explore the pleasures of culinary herbs.

Designing Your Garden

Your vegetable and herb garden can be the focal point of your landscape, or it can be a simple patch tucked away in the backyard. In either case, it should be well-defined, and its design should complement the house and existing plantings. If the garden fits comfortably into the landscape, it will be both functional and pleasing to the eye.

The first question to answer is "Where will my garden be?" From the largest estate to the tiniest condominium garden, any home landscape should be divided into three areas: public, private, and service. You can have a vegetable or herb garden in any one of them, but all three areas do not require the same care.

Would You Dare Put the Garden Out Front?

The *public area* is the part of your landscape that is visible to your neighbors and those who pass by your home. It is usually the area in front of the house.

Many gardeners have never considered planting a vegetable garden here. But there is no reason not to use this area, because with some thought given to design you can create a vegetable or herb garden that is a landscape showpiece. Keeping a public-area garden looking good enough for visitors requires constant attention. But if you take pride in maintaining an immaculate garden, why not grow your vegetables and herbs in front of the house?

The public area is also a good place for the garden because of convenient access. On many homesites, it is easier to drop off bags of fertilizer or flats of transplants near the front of the house beside the drive than to carry them to the back of the lot.

If You Prefer Privacy

If your garden is to be a showcase but you prefer privacy, you can locate it inside a courtyard wall, behind a sideyard fence, or in the back of the house. Here, in the *private area* of the landscape, it is as visible to the family as the public-space garden, but it is hidden from passersby. Place it where you can see it from inside the house or adjacent to an area where you cook out or entertain.

Or Keep It Out of Sight

The third possible location is in the *service area*. Everyone has a place where they stack firewood, park the wheelbarrow, or put the boat when the fishing is done. That is the service area. A well-designed one has good access but is screened from view.

Here a growing bed can be left without an edging; in the public area, it would demand an attractive one. The compost pile can be out in the open rather than screened from view. In the service area, you can keep the garden neat enough for good horticultural practices without worrying about its overall "look."

The lack of visibility is a disadvantage, though, since "out of sight, out of mind" can cost you a crop if you do not make the effort to watch the garden. If you see the garden every day, you are more likely to tend it.

If access to the service area is a problem, solve it with a carefully planned design. Just leave space for those few times each season when you might need to move a vehicle near the garden. And keep gates wide enough for wheel barrows, tillers, and other equipment to get through.

No matter which area you choose—public, private, or service—keep the garden neat, well organized, and well-defined.

A garden in front of the house in full view of passersby can be a showpiece. Just keep it neat and well organized.

This garden in the private area of the landscape is screened from the view of the neighbors. Brick paving and edging for raised beds make it an attractive setting for family entertaining. Owners: Mr. and Mrs. Mark Ferguson, Bryan, Texas.

Permanent growing beds save you the effort of reorganizing your garden each season. The serpentine brick wall and brick-columned terrace define the garden and set off its design. Owner: Dr. Stuart Peery, Charlotte, North Carolina.

Think Sunshine

Your vegetable garden needs plenty of sunshine. Ideally, you want a location that is not shaded by house or trees. If your site is partially shaded, you must make the best of the sunlight you do have, since vegetables need six to eight hours of sunlight daily.

Look first to the south side of the house, since it receives more year-round sun than any other part of the landscape. It is a prime location for your garden if the sun is not blocked by trees or the walls of a neighboring house.

Second choice should be the east or west side of the house. If there are no light-blocking obstructions, either location should receive enough sun for the vegetable garden. Be careful not to put the garden too close to the house, though, or your home may cast its own shadow on the garden. A good guideline is to keep planting areas at least 6 feet away from the walls.

The north side of the house is the last choice for the garden. But it can work if you place the beds at least 8 feet away from the walls. Closer than that, beds will not receive enough sunlight even if the house is only a single story high. Also remember that the sun will be lower in the sky in early spring and late fall, casting longer shadows. That means that if your garden is on the north side and close to the house, you may be limited to growing vegetables only in the summer months when shadows are shortest.

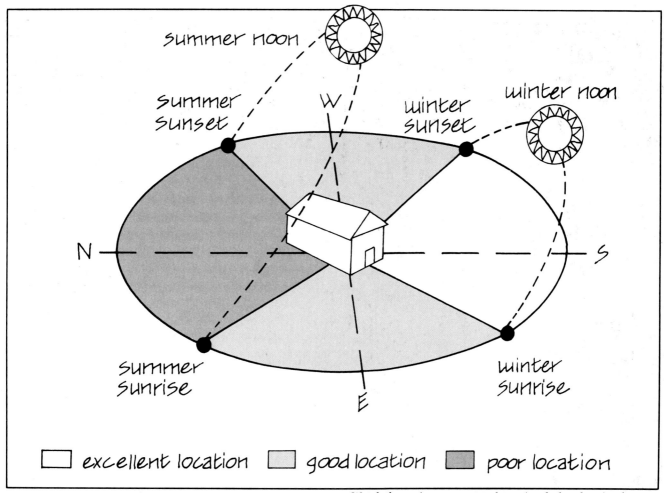

summer noon

summer sunset

W

winter sunset

winter noon

N

S

summer sunrise

E

winter sunrise

☐ excellent location   ▢ good location   ■ poor location

Watch the sun's movement to determine the best location for your garden.

Gauge your sunshine before laying out the garden. Beginning in late winter, make notes or simple sketches of the sun's movement across the sky. Also stake out possible garden locations so that it will be easier to note potential problems with shadows. After observation, you will have a good idea of which locations will provide the most sun for your garden.

If you have a place that receives six to eight hours of sun daily, your garden is off to a good start. If not, you may have to consider moving a tree or two. Fruiting crops such as tomatoes and squash prefer eight hours of sun, while leafy crops such as lettuce can get by with six.

Also consider that at certain times of the day, the sun is more intense than at others. A garden that receives sunshine between 9 A.M. and 3 P.M. should have enough. But if the brightest hours are only in the early morning or late afternoon, there is probably not enough sun for a good vegetable garden.

A fall garden at Old Salem in Winston Salem, North Carolina.

Designing Your Garden   15

The Site Must Be Well Drained

Surface drainage is as important as sunlight to vegetables and herbs. On sites with too little slope, the soil may stay soggy, and seeds and plant roots will rot. On too steep a slope, runoff will wash seeds away. A gentle slope with friable (easily crumbled) soil, little erosion, and no standing water is ideal. But if you do not have the ideal spot, you can improve the drainage in a number of ways.

A sloping site that is terraced can provide plenty of room for a vegetable garden. Here the garden is laid out in rectangles of various sizes with a different vegetable growing in each. Owner: Raymond Deibert, Hoover, Alabama.

Planting across the slope helps reduce runoff and erosion. Diagonal plantings in this garden in Old Salem, North Carolina, are an attractive alternative to the usual.

To determine the slope of your property, use a line level, stake, and string. Place the stake at the highest point, tie the string to it at ground level, and stretch the string from the stake out over the lowest point of your property. The line level will help you keep the string horizontal. Measure the string's length and its height above the ground at the lowest point of your property. (*See Figures 1, 2, and 3.*) If the property drops less than 2 feet in 50 (a 4 percent slope), too little drainage could be a problem. The simplest alternative is to raise the beds above the ground.

If your land slopes more than 5 feet in 50 (greater than 10 percent slope), plan to terrace the garden or to choose a more level site. On a steep slope, terracing creates several tiers down the slope like giant steps, providing well-drained, flatter areas for the planting beds. The soil is held in place by low retaining walls made from railroad ties, concrete blocks, stones, or similar materials.

On a moderate slope that is subject to washing only when rains are heavy, terracing is helpful but not necessary. Planting your crops across the slope (with the contours) to slow runoff, rather than down the hillside, and mulching with a 3-inch layer of pine straw or hay should be an adequate solution.

In addition to adequate surface drainage, the garden should have soil that drains well internally. This is affected by soil structure. (*See Page 60, Soils.*)

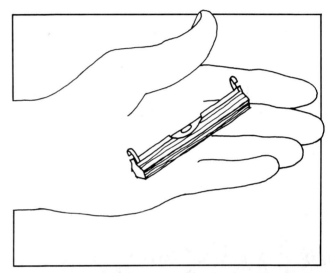

Fig. 1. *You will need a line level to determine the slope of your property. You can find one at a hardware store or building supply company.*

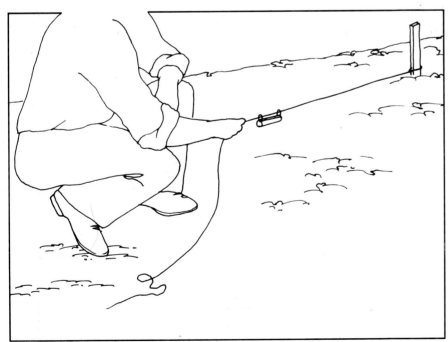

Fig. 2. *Drive a stake into the ground at the highest point of your property. Stretch a string from the stake to the lowest point, using the line level to keep the string horizontal.*

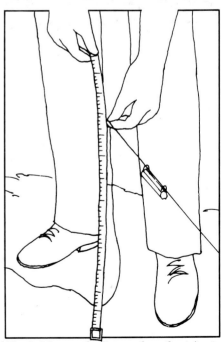

Fig. 3. *Measure the distance from the string to the ground at the lowest point of the property. Also measure the string's length.*

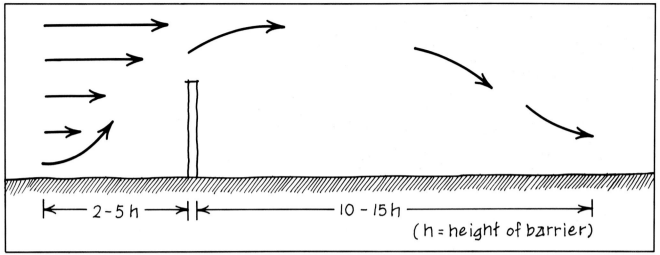

Fig. 1. *A barrier, such as a fence or shrubs, helps control the wind on the leeward side for a distance of ten to fifteen times the barrier. On the windward side, the effect of the wind is diminished for a distance of two to five times the height of the barrier.*

Fig. 2. *Trees and shrubs can reduce the speed of the wind up to 75 percent close to the house. The natural barrier slows the wind for a distance two times the height of the barrier.*

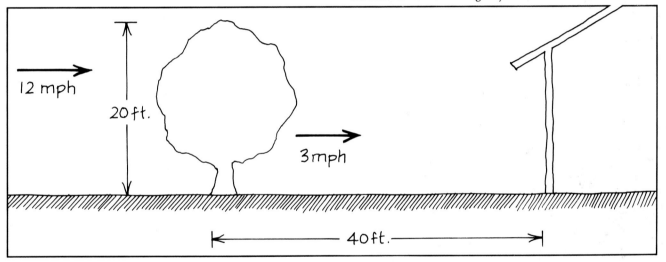

Stay Clear of Tree Roots

Although shading is the main reason to avoid planting near trees, the roots also present problems. They make digging difficult, and will compete with vegetables for valuable nutrients and moisture.

The root system of a mature shade tree may extend far beyond the tree canopy. While the tree might survive the loss of a few roots to make room for the garden, cutting a large area of the root system could weaken or kill the tree.

You can grow plenty of vegetables and herbs in a small garden if you use space efficiently. A picket fence provides some privacy and keeps animals out, but does not interfere with good air circulation. Owners: Mr. and Mrs. Van Chaplin, Birmingham, Alabama.

Good Air Circulation Is a Must

In a garden where air moves freely about the foliage, the vegetables can dry after a good rain or watering. If the air is stagnant, moisture evaporates more slowly, remaining on the plants long enough to encourage diseases.

If you screen the garden from view (as in the service area of the landscape), be sure to use a style of fencing that allows air to move through it. Or plant fairly loose shrubs that will allow air movement through the garden.

Wind can be a problem, however. In an open garden in a windy area, you will need to protect plants from blowing over or becoming overly dry. Use a windbreak of fencing or shrubs. (*See Figures 1,2.*)

Designing Your Garden   19

Consider creating an ornamental effect by using the vegetables as elements in the design, as in this garden in Old Salem, North Carolina.

Remember Utility Lines and Septic Tanks

Utility companies run everything from natural gas lines to cable TV underground, and disturbing an underground utility line can be costly and dangerous. Your utility companies will generally locate and stake out underground lines free of charge if you notify them that you will be digging a garden. If you do not, the companies hold you responsible for any damage.

A septic tank and its drain field also should be located in advance, since piping could obstruct digging your garden. Ask your building contractor or a previous owner of the house for this information.

Keep Equipment and Compost Nearby

When you choose the garden site, remember that you will need a place to store tools and equipment near the garden. For most gardeners, the garage or utility room is a good storage area. They are convenient for unloading bulky items like fertilizer bags from the car. And both areas are usually dry, which is important for storing bags of fertilizer and tools that can rust.

If you do not already have a convenient storage area, a storage shed or tool house is a good project to add to your garden. It can also become an attractive focal point in the landscape. Be sure it provides room for all of your gardening supplies and equipment, and try to place it on the north side to prevent shading the garden.

Also consider the location of your compost bin. It should be convenient to both the garden and the kitchen. If the bin is in the public or private areas, plan to build an attractive structure. Otherwise, locate the bin within the service area of the landscape. With regular addition of garden and kitchen refuse, the compost will be somewhat unsightly, but it should not produce odors if properly turned.

Formal vegetable gardens like this one at Colonial Williamsburg are both ornamental and functional.

Once You Have Picked the Spot

When you have chosen a site for your garden, it is time to design it. Shape is a big factor to consider when you reach this point. Shape is often dictated by the "lay of the land." Once you establish it, you must define the paths and growing areas within the garden that will make the best use of space. Although most people make their gardens rectangular, other shapes such as L-shape, triangular, or free-form offer advantages.

A rectangular garden lends itself to neatly organized paths and beds. But on a sloping site, you may find that a free-form garden that sweeps across the contours is better. By bending the garden around a hillside, you will minimize erosion and save garden soil.

The L-shape is suitable to many lots and divides the garden into distinct areas. For instance, you might plant perennial vegetables and herbs in one leg of the L and seasonal vegetables in the other. The triangular garden adds a dynamic look to the landscape and will fit across a corner or into other spaces where you might not think a garden could go. If you are an avid gardener with a fairly large lot, try a double garden: a small garden just outside the kitchen door for salad vegetables and herbs, and a larger garden, perhaps in the service area, for other crops.

Designing Your Garden 21

Keep planting beds wide to make the best use of space. The major paths should be durable, while narrower ones between beds can simply be mulched. Owner: Dr. Stuart Peery, Charlotte, North Carolina.

Even a sunny courtyard like this one at the Cochran residence in Charlotte, North Carolina, can provide a spot for growing small vegetables such as leafy greens and root crops.

The Growing Areas

From a design point of view, it is easiest to plan on permanent beds for growing the vegetables—ones defined by borders, paths, or edgings of some kind. That way, once the beds are established, you can turn your attention to growing vegetables instead of working out how to rearrange the garden each season. First-time gardeners should start with a few beds and add more as your expertise and enthusiasm grow.

Even if you prefer not to establish permanent growing beds, you can still apply some of the same principles concerning good use of space. The most efficient garden devotes a maximum area to beds and a minimum area to paths. Bed width should be determined by the length of your reach: Plan the beds so that you can comfortably reach to the center of the bed from either side. For most people, this means a bed width of 4 to 5 feet. Narrower beds, such as 1½ to 2 feet, may feel more comfortable; but remember that they use garden space less efficiently.

These beds are wide enough so that you can reach into the middle from either side without walking into the beds, which compacts the soil. Paths are wide enough to move garden equipment easily. Gravel paths let water drain through and are relatively inexpensive. Paca House, Annapolis, Maryland.

When you plan the size of the beds, it is a good practice to keep their area in a simple-to-figure number of square feet. For example, beds 5 x 20 feet long total 100 square feet. This makes it easy to figure how much fertilizer or mulch you will need. In a smaller garden a bed that is 2 x 5 feet (for a total of 10 square feet) makes garden calculations simple.

An advantage to having permanent beds is that structures such as trellises and fences can be permanent as well. This allows you to build them for the long run out of durable materials such as pressure-treated pine, redwood, cypress, or cedar. And you save the time of constructing them every year.

To improve drainage and garden neatness, beds can be raised with brick, rot-resistant lumber, landscape timbers, railroad ties, or concrete blocks. Railroad ties lend themselves especially well to stacking for beds as high as 1 to 3 feet. This reduces the distance you have to stoop. And when combined with wide, hard-surfaced paths, such high beds make gardening possible for those confined to a wheelchair.

Designing Your Garden   23

One disadvantage to permanent, hard edgings occurs when you plan to use power tilling equipment. In tight corners and along the edges you may have to hand-turn the soil.

Here are a few pointers on each type of raised edging.

Wood—Whether you use landscape timbers or dimensional lumber (2 x 4, 2 x 6, for example), be sure it is pressure-treated for ground contact or that it is a rot-resistant type. (Make sure wood has not been treated with a preservative that is toxic to plants, such as creosote.) Avoid lumber in 1 x - dimensions, such as 1 x 2, 1 x 4, and 1 x 6. It will warp under the strain of supporting the soil over a long period of time. Anchor lumber firmly into the ground with stakes driven at least 18 inches deep and no more than 4 feet apart.

Miter corners and nail in both directions (as you would a picture frame) for maximum strength.
Railroad ties—Use old, weathered ties, because much of their toxic creosote will have leached out. A single layer does not need staking for support but should be sunk into the ground 1 or 2 inches. To stack ties, bore holes through them (you will need to rent an industrial drill). Drive sections of galvanized pipe through the holes into the ground with a sledge hammer; overlap corners of stacked ties for strength. Cut ties with a chain saw; be sure to wear safety goggles and ear protection, and watch out for nails.
Concrete blocks—These are especially good for temporary beds. Filled with earth, blocks in a single course or level row make a stable edging. They are also a good place to grow herbs, which benefit from the alkaline lime that leaches from the blocks. Stacked blocks must be mortared together to form a stable permanent edging.

Cross ties make an excellent edging. Be sure the ties are old so that the caustic creosote will have leached out. Owners: Don Morris and Harry White, San Antonio, Texas.

Brick—Although one of the most expensive edgings, brick is also one of the most attractive, and a single row set on end is fairly easy to install. If stacked, the brick must be mortared together. If you choose brick for building raised beds, order grade SW (severe weathering) in the Upper and Middle South and grade MW (moderate weathering) in the Lower South. Grade NW will not hold up outside.

The Paths

No matter what size beds you have, you must have a convenient way to get to the crops. Permanent pathways separate beds and take the majority of the garden traffic, so you avoid walking in the beds and compacting the soil.

Width is the key consideration in designing garden paths. Major paths leading into and out of the garden should be wide enough to handle a garden cart or wheelbarrow; 3 feet should be the minimum. Other paths (between rows and beds) may be as narrow as 18 to 24 inches.

There are many suitable materials for pathways. Brick is costly in comparison to others, but it is among the most handsome and durable of garden path surfaces. Gravel works well if your wheelbarrow has an air-filled tire that will not bog down in it. Railroad ties and concrete stepping pads are good also. (Space stepping pads no more than 2 to 3 inches apart so that you can easily wheel a wheelbarrow over the path.) For a simple, inexpensive path, use mulch.

Raised beds of treated lumber and gravel paths are both effective and attractive. Herbs form an edge for the broccoli. Paca House, Annapolis, Maryland.

In many gardens, the best combination is a strong, hard-surfaced path down the center of the garden and perhaps around the perimeter of large ones. For the lesser-traveled paths between interior beds, use a lighter material such as straw, pine straw, or pine bark. This arrangement gives you a hard surface on which to run equipment but saves the expense and effort of laying permanent paths where they may not be necessary.

Your Garden Needs Fencing

Fencing can serve several purposes. It protects vegetables from rabbits and other animals by providing a strong, continuous barrier around the entire garden. It can serve as a trellis or support for vining crops. It may also have an ornamental purpose, setting off the design and providing a backdrop for the vegetables and herbs. And it can provide privacy, screening the garden from view.

Here a formal pattern is used with raised beds and wide paths that can support equipment. Owners: Don Morris and Harry White, San Antonio, Texas.

A garden does not have to be elaborate to be attractive. This one has a simple post and rail fence, raised beds of rot-resistant lumber, and paths of mulch. Owner: Martha Riddle, Nashville, Tennessee.

In Old Salem, North Carolina, fencing defines this garden, separating it from surroundings and protecting it from animals.

If it is for protection, build it at least 3 feet high to keep rabbits and dogs out of the garden, and taller if deer are a problem. It should also reach low enough to keep out burrowing animals. This may mean burying wire mesh a few inches deep at the base of the fence.

A tall privacy fence may be in order if you intend to screen the garden from view, while a lower picket fence is appropriate if you want to show off the garden. With either type, consider the shadows they may cast, and be sure they allow for air circulation.

The most common materials for garden fences are wire and wood. A brick wall is attractive, but more expensive.

Permanent Trellising

Trellises may be permanently installed to save you from having to erect them every year. However, permanent installation does mean that you will have to pay special attention to rotating trellised beans, English peas, and cucumbers.

Before choosing a fixed location for the trellis, study the movement of the sun so that you do not place the trellis where it will shade other vegetables. Also be aware of views. Do not let the trellis block your view of the garden from indoors; but you can use it to create privacy by screening your garden from the view next door.

Trellised vegetables can form a privacy screen — or they can block the light. Keep this in mind as you plan your garden.

Free-form beds at Mount Vernon are separated by paths of clover and lawngrass.

A vegetable or herb garden close to the kitchen is easy to water and care for. Harvesting will also be convenient.
Owner: Jody Slaymaker, Nashville, Tennessee.

Irrigation

Be sure that getting water to the garden is convenient, because watering is one of the most frequent maintenance tasks. If the garden is located far from the water source, it is a good idea to run an underground line out to the garden and install a spigot on the site.

Another alternative if you have permanent beds is an underground irrigation system. You can even set it with an automatic timer to water regularly if you are away a few days.

In a vegetable garden, the most useful system is usually one with permanent risers (pipes) several feet tall with sprinkler heads. These are installed at strategic points so that their spray covers every square foot of the garden. And they can be high enough to water from overhead even tall crops such as corn.

For a permanent irrigation system, it is best to consult a local irrigation contractor. A contractor can design one to fit your gardening needs and specify the valves, sprinkler heads, piping, and controls that you will require. Be sure to install the irrigation system before you begin garden construction. (*See page 107 for information on portable irrigation systems such as movable sprinklers, hoses, and drip irrigation.*)

Try using a bushel basket lined with plastic to grow large or rambling vegetables such as winter squash.

Container Gardening

If the only sunny spot you have is a patio or deck, you can still grow vegetables and herbs by growing them in containers. Container gardening can also be a practical alternative if your soil is too soggy and poorly drained for vegetables to grow well. And it can be a convenient way to supplement a small garden.

You can harvest a surprising amount from a container garden. In fact, yields may equal those you would expect from plants grown in the ground, or even be higher because nematodes and soilborne diseases are not a problem. If you are determined and inventive, you can find a way to grow almost any vegetable in containers. Some crops, however, are easier and more practical than others and will give a higher return-per-square-foot of space. Lettuce, radishes, and root crops are well suited to container growing, as are tomatoes, eggplant, Irish potatoes, and peppers. Pole beans, most cucumbers, melons, and squash, on the other hand, grow rampantly and will require sturdy trellises for support. When possible, choose dwarf or bush selections of vegetables for growing in containers. (*See page 35 for recommended selections as well as container sizes required.*)

Try mixing flowers and leafy greens in large containers.

To make sure your container garden is an attractive addition to your deck or patio, choose containers that complement your home or outdoor furniture. Clay pots, wooden barrels or boxes, and some types of plastic pots are good choices. In less public locations, you can simply convert plastic trash cans, bushel baskets, or cut oil drums to planters. (Line the bushel basket with a plastic trash bag.) To provide drainage in these improvised containers, drill or punch 4 or more ¼-inch holes around the sides ½ inch from the bottom. Also put 1 inch of gravel in the bottom of the containers.

Use a commercial soilless mix rather than garden soil, which is too heavy and may contain diseases and weed seeds. The soilless mix should be lightweight and well drained, yet able to hold moisture and nutrients. Look for a mix that contains both organic materials such as peat moss or pine bark and inorganic materials such as vermiculite, perlite, or sand. A good mix should contain some lime, too.

Leaf lettuce is one of the easiest vegetables to grow in pots. Sow seeds directly in the containers or put out transplants for an instant effect.

You can also prepare your own soilless mix. One such mixture consists of equal parts of vermiculite or builder's sand, peat moss or compost, and finely ground pine bark; to each bushel of this mixture, add 1 cup of lime, ½ cup of 5-10-10, and ¼ cup 20 percent superphosphate.

Moisten the medium before putting it in the container. Fill containers to within 1 inch of the top, and plant seeds or transplants as you would if sowing or planting directly in the ground. In boxes or pots in which you plant rows of vegetables, be sure to plant at the proper spacing.

When planting Irish potatoes in containers, fill the container only ¼ to ½ full of the mix and plant 2 seed pieces per 5-gallon container. Cover with 2 inches of the mix and as the plants grow, add mulch or soilless mix to encourage tubers to form in the top ½ to ¾ of the container.

Vegetables grown in containers may need water daily in sunny, hot weather and less often during cool, damp periods. When soil is dry to a depth of ½ inch, water the plants well.

Frequent watering washes the fertilizer out of the soil more quickly, so you will also need to fertilize more often. Use a soluble fertilizer such as liquid 20-20-20 diluted to 1/5 the amount recommended on the label and apply every other time you water. Or apply 1 teaspoon of 5-10-10 per square foot of soil every 3 weeks, beginning when plants have 2 true leaves.

Container-grown vegetables are more sensitive to changes in air temperature than those planted in the ground. The soil warms up faster in spring and summer, so you can expect plants to grow and mature faster then. In fall or winter, the soil will probably freeze in containers before the ground does. You will have to bring containers indoors when a freeze is predicted, or harvest and store the vegetables.

Gardening In Containers

Use the Amount to Plant information in the "At-A-Glance" for each vegetable as a guide for planting. Except where indicated, space plants as you would vegetables growing in the ground, or a few inches closer.

Vegetables	Depth of Container (inches)	Recommended Selections
Beans, bush	8	any
Beets	8	any
Broccoli	10; 1 plant/3-gallon pot	any
Cabbage	8	any
Carrots	8	any short or medium length selection
Chard	6-8	any
Cucumbers	10; 1 plant/3-gallon pot	Bush Champion, Spacemaster
Eggplant	11-12; 1 plant/4-5-gallon pot	any
Kohlrabi	6-8	any
Lettuce, leaf	4	any
Lettuce, head	8	any
Onions	8	any—use as scallions
Peppers	8-11; 1 plant/2-4-gallon pot	any, especially short selections
Potatoes, Irish	2 seed pieces/5-gallon pot	any
Radishes	4-6	any small round selections; White Icicle and long types in 6-inch pots
Spinach	4-6	any
Tomatoes	12; 1 plant/5-gallon pot	Patio Hybrid, Small Fry, large-fruited selections
	8; 1 plant/2-gallon pot	Pixie Hybrid, Cherry types
Turnips	8	any
Herbs		
Basil	8	
Bay	12	
Chives	8	
Marjoram	8	
Mint	8	
Parsley	12	
Rosemary	12	
Sage	12	
Savory, summer	8	
Savory, winter	12	
Tarragon	12	
Thyme	8	

By using containers, you can grow vegetables in any sunny spot available.

Planning

One of the greatest benefits of gardening is being able to say "We grew it ourselves." For many people, gardening is recreational, too, providing enjoyable physical exercise as well as fresh vegetables.

It is also a project in which the entire family can participate. Small children delight in watching seeds grow. If yours is to be a family garden, plan it so that everyone can work together comfortably and each person can tend a favorite vegetable.

To be sure your efforts pay off, start with a written plan. The first step in making the plan is to determine the garden's size.

What Size Do You Make the Garden?

Given the amount of suitable land you have available, you will need to consider three things: the garden's purpose, the amount of time you have to work in it, and your gardening experience. If saving money on grocery bills is the objective, you may plan a large garden that produces year-round. If you only want fresh salad ingredients, a few feet for lettuce, tomatoes, radishes, scallions, and other favorites are all that is needed.

If the time you can spend in the garden is limited, keep this in mind when you plan. There are ways to reduce maintenance; but every square foot of the garden will require your time as you prepare the soil, plant, and fertilize. Many gardeners figure on spending an average of an hour in the garden each day. Of course, this varies from all day during the planting season in a large garden to just a few minutes at harvesttime in a small salad garden.

Finally, if you are a beginning gardener, start small. Planning is easier and the work not overwhelming. Even from a space only 10 feet by 10 feet, you can harvest plenty of tomatoes, squash, salad greens, and other high-yield vegetables.

A well-planned garden not only uses space efficiently but generally produces more vegetables. Owners: Mr. and Mrs. George Adams, Charlotte, North Carolina.

Starting with a garden plan makes the job of putting in the garden much easier. You decide ahead of time where to plant each vegetable and how to use the space best. Keeping records from year to year will help you plan better.

Choosing Which Vegetables to Grow

Deciding what to plant depends on the overall purpose of your garden and its size, as well as your preferences. If economy is your main interest, choose vegetables that are expensive at the grocery, such as asparagus, along with those that are most productive, such as tomatoes and squash. Also select vegetables that may be frozen or canned, so that you can avoid paying high out-of-season prices at the grocery later. Annual herbs that you use in large quantities are also a good choice for this type of garden.

The size of your garden also affects your choice of vegetables. Pumpkins, vining types of winter squash, corn, and sweet potatoes are impractical for small gardens because they require so much space. Instead, plant vegetables that are highly productive and space efficient. *(See the box on page 44 for a comparison of the space efficiency of some popular vegetables.)*

Consider which crops will give you an extended harvest season. Collards, kale, and spinach, for example, are extremely hardy, standing in the garden through repeated fall and winter freezes until you are ready to harvest. If properly cared for, a single summer planting of pole beans and vining tomatoes will produce for months.

Freshness, availability, and flavor should also influence your decision on what to grow. Fresh herbs, for example, are rare in most markets. And although corn does not produce much compared to the amount of space it requires, it is impossible to buy corn as good as the fresh ears that come directly from your garden. For that reason alone, many gardeners find a place for it.

Arranging the Vegetables

Once you decide on the garden's size and which vegetables you want to plant, you are ready to put a plan on paper. A large part of planning involves deciding how to arrange the vegetables in the garden. If the garden is on a slope, the rows or beds should run across the slope to help reduce erosion.

Determine the best orientation for the rows or beds: Watch the sun as it moves across the garden. You will need to run the rows or beds in the direction that will give the plants the most even exposure to the sun; it may be north to south, east to west, or something in between. Also keep in mind that the sun shifts through the seasons. Plan for tall crops, such as corn, pole beans, or staked tomatoes, to be toward the north end or along the edge of the garden so they do not shade shorter vegetables.

Planning   37

Single Rows or Wide Rows?

Traditionally, vegetables are planted in a single row, with an aisle or path between each row. The disadvantage of single rows is that a lot of garden space is devoted to paths instead of vegetables. And all this bare ground requires maintenance.

An alternative to single rows is to plant certain suitable vegetables several abreast in wide rows or beds. Rows may be from 1½ to 2 feet wide; beds may be up to 6 feet wide. The width should be determined by how far you can comfortably reach to get to the middle. Wide rows generally increase the productivity of your garden, because more space is given to growing vegetables. The gain in yield can be two to four times that of a garden laid out in single rows; so it can be an especially helpful planting method for small gardens. Since plants in a wide row may be spaced more closely than in single rows, each plant may yield less than its counterpart in a single row. However, the increase in the number of plants allowed by the wide row can more than make up for the difference. Maintenance is also reduced, because you need less total garden area. And the thicker planting tends to crowd out weeds.

Vegetables That Are Easy to Grow: Safe Choices for First-Time Gardeners	
Beans, pole and bush	Leaf Lettuce
Beets	Mustard
Cabbage	Onions, green
Chard, Swiss	Peas, Southern
Collards & Kale	Radishes
Corn, sweet	Squash, summer
Cucumbers	Tomatoes
Curlycress	Turnips
Kohlrabi	

Vegetables Suitable for Wide-Row Planting	
Beans, bush	Kohlrabi
Beets	Lettuce
Cabbage	Mustard
Carrots	Onions, bulbing
Celery	Potatoes, Irish
Chard, Swiss	Radishes
Collards	Salsify
Greens, unusual	Spinach
Kale	Turnips & Rutabagas

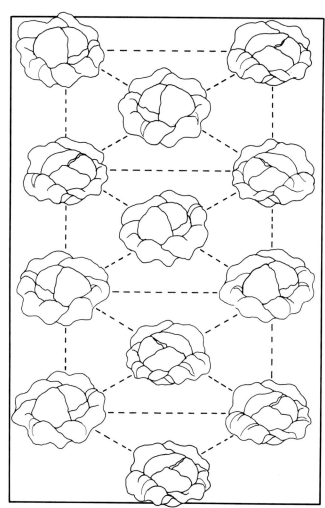

This method of wide-row planting starts with 2 rows spaced the recommended distance apart. Then you stagger the 3rd row down the middle, so that each center plant is equidistant from the 4 on the outside rows.

Diagramming the Garden

A scale drawing of your garden will help you avoid many mistakes. The location of each vegetable is plotted on the diagram, and all you have to do is follow it. Without a plan, you may end up with too much of one vegetable and too little of another.

Draw your diagram to scale. (In our example, each square represents 1 foot.) Then measure off the dimensions of your garden and begin designating areas for each vegetable.

The "Amount-to-Plant-per-Person" in the "At-A-Glance" for each vegetable (*beginning on page 126*) will help you decide how much of each vegetable you want to grow. Use these figures and the spacing information given under each vegetable to determine the size of the beds or rows and the distances between them.

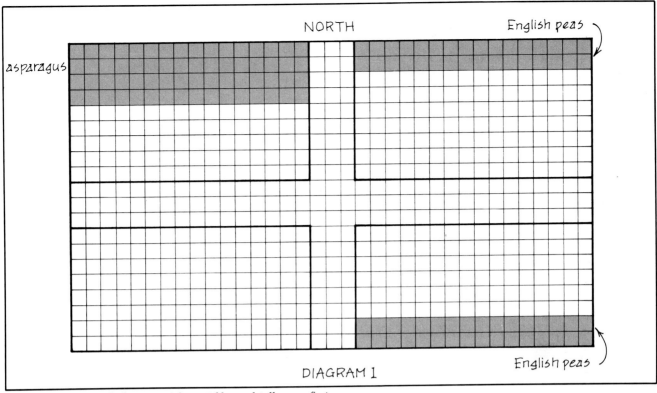

NORTH

asparagus

English peas

English peas

DIAGRAM 1

On graph paper, mark the perennial vegetables and tall crops first.

First draw the permanent beds for perennial crops, such as asparagus and rhubarb, and tall crops, such as trellised English peas or corn. (*See Diagram 1.*)

Then group the rest of the vegetables according to similar planting times and harvest dates.

That way a large area for planting the next season's crops opens up when the current vegetables come out. (*See Diagram 2.*) With several seasons of experience, you will know the length of harvest for each vegetable, and grouping will be easier.

Group remaining vegetables according to similiar planting times and harvest dates.

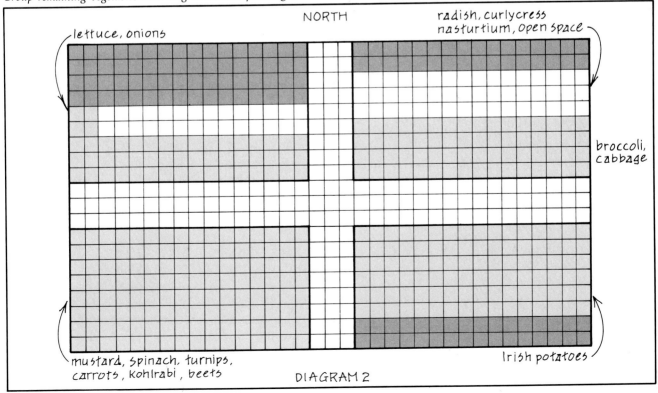

NORTH

lettuce, onions

radish, curlycress
nasturtium, open space

broccoli,
cabbage

mustard, spinach, turnips,
carrots, kohlrabi, beets

Irish potatoes

DIAGRAM 2

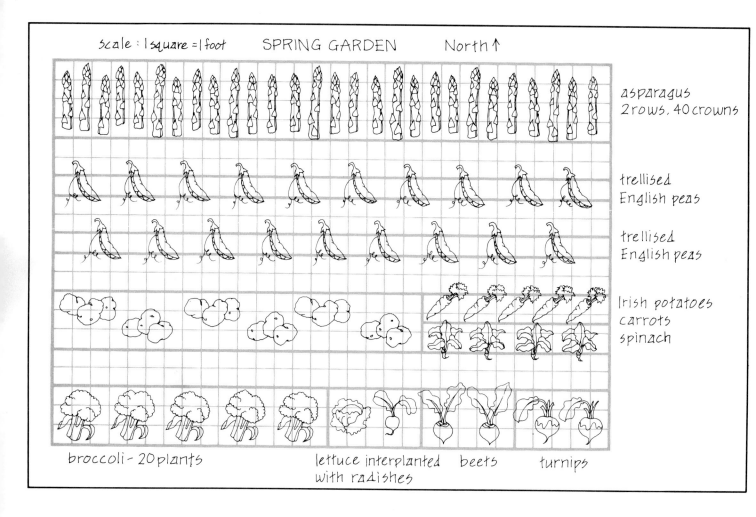

Scale: 1 square = 1 foot   SPRING GARDEN   North ↑

asparagus
2 rows, 40 crowns

trellised
English peas

trellised
English peas

Irish potatoes
carrots
spinach

broccoli — 20 plants

lettuce interplanted
with radishes

beets

turnips

Keep the Garden Going

For a garden that produces all year, plan for the summer and fall gardens when you diagram the spring garden.

To do this, you must know which vegetables grow best in spring and fall (cool weather vegetables) and which grow best in summer (warm weather vegetables). When spring cabbage is harvested, what can you plant in its place for summer? Bush beans are one possibility. And what can you grow in that same spot again in fall? Spinach is a good choice. The best season for each vegetable is indicated in the "At a Glance," beginning on page 126.

Timing is critical to the garden's progress too. When it is time to plant squash, beans, corn, okra, and peppers, much of the garden may still be occupied by cool weather vegetables such as cabbage, collards, broccoli, and lettuce.

If you do not have the space to plant everything at once, you need to know which vegetables can wait until space is available. For example, squash should be planted as early as possible after frost to produce before squash

vine borers become numerous. And peppers and other transplants should be planted at the earliest safe date to minimize the time they stay in flats. Others, such as corn, okra, Southern peas, and beans, can wait a few weeks.

To plan a sequence of plantings that will keep your garden producing in spring, summer, fall, and winter, refer to the planting guide on page 72 for planting dates. Mark these on the diagram or on a calendar, along with the number of days to maturity and the period of expected harvests for each crop. Then choose a replacement crop with the appropriate planting date to put in the place of each harvested vegetable.

Tips for a Garden that Spans the Seasons

• Use early-maturing selections of cool weather crops such as cabbage, cauliflower, and kohlrabi. Since they provide only one harvest, the sooner they are ready in spring, the sooner you can plant another vegetable in that space. With repeated use of early-maturing selections through the seasons, you may gain enough time to harvest an additional crop from that space.

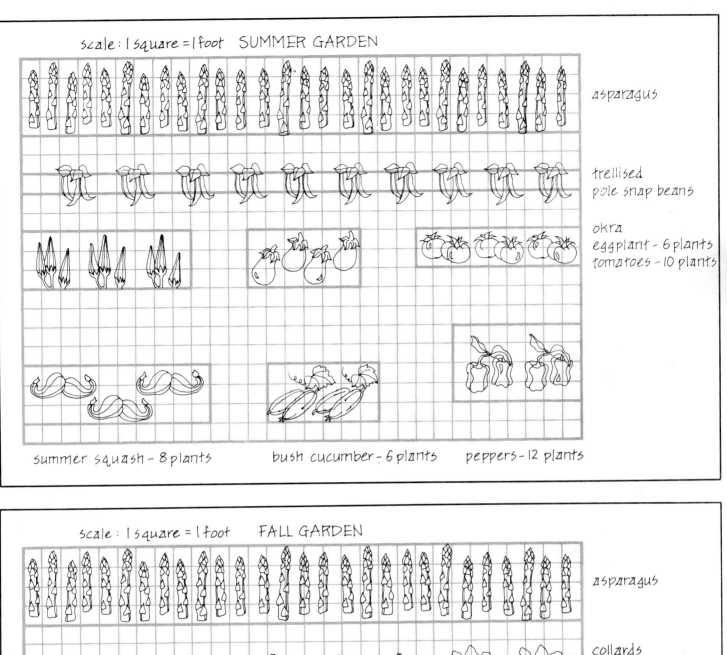

scale: 1 square = 1 foot   SUMMER GARDEN

asparagus

trellised
pole snap beans

okra
eggplant - 6 plants
tomatoes - 10 plants

summer squash - 8 plants   bush cucumber - 6 plants   peppers - 12 plants

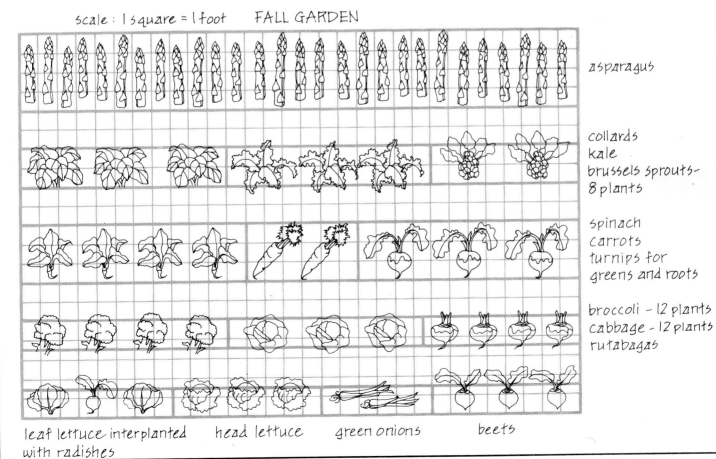

scale: 1 square = 1 foot   FALL GARDEN

asparagus

collards
kale
brussels sprouts-
8 plants

spinach
carrots
turnips for
greens and roots

broccoli - 12 plants
cabbage - 12 plants
rutabagas

leaf lettuce interplanted   head lettuce   green onions   beets
with radishes

For example, if you plant early-maturing cabbage or cauliflower the first week of March, you can harvest in mid-May. Then follow with early-maturing bush beans, which will finish producing by the last week in July. Then make another planting of bush beans, which will finish by mid-October. In the Middle South, you will still have time to follow the beans with a hardy crop such as spinach or fast-maturing radishes and curlycress. In the Lower South, there is still time to plant most cool weather vegetables. The shorter growing season in the Upper South may limit the extra crop, unless you have a warm year or can provide cold protection for plants.

• Extend the harvest with early-, mid-, and late-season selections. For a constant supply of long-standing vegetables such as tomatoes and corn, plant selections with staggered maturity dates. That way you can avoid the "feast or famine" of having more corn than you can use fresh one week, and no harvest at all the next. To prevent overlapping, wait two to three weeks between plantings of different tomato selections.

• Extend harvests with successive plantings. If the only selection of sweet corn that you like is a late-season type, such as Silver Queen, you can sow part of the crop on the earliest possible date, then make a second planting when the first corn has three or four leaves, and continue planting at this interval through the favorable planting season. You can stagger plantings of tomatoes, squash, cabbage, and other crops in a similar manner.

This method is especially useful for crops such as radishes, beans, and lettuce, which you use continuously but in small quantities. (*See individual vegetables to determine how much time to allow between successive plantings.*)

• Always be ready to replant. If tomatoes follow onions on your garden plan, be sure you have tomato transplants on hand the day you harvest the onions. This pays off in a highly productive garden because you never have an idle space. To be sure you have seeds or transplants when you need them, plan ahead. Order enough seeds for continuous planting, and be prepared to grow your own transplants for summer planting.

• Start with transplants when possible. Vegetables such as broccoli, cabbage, tomatoes, and peppers mature about a month earlier if started

Try sowing pole beans between the corn for a late crop. After you harvest the corn, use the stalks as supports for bean vines.

from transplants rather than from seeds sown directly in the garden. This head start is often essential if you are to harvest before the weather becomes too hot or too cold for good growth.

• Interplant to make the best use of space. One way to do this is to plant fast-maturing vegetables in the same row with slow-maturing ones. Vegetables such as lettuce, spinach, and radishes, which mature in a short time, can be planted between crops such as broccoli and cabbage, which stand in the garden longer. The fast-growing vegetables are harvested by the time the others need the space.

Be sure the vegetables have compatible growth habits so they do not compete with or crowd each other. For example, broccoli grows tall while lettuce stays low. In late spring, the lettuce also benefits from the shade. Similarly, tomato transplants may be planted alongside cabbage. This is also one way to "double up" when many cool weather vegetables are still in the ground at planting time for warm weather crops. Other popular combinations include parsley with tomatoes, dill with cabbage, lettuce with onions, and spinach with broccoli or collards. Experience will teach you other combinations for your garden.

When planning the garden, set aside a spot for your children to raise some vegetables on their own.

When the Children Garden

Give the children a small section of the garden. That way they will be encouraged to tend the garden themselves instead of relying on you.

Choose vegetables that are simple and fast growing. Good crops to start from seed include beans, radishes, cucumbers, and squash. Start eggplant, tomatoes, and peppers from transplants. (The children can start their own transplants, too.)

Do your best to provide every chance for success. Supply the young gardeners with well-tilled soil in a sunny spot, fresh seeds, and good quality transplants. Take time to teach proper techniques for planting, thinning, weeding, mulching, and watering.

Check garden supply stores for child-size tools, or cut down the handles of lightweight, normal-size implements. Be sure to discuss tool safety and care before beginning any work in the garden.

To ease the wait between planting and harvest, plan activities such as making scarecrows and watching bees pollinate the squash. Older children can also take photographs of the garden and keep garden diaries.

Children learn responsibility from caring for their own garden. The harvest is especially exciting, so along with fast-maturing crops, include some long-bearing vegetables such as eggplant to prolong the rewards.

Space Efficiency of Popular Vegetables

This list, from a survey conducted by the National Gardening Bureau, is one way to compare the value of many vegetables. The vegetables are rated from 0 to 10, considering their total yield per square foot, average value per pound, and planting-to-harvesttime. This may help you choose vegetables that give a high return.

Tomatoes, grown on supports	9.0
Onions, green (bunching)	8.2
Leaf lettuce	7.4
Turnips, for greens and roots	7.4
Summer squash: zucchini, scallop, yellow types	7.2
Onion bulbs, for storage	6.9
Peas, edible podded	6.9
Beans, pole	6.8
Beets, for greens and roots	6.6
Beans, bush	6.5
Carrots	6.5
Cucumbers, grown on supports	6.5
Peppers, sweet	6.4
Broccoli	6.3
Chard, Swiss	6.3
Kohlrabi	6.3
Mustard	6.2
Spinach	6.2
Beans, lima (pole type)	6.1
Radishes	6.1
Cabbage	6.0
Leeks	5.9
Collards	5.8
Okra	5.7
Kale	5.6
Cauliflower	5.3
Eggplant	5.3
Peas, English	5.2
Brussels sprouts	4.3
Celery	4.3
Peas, Southern	4.3
Corn, sweet	4.1
Melons	3.8
Squash, winter vining types	3.8
Pumpkins	1.9

Keep A Gardening Record

One of the most valuable tools of vegetable gardening is a record of your activities. It improves your gardening by providing a written account of each season's successes and failures.

The first step in record-keeping is to label each plant or row with the name of the selection and the date it is planted. Then you can identify and record the performance of each. Next year, this information will help eliminate the guesswork when you decide which vegetables to plant.

You can buy plant labels or make your own using wooden popsicle sticks. For writing on the labels, choose an indelible marker or a No. 2 pencil. Both withstand weathering.

Record your observations on each selection in a notebook. Here are some things you will want to note.

• Whether you started from seeds or transplants, the planting date, the date each selection began bearing, and when production stopped. This will help you plan for successive harvests next year.

• Disease resistance, heat resistance problems, fruit size, yield, flavor, and texture of each selection. If you are trying several selections of a vegetable, these notes will allow you to make comparisons.

• The date of insect and disease outbreaks in your garden. This will help you anticipate their occurrence next year. In case of certain foliage diseases, such as early blight and late blight of tomatoes, you can often prevent infection by spraying just before the time the diseases usually appear.

Hot peppers.

Kale.

Red onion.

Red cabbage (Red Acre).

Kohlrabi.

Getting Started

The hundreds of vegetable selections available today may make choosing what to grow seem more complicated, but they also make gardening easier. Vegetable breeders have developed plants with increased yields, improved disease resistance, and adaptation to specific climates. All of this means that when you plant a seed, your chances for success are good.

How Do You Choose Selections?

There are many qualities to consider when you choose vegetable selections; the most critical is adaptability—that is, whether a specific selection grows well in your area. Adaptability is important, because a tomato that grows in California may not be resistant to the nematodes and wilt diseases that quickly kill plants in the South. In the discussion of each vegetable, you will find a list of selections recommended for the South. Also, check with your county Extension agent, a local nursery, or other gardeners.

The Extension service recommends only those selections that have been tested. Other selections that have not been observed in local trials may be equally well adapted: If the description in the seed catalog fits the profile recommended for your area, go ahead and try it. But plant only enough for a trial so that you do not risk your entire harvest.

The way you plan to use a vegetable also influences your choice. For example, certain tomatoes are better suited to canning; pickling cucumbers are smaller than slicing types; and some onions are better for storage than others.

Plant size and growth habit are especially important in a small garden. Where every square inch counts, you want to maximize yield with the most compact, highly productive selections, and those that can be trellised.

Maturity date is important too. The relative earliness or lateness of selections helps you plan the succession of the garden.

What a Seed Catalog Can Tell You

Seed catalogs are often a gardener's first reference for information about specific selections. Look for the following information:

Days to maturity: For most vegetables, this is the time from sowing seed until the first harvest. However, for cabbage, broccoli, tomatoes, eggplant, peppers, and other vegetables commonly started from transplants, the number of days usually refers to the time from transplanting. Catalogs usually state this.

Disease resistance: Diseases to which a selection is tolerant or resistant are usually listed in the description. Your county Extension agent can tell you which diseases are common to your area.

Outstanding features: Look for features such as high productivity, compact growth habit, slowness to bolt (for crops such as spinach and lettuce), or hardiness (for fall crops such as cabbage). Remember to evaluate these character-

Pak Choi Chinese cabbage.

Seed catalogs are packed with information that will help you plan and plant your garden successfully. Be sure to order catalogs in December or January so that you can order seeds in time for spring planting.

Adaptability: Selections with a wide or regional adaptation are often noted.

Size of a packet: Most catalogs either give the number of seeds contained in a packet, or the feet of row a packet will plant. This information is essential for you to know how much to order.

Charts, keys, and special symbols: Since so much information must go into a catalog, it is often condensed with the use of charts and symbols. Do not overlook them.

What is an All America Vegetable?

In seed catalogs you will find some vegetable selections described as All America Selections or All America Winners. This means that they are hybrids that have been tested in trial gardens across the country and judged superior.

The hybrids are usually developed and submitted by seed companies, but entries also come from government institutions and private plant breeders. The testing is administered by a volunteer organization called All America Selections, and the judges are breeders, horticulturists, and experienced gardeners. Each new hybrid is grown beside an older comparison selection, which is suggested by the breeder and approved by a panel of experts. The choice of the comparison is important because each new vegetable is given award points on the basis of its superiority over the older selection.

The judges evaluate the advantages and disadvantages of each vegetable from the viewpoint of the home gardener. They score vegetables on taste, texture, total crop yield, plant size, and disease resistance.

The council usually gives 6 to 10 awards every year, assigning a gold, silver, or bronze award. Although an All America Selections winner may not be equally well adapted to all areas of the country, it is more likely to give you good results than a selection picked at random.

Days to Maturity

You may find that various catalogs list different maturity dates for the same vegetable. One reason is that seed producers or companies with their own trial gardens report the days required to reach maturity in their particular climate.

istics as they apply to your garden. Some features, such as extraearliness in tomatoes, are necessary for areas with a short growing season. But such a selection does not offer Southern gardeners any advantage, and the tomatoes may not be as flavorful as ones that are well suited to the South but take longer to mature.

Hybrid selections: Hybrids often combine the good qualities of several selections, resulting in a plant that is more vigorous, disease resistant, productive, and earlier maturing than standard selections. Hybrid seeds are more expensive, but most gardeners will pay more for hybrid selections they consider superior.

Plant growth characteristics: The description of growth habit will give you a clue as to whether the plant requires staking or trellising, or whether it will even fit into your garden. Vining squash, for example, will take over a small garden, but bush squash requires much less space. To help avoid wind damage in windy areas, you may choose shorter-growing corn selections.

The days to maturity also vary with weather, soil, day length, and other factors. In general, spring and summer crops may mature a few days to a couple of weeks faster in the South than indicated in many catalogs because of our warm weather. In fall, vegetables may take longer to mature than the catalog suggests because the days become progressively shorter and cooler. "Days to maturity" figures usually refer to spring and summer growing conditions.

The figures in catalogs are useful, because they give you a general idea of when to expect harvests. And they let you compare relative earliness and lateness among selections. But the best way to get accurate days to maturity is to record the number of days between planting and the first harvest in your own garden.

Should You Start from Seeds or Transplants?

There are two ways to start vegetables: Sow seeds directly in the garden or set out transplants. Starting with transplants reduces the time until harvest by a month or more. It is the best way to grow vegetables such as broccoli, cabbage, cauliflower, and onions, which provide only one major harvest. That way, they tie up garden space for the shortest possible time. Tomatoes, eggplant, and peppers started directly from seed take about six weeks longer to begin producing than if started from transplants. Since these vegetables produce for an extended period, you can begin harvesting sooner if you start with transplants. Herbs that can be started from transplants include basil, chives, parsley, and summer savory.

On the other hand, vegetables such as root crops may be stunted if transplanted and should always be started from seed sown directly in the garden. Starting from seed is also easier and more practical for plants that grow quickly or do not transplant easily. These include corn, squash, melons, cucumbers, beans, and peas. Some herbs have deep taproots that make transplanting them difficult, so it is best to start them from seed too. These include dill, burnet, coriander, and fennel.

For best results, use fresh seeds every year.

Starting cabbage and other cole crops from transplants lets you begin harvesting earlier.

Choose young, stocky transplants that are not rootbound. Those that are already flowering or bearing fruit will not grow or produce as well.

If You Start from Seeds

For the best start, buy fresh seeds from a reputable nursery, farm supply store, or mail-order source. Selections offered locally are usually the established ones, and you should buy early for the best choice. Mail-order sources offer a greater variety, more hybrids, and the convenience of ordering from home; but you must allow time for processing and shipment of your order.

Only the freshest seeds are likely to give good results because age and exposure to moisture cause seeds to lose their ability to germinate. Use seeds left over from the previous season only if they were properly stored. (*See page 57 for storing.*)

Seed Packaging

It is more economical to purchase seeds in measured quantities from a nursery or farm supply store because you can buy only the amount you need. Since it is scooped from a bin into a paper bag, be sure to protect the seeds from heat and moisture. If you are unsure of how much to buy, the clerk can probably guide you.

For the "lazy gardener," there is a seed tape that makes quick work of planting a row. All you have to do is unfold the strip and bury it at the recommended depth. The seeds are in the tape and prespaced to allow the correct amount of space for early growth. This prespacing also makes thinning easier. The tapes are easy to handle; but before planting, be sure to smooth out the folds that occur from packaging. Otherwise, the tape may push out of the ground.

If You Buy Transplants

Buy transplants from a local nursery or farm supply store early in the planting season to be sure of getting the best quality. Look for sturdy, compact plants that are a healthy green color. No matter what the price, a poor transplant is no bargain. Avoid tall, spindly plants with weak, thin stems and yellow leaves.

Young transplants give the best results. Large plants that are in flower or bearing fruit will lag behind vigorous leafy transplants when set out in the garden.

Also, avoid root-bound transplants. Some healthy, white roots should be visible through holes in the bottom of the pack or flat; but if roots are growing out of the holes, the plants may be stunted.

Examine the plants closely for leaf spots or other signs of disease. Also, look for insects, checking the leaf undersides carefully. If you see whiteflies, mites, other insects, or diseases, do not buy the plants.

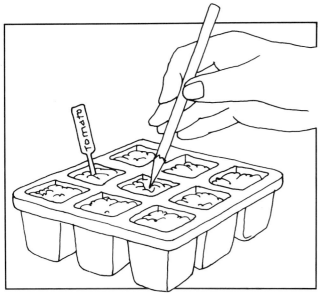

One-Step Method for Starting Transplants: *Sow seeds directly into containers where they will grow until ready to transplant into the garden. For fine seeds, use tweezers or a pencil point to place the seeds in the containers.*

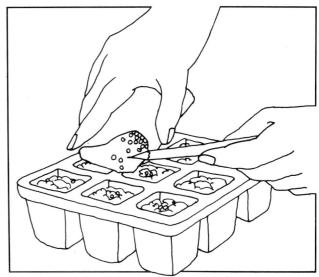

To make sure no container is empty because of poor seed germination, sow two seeds in each container. Be sure to label each pot or flat of pots with the name of the vegetable selection or herb.

Water gently with a fine mist of warm water. (To conserve moisture, you can place the containers in clear plastic bags. Do not use plastic bags if you put pots on a warm surface.)

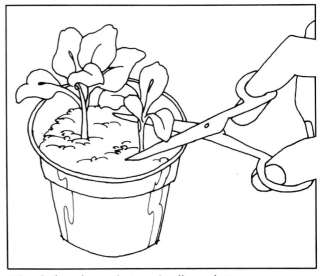

When both seeds germinate, snip off one plant.

How to Grow Your Own Transplants

You can grow healthy transplants at home if you provide the proper temperatures and adequate moisture and light.

Temperature: Seeds of most vegetables and herbs for which you start transplants germinate at a soil temperature of 65 to 70 degrees. Eggplant, tomatoes, and basil prefer a warmer soil of 70 to 75 degrees. These temperatures are easy to achieve indoors on top of the refrigerator, hot-water heater, or in other safe locations where temperatures are consistently warm. Or you can use special electric soil-heating cables in the bottom of the flat to warm the soil. After the seedlings emerge, move them to a windowsill, cold frame, or greenhouse. Seedlings need cool nighttime air temperatures (60 to 65 degrees); high night temperatures result in leggy growth.

You can also start transplants in a cold frame or unheated greenhouse, but additional heat from a soil-heating cable may be necessary. This requires that electricity be provided to the cold frame or greenhouse.

Moisture: Water seeds and seedlings with a gentle stream of water. Large, heavy drops can

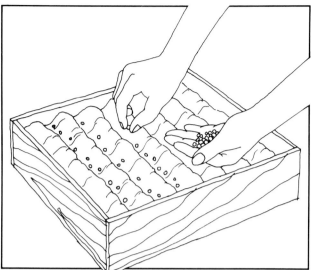

Two-Step Method for Starting Transplants: *Sow seeds thinly in shallow furrows in a flat. Generally seeds should be planted at a depth that is 2 to 4 times their width. Some seeds, such as lettuce, savory, and lemon balm, need light to germinate. Simply pat them into the soil.*

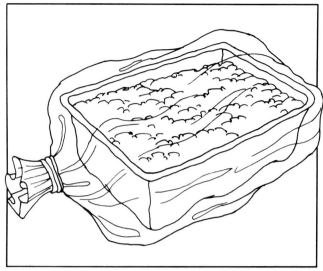

Water gently to conserve moisture; enclose the tray with a clear plastic bag. (Do not use a bag if you also use a soil-heating cable or place the tray on a warm surface, such as the hot-water heater.)

When the first true leaves appear, carefully lift the seedlings with a fork or popsicle stick and plant each seedling in its own container.

displace seeds or uproot tiny seedlings. Use a watering can with fine holes; for seeds and seedlings in a cold frame or greenhouse, you can also use a hose end nozzle adjusted to a fine mist.

To conserve moisture in seed-starting containers indoors, place them in a clear plastic bag or cover with clear plastic wrap. Remove the plastic as soon as seeds germinate or they could be quickly killed by disease.

Light: As soon as the first leaves begin to poke through the soil, move the tiny seedlings to a sunny windowsill to provide the light they need. The best exposure is to the south. If your windowsill is too small, use an old table. By placing the table on casters, you can move it to follow the sun and provide the 10 to 12 hours of sunlight necessary to grow stocky seedlings.

To maximize light, place reflectors made from cardboard covered with aluminum foil (shiny side out) alongside the plants, making sure they do not shade them. If the plants are on a sill, raise them to the level of the windowpane. Turn the seedlings every day to keep them straight; otherwise, they will lean toward the light.

In prolonged cloudy weather or when you cannot provide an adequately sunny location indoors, you will need to supply supplemental lighting or grow the transplants outdoors in a cold frame or greenhouse. (*See page 92 for information on cold frames.*)

Growing Transplants Under Lights

You can grow transplants indoors under 40-watt, cool white fluorescent lights. Seedlings grown under lights for 16 to 18 hours a day should produce strong transplants.

You need a waterproof surface on which to place the transplants. An old bench, work table, or even two sawhorses with plywood placed across them will do. The lights must be 3 to 6 inches above the plants, so you will need an adjustable support that allows you to move the fixture up as the seedlings grow. Use two tubes

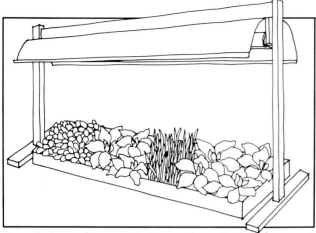

Transplants can be grown indoors under cool white fluorescent lights. Leave them on for 16 to 18 hours a day.

to illuminate an area the length of the tubes and 12 to 18 inches wide. To make the most of the light, place aluminum foil-covered cardboard reflectors beside the plants. Use a timer to help you regulate the lights.

Prefabricated fluorescent light units are also available. Two common types are shelflike units several feet high with built-in trays and lights, and tabletop light stands designed to be placed over the plants.

Materials for Growing Transplants

Containers: Containers must have drainage holes to let water run out, or the seedlings may rot. They must also be clean to prevent disease. Containers for individual transplants should be 1½ to 2 inches in diameter and 2½ to 3 inches deep to allow good root development.

You can use household items such as milk cartons, plastic foam cups, or plastic foam egg cartons to start seeds, provided you punch drainage holes in the bottom of the containers. Place them in a pan to catch water that drains through, and always pour off excess water. Seedlings started in egg cartons must be transplanted to a larger container as soon as the first true leaves develop, because egg carton sockets are too small for good root development.

Several commercial containers are also available for starting transplants. Peat pots are round or square containers made of peat and wood fiber. You fill them with soil and sow 1 or 2 seeds per container. Plant roots can grow through the pot, so when you set out the transplant, you also plant the container.

Plant roots can grow through peat pots, which makes these containers especially convenient to use. You simply plant the pot along with the transplant.

Place a few seeds on each moist pellet; then push the seeds into the pellet with a tapered instrument.

Place peat pellets in a small tray or shallow glass bowl. Add water to make the pellets swell and expand.

Peat pellets are made of compressed peat that expands when moistened to form a container held together by plastic netting or a binding agent in the peat. You sow the seed directly in the pellet; there is no need for soil. Roots grow through the pellet, so you plant them like peat pots. Pellets may dry out quickly, so check them regularly.

Cell packs are small planting trays sectioned into several compartments, one for each plant. Vegetable and bedding plants are often sold in cell packs. The plastic is flimsy, but with a little care, you can reuse them.

Flats or trays made of wood, peat, or plastic are fine for germinating seeds. Fill with soil mix and use a pencil to scratch out shallow furrows about 2 inches apart in the container. Then sow the seeds thinly in the furrows. When seedlings begin to develop their first set of true leaves, transplant each into an individual container.

Flats are also used to hold groups of cell packs or other containers for convenient handling.

Soil: The soil in which you grow transplants must be light, so that sprouting seeds can break through the surface easily. It must also be sterile to prevent damping-off, a disease that kills seedlings shortly after they come up. Synthetic soilless commercial mixes meet both requirements. These mixes consist of a combination of organic materials such as vermiculite, perlite, or sand. You can find them in nurseries and garden shops or purchase them by mail order.

You can also use a light, sterile potting mix, such as one used for houseplants. (Do not use a heavy mix that forms a surface crust or shrinks as it dries.) Or you can make your own mix by blending equal parts of peat moss and vermiculite. Dampen the mixture if the peat moss is dry. It is best not to use compost or garden soil, because they may carry diseases and are usually heavier than the special mixes.

Fertilizer: After seeds germinate, you will need to fertilize regularly; soil mixes contain few or no nutrients. A soluble houseplant fertilizer such as 20-20-20 or 18-18-18 is excellent for growing plants. Apply according to label directions.

When Do You Start Transplants?

Transplants of cool-weather vegetables such as cabbage and broccoli are started in midwinter for early spring planting and again in summer for the fall garden. Warm-weather vegetables such as tomatoes and eggplant are started indoors in late winter or early spring.

To determine the date to start transplants, take the planting date and count back the number of weeks it takes to grow a plant to transplant size (*see chart*). Use the frost maps on pages 58-59 and the planting date charts on pages 72-75 to determine the starting date for your area.

What to Do with Leftover Seeds

If you store leftover seeds properly, you can use them for a later planting. Do not leave seeds in a drawer or other area where they are unprotected from heat and moisture. Such conditions cause seeds to deteriorate rapidly. Under cool, dry conditions, however, seeds will remain viable (able to germinate) for 1 to 5 years.

Place seeds (either in packets or loose) in a sealed container, such as an airtight plastic carton, glass jar, or freezer bag, and place the container in the refrigerator. Be sure seeds, packets, and containers are dry. Any moisture during storage will cause seeds to deteriorate even faster than if left dry in a kitchen drawer.

To help absorb excess moisture, add 2 teaspoons of powdered milk or silica gel to each container. You may want to place these powdery materials in a small square of thin fabric to keep the seeds clean. Do not use dry milk or silica gel with corn, okra, or bean seeds, as overdrying may result.

Testing for Germination

Before planting seeds that you have stored, be sure to test their viability. Place 10 seeds on a wet cloth towel or on a layer of wet paper towels. Place another wet towel over the seeds and carefully roll the towel up. Put the roll in a plastic bag secured with a twist tie and keep it where temperatures remain evenly warm, such as on top of a refrigerator. After 7 to 10 days, check the seeds and count the number that have sprouted tiny healthy roots. If less than 6 out of 10 germinate, it is best to buy new seed. If 6 to 8 out of 10 sprout, sow the seeds more thickly in the garden to assure a good stand.

Starting Transplants from Seeds	
Vegetable/Herb	**Weeks to Transplant Size from Time of Sowing**
Asparagus**	10-12
Basil	6
Broccoli	6-8
Brussels Sprouts	6-8
Cabbage	6-8
Caraway	4-6
Cauliflower	6-8
Celery**	10-12
Chard, Swiss	4
Chives	5-8
Collards	6-8
Eggplant	6-8
Endive & Escarole	6-8
Fennel	4
Kale	6-8
Kohlrabi	6-8
Lettuce*	4-6
Marjoram, sweet**	8
Onions & Leeks	8-10
Oregano**	8
Parsley**	6-8
Peppers**	6-8
Sage	8-10
Savory, summer*	4
Savory, winter**/*	8-10
Thyme**	6-8
Tomatoes	6-10

* Seeds need light to germinate. Pat into the soil; do not bury deeply.

** Seeds are slow to germinate, require more than two weeks.

Average Date of Last 32-Degree Freeze in Spring

Use these maps as a starting point for determining when to plant. The line (isotherm) closest to where you live will indicate your average first or last freeze date; find that date on the planting chart to determine the range of safe planting dates for each vegetable and herb. If you live in an area between 2 isotherms, your average freeze date is likely to occur sometime between the dates indicated by those 2 lines.

Remember that the average dates mean that a freeze is likely to occur earlier than that date half the time and later than that date half the time. It may vary by as much as 10 days in either direction.

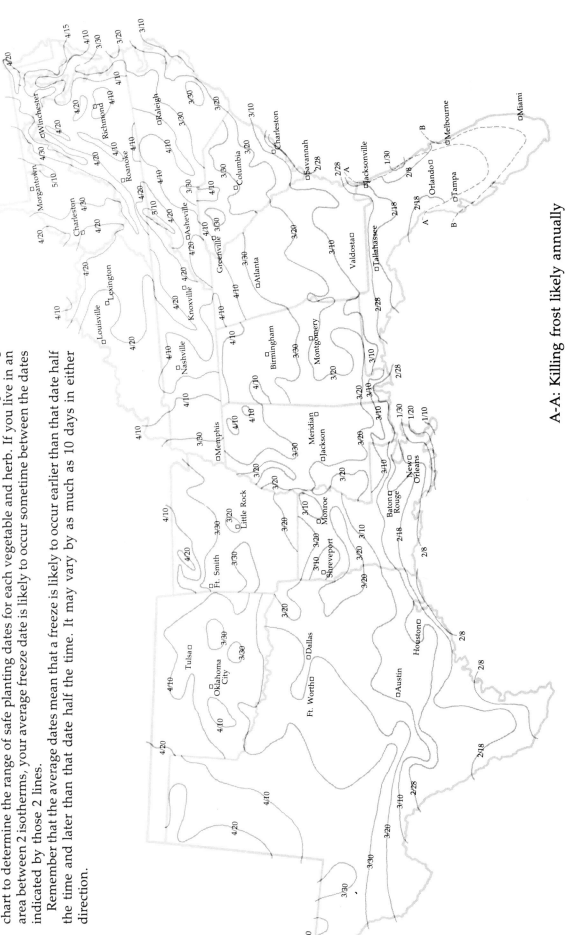

A-A: Killing frost likely annually

B-B: Killing frost likely half the years

Average Date of First 32-Degree Freeze in Fall

Your particular microclimate will affect whether you get frost earlier or later than the average. For example, cold air drains into river valleys and low-lying areas, so a freeze may occur later in spring and earlier in fall than the isotherms indicate. On a warm ridge or south-facing slope, the growing season may be longer.

Air temperatures between 28 and 32 degrees are classified as a light freeze, which injures warm season plants. Temperatures between 25 and 28 degrees are defined as a moderate freeze, which can injure most plants; 24 degrees or below is considered a severe freeze.

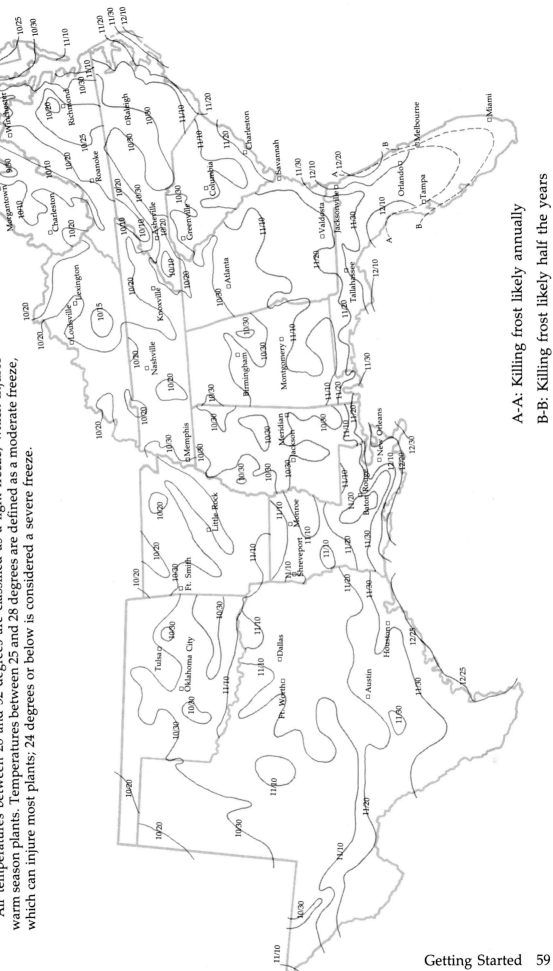

A-A: Killing frost likely annually

B-B: Killing frost likely half the years

Soils

A garden is only as good as the soil in which it grows. In loose, fertile soil, plants can send roots deep into the ground to bring up life-giving water and nutrients. As a result, plants are healthier and more productive. In soils with poor texture and low fertility, growth is limited.

Gardeners generally start with a soil that is less than ideal. Sandy soil is loose and well drained, but also infertile and dries out quickly. Clay soil becomes hard as brick when dry, and sticky when wet. Although clay retains nutrients well, it drains poorly.

The "ideal" soil, described as loam, is the perfect combination of sand, clay, and silt (fine particles halfway between sand and clay) and is rich in organic matter. It sticks together if you squeeze it in your hand, but crumbles readily. Loamy soil retains moisture and nutrients well, but also drains well.

Have the Soil Tested

The first step in preparing the soil is to have it tested. A soil test measures the levels of many vital nutrients available to plants and gives specific recommendations on how to adjust the nutrients if necessary.

The test also measures the pH, which is the degree of the soil's acidity or alkalinity. Vegetables grow best in a pH range of 6.0 to 6.8, while herbs prefer 6.5 to 7.0. In soils that are either strongly acid or alkaline, essential nutrients become tied up chemically so that plants cannot absorb them. If the pH needs adjusting, the test will recommend adding either lime or sulfur. (*See below*).

You can test the soil anytime before planting, but the best time is in late summer or fall. That way, if you add lime or sulfur to change the pH, the material has time to take effect. For the first two or three years, it is a good idea to test the soil every fall to help you develop a program for liming in fall and fertilizing in spring. After that, every three years is usually enough.

The Cooperative Extension Service offers soil testing services through its county offices or your state's land grant university.

Do-it-yourself kits are available from mail-order sources and some nurseries. If you have a streak of the scientist in you, the kits may be an interesting project. However, you must follow directions to the letter or the analysis could be inaccurate.

Changing the pH

If your soil is too acid for good vegetable growth (pH below 5.5 for vegetables and pH below 6.5 for herbs), you will need to raise the pH by adding lime. The soil test results will tell you how much to add. There are several liming materials available, but the safest and most frequently used is ground limestone. Besides raising the pH, it adds calcium to the soil; dolomitic limestone also adds magnesium. Ground limestone may take weeks to affect the pH.

Vegetables and herbs have a difficult time growing in hard, chunky clay soil (right). Loose, crumbly soil (left) holds moisture yet drains well, and allows roots to penetrate deeply in search of water and nutrients. Adding organic matter makes the difference.

Quicklime gives faster results but is more caustic, and applying too much may make the soil so alkaline that plants will not grow in it until the effects wear off.

Pelleted products, which are a combination of quicklime and ground limestone, contain enough quicklime for some immediate results, but not enough to risk burning plants unless heavily overapplied.

If your soil is slightly alkaline, you may need to add sulfur to make it more acid. Again, look to your soil test for the specific amount. Sulfur is available in several forms. Elemental sulfur can be worked into the soil as a dust or in granular form. Wettable sulfur, which is often recommended as a pesticide, is mixed with water for application to the soil. Aluminum sulfate also lowers pH, but overusing it can result in aluminum levels that are toxic to plants.

Changing the Soil Structure

Organic matter is basic to a productive garden. Experienced gardeners use it by the truckload to improve drainage and aeration of clay soils and to increase the capacity of sandy soils to hold moisture and nutrients. Organic matter also makes phosphorus and potassium stored in the soil available to plants, and it contributes nitrogen when it decomposes.

Work organic amendments into the soil in late winter before planting the spring garden and in late summer when you plant the fall garden.

Apply at least a 4-inch layer of organic matter each time and work it into the soil to a depth of 8 to 12 inches. As organic matter continually decomposes, you must add it regularly.

Types of Organic Materials

Following are some readily available organic materials to use for improving your soil.

Compost

Compost, which is decayed organic matter, is the best soil amendment you can use. Besides improving soil structure, it adds small amounts of essential nutrients.

Good ingredients for compost include cooled wood ashes, kitchen refuse (fruit and vegetable peelings, eggshells, coffee grounds), and garden waste (leaves, grass clippings, and spent vegetables, herbs, and annual flowers).

Do not compost grass clippings from a lawn that has been treated with an herbicide or has gone to seed. Also avoid weeds and plants with insect and disease problems.

To begin the pile, spread an 8-inch-deep layer of organic materials in the bottom of the cage or bin. (*See page 91 for types of bins.*) Layer grass clippings and leaves no thicker than 2 to 3 inches or they will form an impermeable mat.

Sprinkle the organic layer with 1 cup of nitrogen fertilizer such as 10-10-10 per 10 to 15 square feet to aid decomposition. Or apply a 2-inch layer of manure, blood meal, or cottonseed meal. Then add another 8-inch layer of organic matter. Top it with 2 inches of soil to introduce the bacteria that decompose the organic materials, and dust the soil with lime. Lime helps maintain the proper level of acidity for the bacteria. (If you regularly compost wood ashes, reduce the amount of lime you add by one-quarter to one-half.)

Repeat these layers, dampening each layer as you build the pile. Compost needs moisture, but should never be soggy, as this stops decomposition. If your pile is sheltered from rain or located in the sun, dampen it weekly.

Every four to six weeks, turn the pile to mix the ingredients and provide the air that bacteria need. A bad odor means the pile needs turning. Move materials from the top and sides of the pile to the center where they will decompose faster. After a few months, most of the compost should be ready to use.

In hot weather, remember that decomposition is rapid; in winter, it is slow. Be aware that compost can catch fire if heat produced during decomposition becomes sufficiently intense. Although this is rare, check with your fire department for advice on prevention, and be careful not to apply too much high-nitrogen fertilizer to the pile.

Leaf Mold

To make leaf mold, simply compost leaves. Shredding or chopping them with a lawn mower will speed the process. You can also work shredded leaves directly into the soil, but you must add fertilizer to supply nitrogen for decomposition.

Peat Moss

Peat moss is excellent for increasing the nutrient- and moisture-holding capacity of sandy soils. But it is expensive and not as rich in nutrients as compost and leaf mold, so use it with other amendments. Sphagnum peat moss is best, because it is more absorbent and breaks down more slowly than sedge peat, which is usually sold as Michigan peat or humus peat. For a 10- x 10-foot area, 1½ bales (6 cubic feet each) will make a layer 1 inch deep.

Sawdust

Well-rotted sawdust is a good source of organic matter. Fresh sawdust can be used; but because it requires nitrogen to decompose, you may need to double the amount of nitrogen fertilizer you apply and fertilize more often during the season. Be sure to avoid sawdust from chemically treated lumber.

Pine Bark

Finely shredded pine bark can be purchased in 3-cubic-foot bags. Some nurseries also sell it by the truckload, and large quantities may be available locally from lumber or pulp mills. Like sawdust, pine bark requires additional fertilizer to support decomposition.

Manure

The most commonly available types are dehydrated and composted cow manure, which are usually sold in 50-pound bags. Do not apply fresh manure to the soil just before planting, because it can burn seeds and seedlings. Work it into the soil in late fall. Or compost it with other materials or alone.

Amending the Soil with Sand

Sometimes adding coarse builder's sand to clay soil helps loosen it, provided you also work in plenty of organic matter. (If you add sand to clay without also adding organic matter, it can compact as hard as concrete.) Spread a 2-inch layer of sand over the amended soil and work it in. Sand is usually sold by the yard (27 cubic feet), which is about 2 or 3 loads for a small pickup truck. One yard of sand will make a 2-inch layer over an area about 10 x 16 feet.

Cover Crops

A cover crop is grown for the purpose of turning it back into the soil to add organic matter and nutrients. Plant tissues absorb nutrients, keeping them from leaching out of the soil. When turned under, the decomposing plants return the nutrients to the soil. Legumes such as clover and hairy vetch also add nitrogen.

Cover crops help prevent erosion, too. The roots hold soil in place and the foliage protects the soil from splashing rain. And the roots penetrate deeply to help keep the soil loose. Finally, cover crops provide an attractive green cover during the winter when much of the garden would otherwise be bare.

Alfalfa, lespedeza, wheat, and other grains may be used as cover crops in large gardens. But annual ryegrass, buckwheat, clover, and hairy vetch are suited to any size garden. Seeds are usually available from local farm supply stores and some mail-order sources.

How To Use Cover Crops

You can use cover crops in two ways: between peak gardening periods, to help rebuild the soil; and year-round to improve poor soils.

For rebuilding soil, cover crops are most often planted in fall when the most garden space is vacant. Sow clover, rye, or vetch as space becomes available. In the Lower and Middle South, you can sow rye or clover around broccoli, collards, and kale in late November. Because the cover crop is sown late, it does not grow large enough to choke out the vegetables, but provides a low green cover under them. (In Florida and the Gulf South where winter days are warm, however, the cover crop could grow large enough to compete with the vegetables.) In the Upper South sow rye and vetch in September and crimson clover in August.

You can also plant a midsummer cover crop between the summer and fall gardens. Buckwheat grows quickly, so you can plant it in July and turn it under in late August or September.

A year-round cover-cropping program is especially helpful for improving poor soil. If you have a large garden, you can cover crop a part of the garden while vegetables grow in the rest. Each year, rotate the area planted in cover crop.

To build the soil in a new garden, consider growing only cover crops the first year. Follow this seasonal sequence: Plant clover, vetch, or ryegrass in the fall and turn it under at the time of the last spring frost. Follow with buckwheat for summer, turning it under before it produces seed. Plant buckwheat again if there is time for another crop before the first fall frost. Then sow clover, ryegrass, or vetch again in the fall to turn under in late winter before you plant in spring.

Preparing the Soil

The cardinal rule of soil preparation is never to work the soil when it is wet. If you do, clods will form that are nearly impossible to break up. To test the soil, squeeze a fistful into a ball, then drop it from a height of 3 feet. If the ball crumbles, then the soil is dry enough to work.

Organic matter, lime, and other materials can be worked in at the same time. In a large garden, use a rotary tiller to make two passes at right angles to each other to thoroughly incorporate amendments and fertilizer.

Work the soil at least 8 inches deep; 12 inches deep is even better. If, however, you have shallow topsoil with poor, heavy subsoil, it is best not to bring up more than 1 or 2 inches of subsoil each year. Otherwise, you dilute the good topsoil with too much poor soil.

If the soil is not too wet in spring, it is a good idea to turn it once a week for several weeks to expose germinating weed seeds and kill them.

Double Digging

Double digging is the process of preparing the soil to twice the normal depth. The idea is to dig the soil 16 to 24 inches deep, remove the soil, and add organic matter to it; then return it to the growing bed. The advantages of the method include better drainage, deeper root penetration, and improved fertility. In double-dug soil, plants are healthier and more productive.

Shallow bedrock is about the only reason not

To double dig a planting bed, remove the soil to a depth of 16 to 24 inches. Amend it with organic matter, then return it to the growing bed.

to double dig. But the procedure does test even the most devoted gardener. In heavy soils, which benefit the most from double digging, it could take you 6 hours to prepare an area 10 x 10 feet. To make the job more manageable, divide the garden into sections and double dig one each season until the entire garden is done.

If you have distinctly different soil layers, such as heavy clay subsoil, you may want to discard the poorer soil and bring in good topsoil or loads of compost.

How Much Seed to Buy for Cover Cropping	
Cover Crop*	Pounds/1000 square feet
Annual ryegrass	2
Buckwheat	4
Clovers**	
red	1
crimson	1
Hairy vetch**	2

* Broadcast seeds with a seeder to ensure even distribution. Cover by raking the soil lightly.

**Legumes such as clover and hairy vetch require a specific bacteria to be present in the soil for best growth and to enable them to add nitrogen to the soil. This bacteria, or inoculant, is inexpensive. If your seed supplier does not carry it, check page 264 for a source. Inoculants for peas and beans are not effective for these legumes.

Planting

At planting time, the plan you made on paper is finally translated into action. If you have planned carefully and prepared the soil well, the job should go quickly and smoothly.

Building the Rows

First, rake the soil level and smooth to eliminate low spots that collect water. Also remove rocks and break up clods of soil. A bow rake (garden rake with short, stiff metal teeth) is best for the job.

Single Rows

To make sure your row is straight, drive a stake into the ground at each end of the planned row. Stretch a cord from stake to stake to use as a guide when you sow seeds or set out plants.

Some gardeners build the row into a ridge 4 to 6 inches high. This allows earlier warming of the soil for spring vegetables. It also improves drainage, which is helpful in heavy clay soils or in low-lying areas, but is not necessary in fertile, well-drained soils. Use the cord as a guide as you mound the soil with a hoe.

Wide Rows

To mark off rows 18 to 24 inches wide, use four stakes, one at each corner of the planned wide row. Stretch cord around them to form a

box. A wide row can also be built up about 6 to 8 inches high to improve drainage. If you do this, leave the string off one side of the row so that it will not interfere with mounding the soil. Remember that beds this high dry out faster, especially in sandy soils, and may need watering more often.

Planting vegetables on wide raised beds or rows provides better drainage and deeper soil in which plants can extend their roots. Seasonal ones like these are easy to make with a tiller that has a hilling attachment.

Loose, rich soil freshly prepared for planting.

Seed potatoes being cut for planting.

The early-spring garden with lettuce, broccoli, and sugar snaps.

Turning under cover crop and working in amendments to prepare the soil.

Seeds of popular Southern vegetables.

Transplanting tomatoes.

Protecting pepper plant from late frost.

Permanent raised beds can be any height you wish. These were designed to make gardening easier for people with back problems.

Raised Beds

Another way to improve drainage and give the plants a deeper soil in which to sink their roots is to build raised beds. You can construct permanent raised beds with railroad ties or other edging; or simply build seasonal ones that are destroyed when you till the crop under. A seasonal raised bed is similar to the raised wide row, but is even wider: It should be 42 to 48 inches wide at the base, 30 to 36 inches wide at the top, and 6 to 8 inches high. Level the top for planting. This width allows for a comfortable reach to the middle, and the height does not encourage erosion; but you can make the beds as wide and as high as you want them.

A Special Case for Squash and Its Relatives

Squash, pumpkins, melons, and cucumbers are often planted in hills, or mounds of soil. The small mound is quickly warmed by the sun; this helps cold-sensitive seeds germinate more readily. And like mounded single and wide rows, it provides improved drainage and a deeper soil for the plant's roots.

To make hills, mound the soil about 6 inches high and 2 feet in diameter. Gather the soil from all directions using a hoe, then level the top for planting seeds.

Squash is usually planted in hills or mounds of soil, with 2 or 3 plants to each hill.

Underplanting collards with a cover crop of clover.

Starting from Seeds

Sowing seeds directly in the garden has two advantages: It is less work than starting your own transplants, and the seedlings do not suffer from transplant shock. On the other hand it is riskier, because you cannot always provide favorable conditions for germination outdoors. And you must nurture some seedlings along until they are well established.

Make a shallow furrow in which to sow the seeds, using a Warren hoe or the corner of a garden hoe. Or lay your rake or hoe down and step lightly on the handle to push it into the soil, making a shallow depression. For most seeds, the furrow should be no deeper than ½ to 1 inch; otherwise, soil may wash down into the furrow and bury the seeds too deeply. Some vegetables, however, such as corn and leeks, benefit from being planted in the bottom of a trench so that as the plant grows you can mound the soil around the base of the plants.

Take the time to drop seeds into the furrow at the recommended spacing. A little patience at this point will make thinning a lot easier. For gardeners with plenty of experience, seeds seem to shake right out of the packet exactly where they are to go. If you are not so skillful, try coaxing seeds from the packet one at a time with a pencil point. Or use a commercial seeder.

For a wide row, simply broadcast seeds across the row, or plant in several evenly spaced furrows. Plastic herb and spice containers which have lids with holes are helpful for broadcasting seeds evenly; use them as you would a salt shaker. Mixing small seeds with sand can help you distribute them, too.

After sowing, cover seeds to the recommended depth. Where seeds were broadcast across a wide row, rake from the sides of the row to cover them with soil. Lettuce and other seeds that need light to germinate should simply be patted into the soil with your hand or the back of your hoe.

Water the seedbed well after planting. Seeds need constant moisture to germinate and establish roots. Use a sprinkler or water breaker attached to the end of your hose to avoid a strong stream that will wash up the seeds.

Tips for Starting From Seed

• Certain seeds germinate more readily if soaked overnight before planting. These include okra, nasturtium, beets, Swiss chard, and New Zealand spinach.

• When planting cool-weather vegetables such as salsify or lettuce in midsummer, cover the seedbed with a board to keep the soil cool. They may not germinate in warm soil. Check under the board daily, and remove at the first sign of germination. You can also presprout seeds in the refrigerator. Sprinkle seeds on a moist paper towel and cover with plastic wrap or waxed paper. After 4 or 5 days or as soon as seeds sprout, sow them in moist soil in the garden.

• Sow seeds ¼ to ½ inch deeper in sandy soils (except those that need light to germinate). Sandy soils dry out quickly, and sowing deeper helps keep seeds moist.

• In rocky soils or those that crust over as they dry, cover the seeds with sand, perlite, vermiculite, or sterile potting soil. This lets the seedlings push through more easily.

• Seeds need moisture to germinate. Because they are close to the surface, which dries out quickly, you may need to mist or lightly water twice a day to keep the seedbed moist. A light layer of pine straw or other fine material spread so that you can see the soil through the mulch offers some protection from the drying sun.

The Importance of Thinning

Thinning young seedlings is critical to the success of your garden. Crowded seedlings compete for space, water, and nutrients, and none develop properly. By thinning, you provide ample space for the ones that remain. Thin soon after plants come up, before crowding stunts their growth.

You can thin by pulling the plants up, but if seedlings are crowded, this disturbs the roots of adjacent plants. Watering before you thin makes pulling up the plants easier. Snipping off the plants at the soil line with a pair of scissors is even better, because it is less disruptive to the remaining plants.

If your soil crusts over as it dries, cover seeds with sand instead of soil. This lets seedlings emerge more easily. Be sure to water often, because sand dries out quickly.

The best way to thin crowded seedlings is by snipping the foliage of unwanted plants at soil level. That way, you avoid disturbing the roots of remaining plants.

Make the first thinning at ⅓ to ½ the recommended spacing to allow for loss. As the plants become established, thin again to the recommended spacing. You can use the second thinning of leafy greens to toss your first salad.

Setting Out Transplants

If you grew your own transplants indoors or in a greenhouse, you will need to harden them off before planting. Getting them accustomed to the outdoors reduces the shock caused by a sudden change in growing conditions.

Begin hardening off transplants 7 to 10 days before planting time. Unless the weather is severe, place the plants in a cold frame, or move them outdoors to a shaded location for 1 to 2 hours. Lengthen the period by an hour or 2 each day and gradually expose them to more sun. Also reduce watering and fertilization. Slight wilting during the heat of the day is normal. After a week to 10 days, the transplants should be ready for the garden.

Transplants that you purchase may be growing in plastic pots, plastic cell packs, or peat pots, or they may be bare-rooted. If you cannot plant them right away, keep them watered and out of direct sunlight until planting time.

On planting day, keep transplants in the shade until you are ready to set them out. Water container-grown plants thoroughly while they are still in the container. Soak the roots of bare-

Water transplants well just before setting them out.

rooted plants for 1 to 2 hours before planting. This is especially important if they are wilted.

If plants are in peat pots, peel off the rims so that they do not protrude above the ground. If exposed, the rim acts like a wick, pulling moisture away from the plant. Also break up the bottom edge of the pots, provided no roots are protruding.

Remove transplants from plastic or clay containers gently to avoid disturbing the roots. To remove the plant, put your fingers over the mouth of the container and turn it upside down so that the plant slides out. You may need to tap the bottom of the container or gently squeeze its sides to loosen the plant, but do not pull on the plant stem. Keep as much of the soil as possible around the roots to lessen transplant shock; gently loosen potbound roots.

Use a trowel to dig the planting hole and set transplants at the same depth they grew in the container. Firm the soil around the plant with your hands, and remember to label the vegetable with the name of the selection and planting date. Protect the plant from cutworms as suggested on page 96.

After transplanting, water and apply a starter solution. This provides an immediate supply of nitrogen and other elements, and supports growth until roots are well established. Soluble liquid houseplant fertilizers such as 18-18-18 or 20-20-20 make good starter solutions. Dilute according to label directions. This starter solution may also be applied to seedlings when they come up, for a quick boost to growth.

Frost Protection

Even when you plant at the recommended time, a late frost may threaten cold-sensitive ones. If so, be prepared to cover them or the plants may be injured or killed.

Cold protection devices can be as simple as a plastic milk jug with the bottom removed. Even a cardboard box inverted over the plant or tents made from newspapers will do. Or you can purchase hot caps and cloches.

Remember that if the temperature goes below freezing at night and the following day is mild and sunny, you must provide ventilation in the plant protectors, or uncover the plants. Otherwise, they will be killed by the excessive build-up of heat.

| Vegetable/Herb | If the average date of the last frost in your area is | | | | |
| | Jan. 30 | Feb. 8 | Feb. 18 | Feb. 28 | Mar. 10 |
	then the best times to plant are				
Asparagus*	—	—	Jan. 1-Feb. 8	Jan. 1-Feb. 18	Jan. 1-Mar. 1
Basil	Feb. 10-Apr. 10	Feb. 20-Apr. 15	Mar. 5-Apr. 30	Mar. 10-May 5	Mar. 20-May 15
Bay*	Feb. 10-Mar. 10	Feb. 20-Mar. 20	Mar. 5-Apr. 5	Mar. 10-Apr. 10	Mar. 20-Apr. 20
Beans, lima	Feb. 10-Apr. 15	Feb. 20-May 1	Mar. 1-May 1	Mar. 15-June 1	Mar. 20-June 1
Beans, snap	Feb. 1-Apr. 1	Feb. 10-May 1	Feb. 20-May 15	Mar. 1-May 15	Mar. 15-May 15
Beets	Jan. 1-Mar. 15	Jan. 10-Mar. 15	Jan. 20-Apr. 1	Feb. 1-Apr. 15	Feb. 10-May 1
Broccoli*	Jan. 1-30	Jan. 10-Feb. 5	Jan. 25-Feb. 15	Feb. 1-Mar. 1	Feb. 10-Mar. 10
Brussels sprouts*	—	—	—	—	Feb. 10-28
Burnet	—	—	—	Mar. 10-Apr. 10	Mar. 20-Apr. 15
Cabbage*	Dec. 15-Jan. 30	Dec. 25-Feb. 5	Jan. 10-Feb. 15	Jan. 15-Feb. 25	Jan. 30-Mar. 10
Cabbage, Chinese*	Dec. 15-Jan. 30	Dec. 25-Feb. 5	Jan. 10-Feb. 15	Jan. 15-Feb. 25	Jan. 30-Mar. 10
Caraway	—	—	—	Feb. 28-Mar. 25	Mar. 10-Apr. 10
Carrots	Dec. 20-Mar. 1	Dec. 25-Mar. 1	Jan. 10-Mar. 1	Jan. 15-Mar. 1	Jan. 30-Mar. 15
Cauliflower*	Jan. 1-30	Jan. 10-Feb. 10	Jan. 25-Feb. 25	Feb. 1-28	Feb. 10-Mar. 10
Celery*	Jan. 1-30	Jan. 10-Feb. 10	Jan. 15-Feb. 15	Feb. 1-Mar. 1	Feb. 10-Mar. 10
Chard, Swiss	Jan. 1-Apr. 1	Jan. 10-Apr. 1	Jan. 20-Apr. 15	Feb. 1-May 1	Feb. 15-May 15
Chives*	—	—	—	Jan. 15-Feb. 15	Feb. 1-Mar. 1
Collards & Kale	Dec. 15-Jan. 30	Dec. 20-Feb. 5	Jan. 10-Feb. 15	Jan. 15-Feb. 25	Jan. 30-Mar. 10
Coriander	—	—	—	Mar. 10-Apr. 10	Mar. 20-Apr. 15
Corn, sweet	Feb. 1-May 15	Feb. 10-June 1	Feb. 20-June 1	Mar. 1-June 1	Mar. 10-June 1
Cucumbers	Feb. 15-Mar. 15	Feb. 20-Apr. 1	Mar. 5-Apr. 15	Mar. 10-Apr. 15	Mar. 25-Apr. 15
Dill	Jan. 1-Mar. 30	Jan. 10-Apr. 15	Feb. 5-Apr. 30	Feb. 15-Apr. 30	Mar. 1-Apr. 30
Eggplant*	Feb. 10-Mar. 15	Feb. 20-Mar. 30	Mar. 5-Apr. 1	Mar. 10-Apr. 10	Mar. 25-Apr. 25
Endive & Escarole*	Jan. 1-Mar. 1	Jan. 10-Mar. 1	Jan. 25-Mar. 1	Feb. 1-Mar. 1	Feb. 15-Mar. 15
Fennel	—	—	—	Mar. 10-Apr. 15	Mar. 25-Apr. 15
Garlic	—	—	—	—	—
Horseradish	Jan. 1-15	Jan. 10-25	Jan. 25-Feb. 5	Feb. 1-15	Feb. 15-28
Jerusalem artichokes	Jan. 1-30	Jan. 1-Feb. 5	Jan. 1-Feb. 15	Feb. 1-28	Feb. 1-28
Kohlrabi	Jan. 1-Feb. 1	Jan. 10-Feb. 1	Jan. 20-Feb. 10	Feb. 1-20	Feb. 10-Mar. 1
Leeks	Jan. 1-Feb. 1	Jan. 1-Feb. 1	Jan. 1-Feb. 15	Jan. 15-Feb. 15	Jan. 25-Mar. 1
Lemon balm*	—	—	—	Mar. 5-Apr. 30	Mar. 15-May 15
Lettuce, head*	Dec. 20-Feb. 1	Jan. 1-Feb. 1	Jan. 10-Feb. 1	Jan. 15-Feb. 15	Feb. 1-20
Lettuce, leaf	Dec. 20-Feb. 10	Jan. 1-Mar. 1	Jan. 10-Mar. 5	Jan. 15-Mar. 10	Feb. 1-Mar. 25
Marjoram, sweet	—	—	—	Mar. 1-May 1	Mar. 10-May 10
Melons	Feb. 10-Mar. 15	Feb. 20-Mar. 30	Mar. 5-Apr. 1	Mar. 10-Apr. 10	Mar. 25-Apr. 25
Mint*	—	—	—	Mar. 5-Apr. 30	Mar. 20-May 15
Mustard	Jan. 1-Feb. 5	Jan. 10-Feb. 15	Jan. 20-Feb. 25	Feb. 1-Mar. 5	Feb. 15-Mar. 15
Okra	Feb. 5-Apr. 1	Feb. 15-Apr. 15	Feb. 25-June 1	Mar. 5-June 1	Mar. 15-July 15
Onion plants	Jan. 1-15	Jan. 1-15	Jan. 1-15	Jan. 1-Feb. 1	Jan. 15-Feb. 15
Onion seeds	—	—	—	—	—
Onion sets	Jan. 1-15	Jan. 1-15	Jan. 1-15	Jan. 1-Feb. 1	Jan. 15-Feb. 15
Oregano*	—	—	—	Mar. 1-30	Mar. 15-Apr. 10
Parsley*	—	—	—	—	—
Peas, English	Dec. 5-Feb. 15	Dec. 10-Mar. 1	Dec. 25-Mar. 1	Jan. 1-Mar. 1	Jan. 15-Mar. 15
Peas, Southern	Feb. 15-May 1	Feb. 15-May 15	Mar. 1-June 15	Mar. 10-June 20	Mar. 15-July 1
Peppers*	Feb. 10-Mar. 15	Feb. 20-Mar. 30	Mar. 5-Apr. 1	Mar. 10-Apr. 10	Mar. 25-Apr. 25
Potatoes, Irish	Jan. 1-Feb. 15	Jan. 1-Feb. 15	Jan. 15-Mar. 1	Jan. 15-Mar. 1	Feb. 1-Mar. 1
Potatoes, sweet	Feb. 20-May 15	Mar. 1-May 15	Mar. 10-June 1	Mar. 20-June 1	Apr. 1-July 1
Pumpkins	Feb. 15-Mar. 15	Feb. 20-Mar. 30	Mar. 5-Apr. 30	Mar. 10-July 1	Mar. 25-July 1
Radishes (spring)	Dec. 20-Feb. 28	Dec. 25-Mar. 5	Jan. 10-Mar. 20	Jan. 15-Mar. 25	Feb. 1-Apr. 10
Rhubarb*	—	—	—	—	—
Rosemary*	—	—	—	Mar. 1-Apr. 30	Mar. 15-May 15
Rutabagas	Dec. 5-Jan. 30	Dec. 10-Feb. 8	Dec. 25-Feb. 18	Jan. 1-Mar. 1	Jan. 15-Mar. 1
Sage	—	—	—	Mar. 1-30	Mar. 15-Apr. 10
Salsify	Jan. 1-Feb. 1	Jan. 10-Feb. 10	Jan. 15-Feb. 20	Jan. 15-Mar. 1	Feb. 1-Mar. 1
Savory, summer	Feb. 1-Mar. 30	Feb. 10-Apr. 10	Feb. 20-Apr. 25	Mar. 1-Apr. 30	Mar. 15-May 15
Savory, winter*	—	—	—	Mar. 1-30	Mar. 15-Apr. 10
Sorrel	—	—	—	Feb. 1-Mar. 10	Feb. 10-Mar. 15
Spinach	Dec. 20-Feb. 15	Dec. 25-Feb. 15	Jan. 10-Mar. 1	Jan. 15-Mar. 1	Feb. 1-Mar. 10
Spinach, Malabar	Feb. 1-Aug. 30	Feb. 10-Aug. 30	Feb. 20-Aug. 30	Mar. 1-Aug. 30	Mar. 15-Aug. 30
Spinach, New Zealand	Feb. 1-Apr. 15	Feb. 15-Apr. 15	Mar. 1-Apr. 15	Mar. 15-May 15	Mar. 20-May 15
Spinach, Tampala	Feb. 10-Aug. 30	Feb. 20-Aug. 30	Mar. 5-Aug. 30	Mar. 10-Aug. 30	Mar. 25-Aug. 30
Squash, summer	Feb. 1-Apr. 15	Feb. 20-Apr. 15	Feb. 20-Apr. 15	Mar. 1-May 15	Mar. 10-May 1
Squash, winter	Feb. 15-Mar. 30	Feb. 20-Mar. 30	Mar. 5-July 1	Mar. 10-July 1	Mar. 25-July 1
Tarragon*	—	—	—	Mar. 1-Apr. 30	Mar. 15-May 15
Thyme	—	—	—	Mar. 1-30	Mar. 15-Apr. 10
Tomatoes*	Feb. 1-Apr. 1	Feb. 10-Apr. 10	Feb. 20-Apr. 20	Mar. 1-May 1	Mar. 10-May 10
Turnips	Jan. 1-Feb. 15	Jan. 10-Feb. 20	Jan. 20-Mar. 1	Feb. 1-Mar. 10	Feb. 15-Mar. 25

*Started from transplants.

Earliest Dates and Range of Dates for Spring Planting of Vegetables and Herbs Outdoors

If the average date of the last frost in your area is ... then the best times to plant are

Mar. 20	Mar. 30	Apr. 10	Apr. 20	Apr. 30	May 10
Jan. 15-Mar. 10	Feb. 1-Mar. 20	Mar. 1-Apr. 10	Mar. 10-Apr. 15	Mar. 20-Apr. 15	Mar. 20-Apr. 30
Apr. 1-May 30	Apr. 10-June 5	Apr. 25-June 20	May 1-June 30	May 15-June 15	May 25-June 15
Apr. 1-30	Apr. 15-May 15	Apr. 25-May 25	May 1-30	May 15-June 15	May 20-June 15
Apr. 1-June 15	Apr. 15-June 20	Apr. 25-June 30	May 5-June 20	May 15-June 15	May 25-June 15
Mar. 25-May 25	Apr. 1-June 1	Apr. 15-June 30	Apr. 25-June 30	May 1-June 30	May 15-June 30
Feb. 20-May 15	Mar. 1-June 1	Mar. 10-June 1	Mar. 20-June 1	Apr. 1-June 15	Apr. 10-June 15
Feb. 10-Mar. 15	Mar. 1-20	Mar. 15-Apr. 15	Mar. 25-Apr. 20	Apr. 1-30	Apr. 10-June 1
Feb. 20-Mar. 15	Mar. 1-20	Mar. 15-Apr. 15	Mar. 25-Apr. 20	Apr. 1-30	Apr. 10-June 1
Apr. 1-30	Apr. 15-May 15	Apr. 25-May 25	May 1-30	May 15-June 15	May 25-June 15
Feb. 5-Mar. 15	Feb. 15-Mar. 20	Mar. 1-Apr. 1	Mar. 10-Apr. 1	Mar. 20-Apr. 10	Apr. 1-May 15
Feb. 5-Mar. 1	Feb. 15-Mar. 10	Mar. 1-Apr. 1	Mar. 10-Apr. 1	Mar. 20-Apr. 10	Apr. 1-May 15
Mar. 20-Apr. 20	Mar. 30-Apr. 30	Apr. 10-May 10	Apr. 20-May 20	Apr. 30-May 30	May 10-June 10
Feb. 5-Mar. 20	Feb. 20-Apr. 10	Mar. 1-Apr. 20	Mar. 5-May 15	Mar. 20-June 1	Mar. 30-June 15
Feb. 20-Mar. 20	Mar. 1-30	Mar. 10-Apr. 10	Mar. 20-Apr. 20	Mar. 30-Apr. 30	Apr. 10-May 10
Feb. 20-Apr. 1	Mar. 1-Apr. 15	Mar. 10-Apr. 20	Mar. 20-May 1	Mar. 30-May 1	Apr. 10-June 15
Feb. 20-May 1	Mar. 1-May 25	Mar. 10-June 15	Mar. 20-June 15	Mar. 30-June 15	Apr. 10-June 15
Feb. 10-Mar. 10	Feb. 15-Mar. 15	Mar. 1-30	Mar. 10-Apr. 10	Mar. 20-Apr. 20	Apr. 1-30
Feb. 1-Mar. 1	Feb. 15-Mar. 10	Mar. 1-30	Mar. 10-30	Mar. 15-Apr. 10	Apr. 1-May 15
Apr. 1-30	Apr. 15-May 15	Apr. 25-May 25	May 1-30	May 15-June 15	May 25-June 15
Mar. 20-July 15	Mar. 30-July 15	Apr. 10-July 15	Apr. 20-July 15	Apr. 30-July 15	May 10-July 1
Apr. 1-May 1	Apr. 15-May 15	Apr. 20-June 1	May 1-June 15	May 15-June 15	May 25-June 15
Feb. 20-May 15	Mar. 5-May 30	Mar. 10-June 15	Mar. 20-June 30	Apr. 1-June 30	Apr. 10-June 30
Apr. 1-30	Apr. 15-May 15	Apr. 25-May 25	May 5-June 5	May 15-June 15	May 25-June 15
Feb. 20-Apr. 1	Mar. 1-Apr. 10	Mar. 10-Apr. 15	Mar. 20-Apr. 25	Apr. 1-30	Apr. 1-30
Apr. 1-May 1	Apr. 15-May 15	Apr. 20-June 1	May 1-June 15	May 15-June 15	May 25-June 15
—	Feb. 15-Mar. 5	Mar. 1-15	Mar. 5-20	Mar. 20-Apr. 1	Mar. 25-Apr. 10
Feb. 20-Mar. 5	Mar. 1-15	Mar. 15-25	Mar. 20-Apr. 1	Apr. 1-15	Apr. 10-25
Feb. 1-Mar. 20	Feb. 10-Mar. 30	Feb. 20-Apr. 10	Mar. 10-Apr. 20	Mar. 20-Apr. 30	Apr. 1-May 10
Feb. 20-Mar. 10	Mar. 1-30	Mar. 10-Apr. 10	Mar. 20-May 1	Mar. 30-May 10	Apr. 10-May 15
Feb. 1-Mar. 1	Feb. 15-Mar. 15	Mar. 1-Apr. 1	Mar. 15-Apr. 15	Apr. 1.-May 1	Apr. 15-May 15
Mar. 25-May 20	Apr. 5-May 30	Apr. 15-June 10	Apr. 25-June 20	May 5-June 30	May 15-June 30
Feb. 5-Mar. 10	Feb. 20-Mar. 20	Mar. 1-30	Mar. 5-Apr. 10	Mar. 20-Apr. 20	Apr. 1-30
Feb. 5-Apr. 1	Feb. 20-Apr. 10	Mar. 1-Apr. 20	Mar. 5-Apr. 30	Mar. 20-May 15	Apr. 1-May 30
Mar. 20-May 20	Apr. 1-June 1	Apr. 10-June 1	Apr. 20-June 10	May 1-June 15	May 10-June 15
Apr. 1-30	Apr. 15-May 15	Apr. 25-May 25	May 5-June 5	May 15-June 15	May 25-June 15
Mar. 25-May 20	Apr. 5-May 30	Apr. 15-June 10	Apr. 25-June 20	May 5-June 30	May 15-June 30
Feb. 20-Mar. 25	Mar. 1-Apr. 5	Mar. 10-Apr. 15	Mar. 20-Apr. 30	Mar. 30-May 5	Apr. 10-May 15
Apr. 1-July 15	Apr. 10-July 15	Apr. 20-June 15	May 1-30	May 10-30	May 20-June 10
Feb. 20-Mar. 10	Mar. 1-15	Mar. 10-30	Mar. 20-Apr. 10	Apr. 1-30	Apr. 10-30
—	Feb. 1-Mar. 15	Feb. 15-Apr. 1	Mar. 1-Apr. 1	Mar. 5-Apr. 15	Mar. 15-30
Feb. 20-Mar. 10	Mar. 1-15	Mar. 10-30	Mar. 20-Apr. 10	Apr. 1-30	Apr. 10-30
Mar. 25-Apr. 25	Apr. 1-30	Apr. 15-May 15	Apr. 25-May 25	May 1-30	May 15-30
Apr. 1-25	Apr. 15-30	Apr. 25-May 15	May 1-25	May 15-30	May 25-June 5
Jan. 25-Mar. 15	Feb. 5-Mar. 20	Feb. 15-Mar. 20	Mar. 1-Apr. 10	Mar. 5-May 1	Mar. 15-May 15
Apr. 1-July 1	Apr. 15-July 1	Apr. 15-July 1	Apr. 25-June 15	May 10-June 1	—
Apr. 1-30	Apr. 15-May 15	Apr. 25-May 15	May 5-June 5	May 15-June 15	May 25-June 15
Feb. 10-Mar. 15	Feb. 20-Mar. 20	Mar. 1-Apr. 10	Mar. 15-Apr. 10	Mar. 20-May 10	Apr. 1-June 1
Apr. 10-June 10	Apr. 25-June 1	Apr. 30-June 1	May 10-June 10	May 20-June 10	June 1-15
Apr. 1-30	Apr. 15-May 15	Apr. 25-May 25	May 5-May 25	May 15-May 25	May 15-25
Feb. 5-Apr. 15	Feb. 20-Apr. 30	Feb. 28-May 5	Mar. 10-May 15	Mar. 20-May 30	Mar. 25-June 5
Feb. 25-Mar. 5	Mar. 1-15	Mar. 15-30	Mar. 25-Apr. 5	Apr. 1-15	Apr. 15-30
Mar. 25-May 25	Apr. 5-May 30	Apr. 15-June 5	Apr. 25-June 10	May 5-June 30	May 15-June 30
Jan. 25-Mar. 1	Jan. 30-Mar. 1	Feb. 15-Mar. 1	Feb. 20-Mar. 10	Mar. 5-June 1	Mar. 15-June 1
Mar. 25-Apr. 25	Apr. 1-30	Apr. 15-May 15	Apr. 25-May 25	May 1-30	May 15-30
Feb. 15-Mar. 1	Mar. 1-15	Mar. 10-Apr. 15	Mar. 20-May 1	Apr. 1-May 15	Apr. 15-June 1
Mar. 25-May 30	Apr. 1-June 5	Apr. 15-June 15	Apr. 25-June 25	May 1-June 30	May 15-June 30
Mar. 25-Apr. 25	Apr. 1-30	Apr. 15-May 15	Apr. 25-May 25	May 1-30	May 15-30
Feb. 10-Mar. 20	Feb. 20-Apr. 1	Mar. 1-Apr. 15	Mar. 15-May 1	Apr. 1-May 15	Apr. 15-June 1
Feb. 5-Mar. 15	Feb. 20-Mar. 20	Feb. 28-Apr. 1	Mar. 5-Apr. 1	Mar. 20-Apr. 15	Mar. 25-June 15
Mar. 25-July 30	Apr. 1-July 30	Apr. 15-July 30	Apr. 25-July 30	May 1-July 30	May 15-July 30
Apr. 1-May 15	Apr. 10-June 1	Apr. 20-June 1	May 1-June 15	May 1-June 15	May 10-June 15
Apr. 1-July 30	Apr. 15-July 30	Apr. 25-July 30	Apr. 30-July 30	May 15-July 30	May 20-July 30
Mar. 20-May 15	Apr. 1-June 1	Apr. 10-June 1	Apr. 20-June 15	May 1-30	May 10-June 10
Mar. 20-Apr. 30	Apr. 1-May 15	Apr. 10-May 25	Apr. 20-May 25	May 1-May 25	May 10-May 25
Mar. 25-May 25	Apr. 5-May 30	Apr. 15-June 5	Apr. 25-June 10	May 5-June 30	May 15-June 30
Mar. 25-Apr. 25	Apr. 1-30	Apr. 15-May 15	Apr. 25-May 25	May 1-30	May 15-30
Mar. 20-May 20	Apr. 1-June 1	Apr. 10-June 1	Apr. 20-June 10	May 1-June 15	May 10-June 15
Feb. 20-Apr. 1	Mar. 1-Apr. 10	Mar. 10-Apr. 20	Mar. 20-Apr. 30	Apr. 5-May 15	Apr. 10-May 20

Latest Dates and Range of Dates for Fall Planting of Vegetables and Herbs Outdoors				
	If the average date of the first frost in your area is			
Vegetable/Herb	Sept. 30	Oct. 10	Oct. 20	Oct. 30
	then the best times to plant are			
Asparagus*	—	Nov. 1-Mar. 30	Nov. 1-Mar. 30	Nov. 15-Mar. 15
Basil	July 1-30	July 10-Aug. 10	July 20-Aug. 20	Aug. 1-30
Beans, lima	June 1-15	June 1-15	June 15-30	July 1-30
Beans, snap	June 1-July 10	June 15-July 20	July 1-30	July 1-Aug. 15
Beets	July 1-30	July 5-Aug. 15	July 15-Aug. 30	July 25-Sept. 1
Broccoli*	June 1-30	June 15-July 15	July 1-30	July 1-Aug. 15
Brussels sprouts*	July 1-25	July 5-30	July 15-Aug. 15	July 25-Aug. 20
Burnet	Aug. 15-30	Aug. 25-Sept. 10	Sept. 5-20	Sept. 15-30
Cabbage*	June 25-Aug. 5	July 5-Aug. 15	July 5-Aug. 25	July 25-Sept. 5
Cabbage, Chinese*	June 25-Aug. 5	July 5-Aug. 15	July 5-Aug. 25	July 25-Sept. 5
Caraway	Aug. 15-30	Aug. 30-Sept. 10	Sept. 10-25	Sept. 15-30
Carrots	June 5-July 10	June 10-July 20	June 25-July 30	July 5-Aug. 10
Cauliflower*	July 25-Aug. 5	Aug. 1-15	Aug. 15-25	Aug. 20-Sept. 5
Celery*	—	June 1-July 10	June 1-July 25	June 15-Aug. 1
Chard, Swiss	June 10-July 10	June 20-July 20	July 1-30	July 10-Aug. 5
Chives*				
Collards & Kale	July 10-Aug. 5	July 15-Aug. 15	Aug. 1-30	Aug. 5-Sept. 5
Coriander	Aug. 20-Sept. 5	Aug. 25-Sept. 10	Sept. 10-25	Sept. 15-30
Corn salad	July 15-Sept. 1	Aug. 15-Sept. 15	Sept. 1-Oct. 15	Sept. 15-Nov. 1
Corn, sweet	June 1-30	June 1-July 10	June 1-July 20	June 1-Aug. 1
Cucumbers	July 1-25	July 10-30	July 25-Aug. 15	Aug. 1-20
Dill	Aug. 1-15	Aug. 10-25	Aug. 20-Sept. 10	Sept. 5-20
Endive & Escarole*	June 15-Aug. 1	July 1-Aug. 15	July 15-Sept. 1	July 15-Aug. 15
Fennel	—	—	—	—
Garlic	July 15-30	July 30-Aug. 15	Aug. 1-Sept. 15	Aug. 1-Sept. 15
Horseradish	—	—	—	—
Jerusalem artichokes	Aug. 1-Sept. 30	Aug. 10-Oct. 10	Aug. 20-Oct. 20	Aug. 30-Oct. 30
Kohlrabi	July 1-30	July 15-Aug. 15	July 30-Aug. 25	Aug. 1-30
Lemon balm	Aug. 20-Sept. 5	Aug. 30-Sept. 10	Sept. 10-25	Sept. 15-Oct. 1
Lettuce, head*	June 25-July 25	July 1-30	July 15-Aug. 15	July 25-Aug. 20
Lettuce, leaf	June 25-Aug. 15	July 1-Aug. 22	July 15-Sept. 5	July 25-Sept. 10
Marjoram, sweet	—	—	—	—
Melons	—	—	—	—
Mint*	Sept. 1-15	Sept. 10-25	Sept. 25-Oct. 5	Oct. 1-15
Mustard	July 10-Aug. 20	July 15-Aug. 25	Aug. 1-Sept. 10	Aug. 5-Sept. 15
Onion plants	—	—	—	Sept. 1-30
Onion seeds	—	—	—	Sept. 1-15
Onion sets	—	—	—	Sept. 1-15
Oregano*	Aug. 20-Sept. 5	Aug. 30-Sept. 10	Sept. 10-25	Sept. 15-30
Parsley*				
Peas, English	July 10-25	July 15-30	Aug. 1-15	Aug. 1-15
Peas, Southern	June 1-15	June 1-30	June 1-July 15	July 1-20
Peppers*	—	—	—	—
Potatoes, Irish	—	June 10-July 15	June 25-Aug. 1	July 5-Aug. 5
Pumpkins	—	June 10-July 10	June 25-July 25	July 1-30
Radishes				
(spring)	Aug. 20-Sept. 5	Aug. 25-Sept. 10	Sept. 5-20	Sept. 20-30
(summer)	July 25-Aug. 20	Aug. 1-30	Aug. 15-Sept. 10	Aug. 20-Sept. 15
(winter)	Aug. 1-Sept. 5	Aug. 10-Sept. 10	Aug. 20-Sept. 25	Aug. 30-Oct. 1
Rhubarb*	Sept. 25-Oct. 30	Oct. 5-Nov. 10	Oct. 15-Nov. 20	Oct. 25-Nov. 30
Rosemary*	Aug. 20-Sept. 5	Aug. 25-Sept. 10	Sept. 10-25	Sept. 15-30
Rutabagas	July 1-15	July 1-30	July 1-30	July 1-30
Sage	Aug. 5-20	Aug. 15-30	Aug. 25-Sept. 10	Sept. 5-20
Salsify	June 1-15	June 5-20	June 15-30	June 25-July 10
Savory, winter	Aug. 20-Sept. 5	Sept. 1-10	Sept. 10-25	Sept. 15-Oct. 1
Sorrel	Aug. 20-Sept. 5	Sept. 1-10	Sept. 10-25	Sept. 15-Oct. 1
Spinach	Aug. 1-30	Aug. 15-Sept. 10	Aug. 25-Sept. 25	Sept. 1-30
Squash, summer	June 25-July 20	July 1-25	July 15-Aug. 5	July 25-Aug. 15
Squash, winter	—	June 10-July 10	June 25-July 25	July 1-30
Tarragon*	Aug. 20-Sept. 5	Aug. 25-Sept. 10	Sept. 10-25	Sept. 15-30
Thyme*	Aug. 20-Sept. 5	Aug. 30-Sept. 10	Sept. 10-25	Sept. 15-Oct. 1
Tomatoes*	June 5-25	June 10-July 5	June 25-July 25	July 1-30
Turnips	June 25-Aug. 20	July 10-Aug. 25	July 15-Sept. 10	July 25-Sept. 20

*Started from transplants.

Latest Dates and Range of Dates for Fall Planting of Vegetables and Herbs Outdoors

If the average date of the first frost in your area is				
Nov. 10	Nov. 20	Nov. 30	Dec. 10	Dec. 20
then the best times to plant are				
Nov. 30-Mar. 1	Dec. 1-30	—	—	—
Aug. 10-30	Aug. 20-Sept. 5	Aug. 25-Sept. 10	Sept. 10-25	Sept. 20-Oct. 5
July 1-Aug. 15	July 15-Sept. 1	Aug. 1-Sept. 15	Sept. 1-30	Sept. 1-30
July 1-Sept. 1	July 1-Sept. 10	Aug. 15-Sept. 20	Sept. 1-30	Sept. 1-Nov. 1
Aug. 10-Sept. 20	Aug. 5-Sept. 15	Aug. 15-Sept. 25	Aug. 25-Oct. 10	Sept. 5-Oct. 15
Aug. 1-30	Aug. 1-Sept. 15	Aug. 1-Oct. 1	Aug. 1-Nov. 1	Sept. 1-Nov. 1
Aug. 5-Sept. 5	Aug. 5-Sept. 10	Aug. 20-Sept. 20	Sept. 1-Oct. 1	Sept. 10-Oct. 10
Sept. 25-Oct. 10	Sept. 25-Oct. 20	Oct. 1-30	Oct. 15-Nov. 15	Nov. 1-30
Aug. 5-Sept. 20	Aug. 15-Sept. 25	Aug. 20-Oct. 1	Sept. 5-Oct. 15	Sept. 10-Oct. 20
Aug. 5-Sept. 20	Aug. 15-Sept. 25	Aug. 20-Oct. 1	Sept. 5-Oct. 15	Sept. 10-Oct. 20
Sept. 30-Oct. 10	Oct. 10-25	Oct. 15-30	Nov. 1-15	Nov. 5-20
July 15-Aug. 20	Aug. 5-Oct. 1	Aug. 15-Oct. 10	Aug. 25-Oct. 25	Sept. 5-Nov. 1
Sept. 1-15	Sept. 10-25	Sept. 20-30	Oct. 1-15	Oct. 10-25
July 1-Aug. 10	July 10-Aug. 20	July 15-Aug. 30	Aug. 1-Sept. 5	Aug. 5-Sept. 20
July 25-Aug. 20	Aug. 1-30	Aug. 5-Sept. 5	Aug. 20-Sept. 20	Sept. 1-30
—	Oct. 1-30	Oct. 1-30	Nov. 1-30	Nov. 1-30
Aug. 10-Sept. 10	Aug. 25-Sept. 25	Sept. 1-30	Sept. 15-Oct. 15	Sept. 25-Oct. 25
Oct. 1-15	Oct. 10-25	Oct. 15-30	Nov. 1-15	Nov. 5-20
Oct. 1-Dec. 1	Oct. 1-Dec. 30	Oct. 1-Dec. 30	Oct. 1-Dec. 30	Oct. 1-Dec. 30
June 1-Aug. 15	June 1-Sept. 1	Aug. 1-30	Aug. 1-Sept. 30	—
Aug. 15-30	Aug. 20-Sept. 10	Aug. 30-Sept. 20	Sept. 10-Sept. 30	Sept. 20-Oct. 10
Sept. 15-30	Sept. 25-Oct. 10	Oct. 5-15	Oct. 15-30	Oct. 25-Nov. 5
Aug. 1-30	Sept. 1-30	Sept. 1-Nov. 15	Sept. 1-Dec. 31	Sept. 1-Dec. 31
—	Oct. 1-30	Oct. 1-30	Nov. 1-30	Nov. 1-30
Aug. 1-Oct. 1	Aug. 15-Oct. 1	Oct. 1-30	Oct. 1-30	Oct. 1-30
—	—	—	—	—
Sept. 10-Nov. 10	Sept. 20-Nov. 20	Sept. 30-Nov. 30	Nov. 10-Dec. 10	Nov. 20-Dec. 20
Aug. 20-Sept. 20	Sept. 1-30	Oct. 1-Nov. 30	Oct. 1-Nov. 30	Nov. 1-Dec. 10
Oct. 1-15	Oct. 10-25	Oct. 15-30	Nov. 1-15	Nov. 5-20
Aug. 5-30	Aug. 15-Sept. 30	Aug. 20-Sept. 30	Sept. 1-Nov. 30	Sept. 1-Nov. 30
Aug. 5-Sept. 25	Aug. 15-Sept. 30	Aug. 20-Sept. 30	Sept. 1-Nov. 30	Sept. 1-Nov. 30
—	Oct. 1-30	Oct. 1-30	Nov. 1-30	Nov. 1-30
—	July 1-30	July 1-Aug. 30	Aug. 1-30	Aug. 1-30
Oct. 15-30	Oct. 1-30	Oct. 1-30	Nov. 1-30	Nov. 1-30
Aug. 20-Oct. 1	Aug. 30-Sept. 30	Sept. 5-Oct. 15	Sept. 20-Nov. 1	Sept. 25-Nov. 5
Sept. 15-Oct. 15	Sept. 25-Oct. 20	Oct. 1-30	Oct. 15-Nov. 15	Oct. 25-Nov. 20
Sept. 15-30	Sept. 25-Oct. 10	Oct. 1-15	Oct. 15-30	Oct. 25-Nov. 5
Sept. 15-30	Sept. 25-Oct. 10	Oct. 1-15	Oct. 15-30	Oct. 25-Nov. 5
Oct. 1-15	Oct. 10-25	Oct. 15-30	Nov. 1-15	Nov. 5-20
—	Sept. 1-Dec. 30	Sept. 1-Dec. 30	Sept. 1-Dec. 30	Sept. 1-Dec. 30
Aug. 15-30	Aug. 25-Sept. 10	Sept. 5-20	Sept. 15-30	Sept. 25-Oct. 10
July 1-30	July 1-Aug. 10	July 1-Aug. 10	July 1-Sept. 30	July 1-Sept. 30
July 1-30	July 15-Aug. 15	July 15-Aug. 30	Aug. 1-30	Aug. 1-30
July 15-Aug. 20	July 25-Aug. 25	Aug. 1-Sept. 5	Aug. 15-Sept. 20	Aug. 20-Sept. 25
July 15-Aug. 15	July 25-Aug. 20	Aug. 1-30	Aug. 15-Sept. 10	Aug. 20-Sept. 20
Oct. 1-Oct. 15	Oct. 10-25	Oct. 15-30	Nov. 1-15	Oct. 10-20
Sept. 1-Oct. 1	Sept. 10-Oct. 10	Sept. 20-Oct. 15	Oct. 1-Nov. 1	Oct. 10-Nov. 5
Sept. 10-Oct. 15	Sept. 20-Oct. 25	Sept. 25-Nov. 1	Oct. 10-Nov. 15	Oct. 15-Nov. 20
Nov. 5-Dec. 10	Nov. 15-Dec. 20	Nov. 1-30	Nov. 1-30	Nov. 1-30
Oct. 1-15	Oct. 10-25	Oct. 15-30	Nov. 1-15	Nov. 5-20
July 1-Aug. 31	Aug. 1-30	Aug. 1-Sept. 15	Aug. 15-Sept. 15	Aug. 15-Sept. 15
Sept. 15-30	Sept. 25-Oct. 10	Oct. 1-15	Oct. 15-30	Oct. 25-Nov. 5
July 10-25	July 15-30	July 25-Aug. 5	Aug. 5-20	Aug. 15-25
Oct. 1-15	Oct. 10-25	Oct. 15-30	Nov. 1-15	Nov. 5-20
Oct. 1-15	Oct. 10-25	Oct. 15-30	Nov. 1-15	Nov. 5-20
Sept. 15-Oct. 15	Sept. 25-Oct. 25	Oct. 1-30	Oct. 15-Nov. 10	Oct. 25-Nov. 20
Aug. 5-25	Aug. 15-Sept. 5	Aug. 20-Sept. 10	Sept. 5-25	Sept. 10-30
July 15-Aug. 15	July 25-Aug. 20	Aug. 1-30	Aug. 15-Sept. 10	Aug. 20-Sept. 20
Oct. 1-15	Oct. 10-25	Oct. 15-30	Nov. 1-15	Nov. 5-20
Oct. 1-15	Oct. 10-25	Oct. 15-Nov. 1	Nov. 1-15	Nov. 5-20
July 15-Aug. 5	July 25-Aug. 15	Aug. 1-20	Aug. 15-Sept. 5	Aug. 20-Sept. 10
Aug. 5-Oct. 1	Aug. 15-Oct. 10	Aug. 20-Oct. 15	Sept. 5-Nov. 1	Sept. 10-Nov. 5

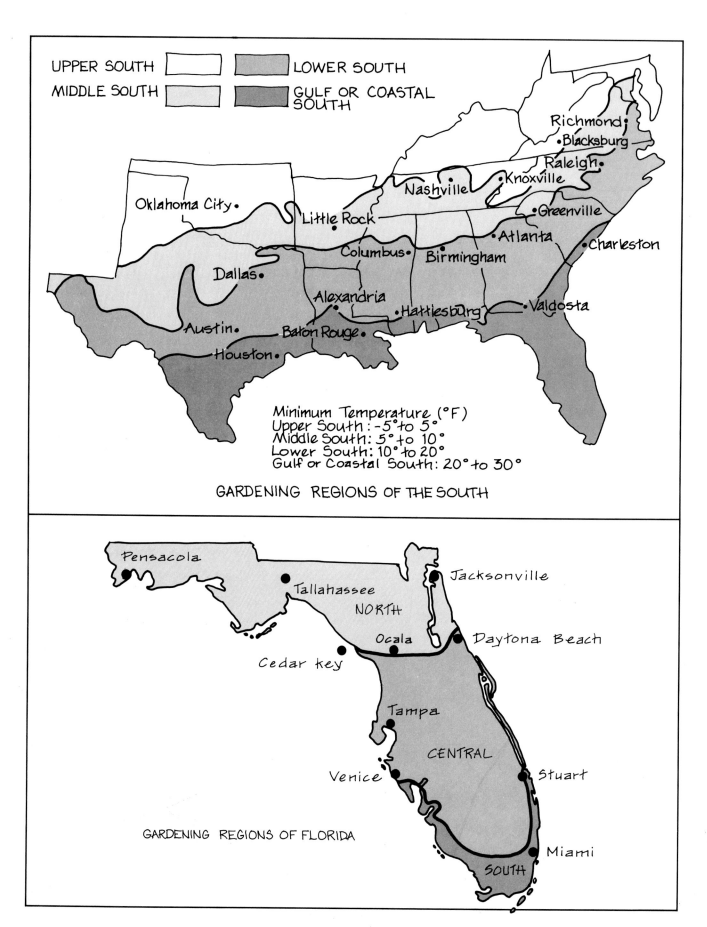

UPPER SOUTH ☐   ▨ LOWER SOUTH

MIDDLE SOUTH ☐   ▨ GULF OR COASTAL SOUTH

Richmond
Blacksburg
Raleigh
Oklahoma City
Nashville
Knoxville
Little Rock
Greenville
Atlanta
Columbus
Birmingham
Charleston
Dallas
Alexandria
Austin
Hattiesburg
Valdosta
Baton Rouge
Houston

Minimum Temperature (°F)
Upper South: -5° to 5°
Middle South: 5° to 10°
Lower South: 10° to 20°
Gulf or Coastal South: 20° to 30°

GARDENING REGIONS OF THE SOUTH

Pensacola
Tallahassee
Jacksonville
NORTH
Ocala
Daytona Beach
Cedar key
Tampa
CENTRAL
Venice
Stuart
Miami
GARDENING REGIONS OF FLORIDA
SOUTH

Cole crops nearing maturity.

Corn beginning to tassel.

Harvesting squash from an early planting.

Late-fall cole crops ready for harvest.

Maintenance

A high-yielding garden is the result of ongoing care—fertilizing, watering, and weeding keep it growing and producing. With the right information and some experience, you can get maximum results with a minimum of effort—and enjoy doing it.

Choosing a Fertilizer

Fertilizers cost money, so you want to get the best buy. But the cheapest is not always the most economical. To buy wisely, you need to know what to look for in a fertilizer.

By law, the contents of every fertilizer must be listed in a guaranteed analysis. The sample fertilizer tag (*on page 82*) will help you interpret the information in the analysis, so that you can choose the fertilizer best suited to your needs. This label is a composite of various fertilizer analyses that you might actually find available. Each line is designated by a number and explained below:

1. Brand name.
2. This is the fertilizer grade. The three numbers represent the percentages of nitrogen, phosphorus, and potassium a fertilizer contains, in that order. Nitrogen is the first element to consider, because it is required in the largest quantity for growth. (You will see in line 4 that it is not only the amount but also the type of nitrogen that is important.)

Phosphorus is important for good root development and all stages of plant growth. If your soil test indicates excessive phosphorus, look for a fertilizer with a low middle number, such as 10-5-10. Since phosphorus tends to accumulate in the soil, excessive application results in undesirably high levels.

Potassium is also essential to the overall vigor of plants, although all of its specific functions are unclear. Some plants require as much of this element as they do nitrogen, so look for a formulation with nearly equal percentages of the two. It is especially important to add potassium in areas with sandy soils, which lose nutrients quickly through leaching.

3. The guaranteed analysis lists the materials in the fertilizer and the percentage of each.
4. This is the breakdown of all the types of nitrogen in the fertilizer. Nitrate nitrogen (line 4a) is a form of nitrogen that is available to plants quickly. However, it is not held by soil particles, so it leaches out with irrigation and rain. A small amount of nitrate nitrogen in a fertilizer is good, but if there is a high percentage, most will be washed away faster than the plants can use it.

Ammoniacal nitrogen (line 4b) is held by soil particles but is converted to nitrate nitrogen by soil bacteria. In warm soil (above 50 degrees) this occurs very quickly, so it too is available almost immediately. If a fertilizer is composed mostly of ammoniacal nitrogen, much of it may leach from the soil faster than plants can use it. Look for a low percentage.

Urea (line 4c) is a concentrated source of nitrogen that becomes available almost as quickly as ammoniacal nitrogen. In warm, moist soil, bacteria may break it down into ammoniacal nitrogen in only one or two days; then it breaks down further into nitrate nitrogen. But urea can be coated (line 4d) to slow its release into the soil. If you want your fertilizer to last more than two to three weeks, look for one that contains a relatively high percentage of a slower-release form of nitrogen, such as coated urea.

Water-insoluble nitrogen (4e) is a slow-release fertilizer that must be broken down by nature into soluble sources in order to become available to plants. However, depending on the materials, an insoluble nitrogen may not be available for months, so look for a vegetable garden fertilizer with a relatively low percentage.

5. Available phosphoric acid is the fertilizer industry's term for the percentage of phosphorus (P_2O_5) in the fertilizer that is available to plants.

6. Soluble potash (K_2O) is the industry's term for the percentage of potassium in the fertilizer available to plants. Before the development of modern fertilizer manufacturing methods, potassium fertilizer was produced by burning wood and plant residues in pots. This left an ash high in potassium, thus the name potash.

7. In addition to nitrogen, phosphorus, and potassium (called the primary nutrients), plants need other nutrients for growth. Calcium, magnesium, and sulfur (called secondary nutrients) are generally already present in soils. They may be ingredients in some fertilizers, however, as "tagalongs" from chemicals that supply other nutrients. They may also be added purposely for use on soils that are deficient. Unless your soil test indicates a deficiency in the secondary nutrients, there is no advantage to buying a fertilizer containing them. (Calcium and magnesium can also be supplied by liming the soil regularly. *See page 60.*)

Micronutrients include boron, chlorine, copper, iron, manganese, molybdenum, and zinc. They are needed in very small amounts for plant growth; but like other nutrients, if one of them were totally lacking, the plants would not grow. Check with your county Extension agent for

Sample Tag

1. Brand "X" Vegetable Garden Food

2. 10-10-10

3. Guaranteed analysis

4. Total nitrogen (N)   10%
   - 4a.   1% Nitrate nitrogen
   - 4b.   1.8% Ammoniacal nitrogen
   - 4c.   1% Urea nitrogen
   - 4d.   5% Coated urea nitrogen
   - 4e.   1.2% Water-insoluble nitrogen

5. Available phosphoric acid (P_2O_5)   10%

6. Soluble potash (K_2O)   10%

7. Sulfur   .5%
   Boron   .02%
   Copper   .05%
   Iron   .5%
   Manganese   .05%
   Molybdenum   .0005%
   Zinc   .05%

8. Plant nutrient sources: Ammonium Nitrate, Urea, Sulfur-Coated Urea, Diammonium Phosphate, Triple Superphosphate, Muriate of Potash, Borate, Copper Oxide, Ferrous Sulphate, Manganese Oxide, Molybdate, Zinc Oxide, Iron Oxide

9. Chlorine, not more than 10%

10. Potential acidity equivalent to 650 lbs. of calcium carbonate per ton

advice on whether soils in your area tend to be deficient in micronutrients.

8. These are the plant nutrient sources, or chemical ingredients that make up the fertilizer.

9. & 10. The percentage of chlorine (usually found on fertilizers sold in Florida) and the calcium carbonate equivalent are regulatory requirements for commercial use. They do not have a practical application in the home garden.

Sources of Nitrogen in Fertilizers

Nitrate sources of nitrogen include ammonium nitrate (NH_4NO_3), which contains about 33% nitrogen, and sodium nitrate ($NaNO_3$), which contains 16% nitrogen. Sodium nitrate or nitrate of soda may be produced synthetically, or it may be a natural product extracted from huge salt deposits in Chile.

Ammoniacal sources of nitrogen are a group of chemical compounds produced from ammonia, including ammonium nitrate (*see above*) and ammonium sulfate [$(NH_4)_2SO_4$]. Ammonium sulfate contains 20.5% nitrogen; it is produced as a by-product of the coking of coal.

Urea [$CO(NH_2)_2$] contains 45% nitrogen and is produced by reacting ammonia with carbon dioxide. Because of the form in which it is marketed, it is not actually an ammonium fertilizer; but it decomposes quickly in the soil to form ammonium. Ammonium may be held by the soil until it is converted into nitrate nitrogen by soil bacteria. However, if you apply urea to bare, moist soil, much of the ammonia may be reduced to ammonia gas, which can be lost through evaporation. Therefore, be sure to work the fertilizer into the soil.

Water-insoluble sources of nitrogen may consist of a urea-formaldehyde compound, isobutylidene diurea (IBDU), or natural organic materials such as sludge, tankage, and manure.

Additional Fertilizer Sources

Fertilizers like the one represented by the sample tag are called complete fertilizers because they supply the three primary nutrients, nitrogen, phosphorus, and potassium. There are also fertilizers that supply only one or two nutrients for more specific uses. Here are a few of the most common ones.

Ammonium nitrate, ammonium sulfate, and nitrate of soda (*see above*) are used to give plants a quick boost. If overapplied, however, they can burn plants. Do not use nitrate of soda on soils with high levels of sodium.

Superphosphate is a source of phosphorus to use when a soil test indicates a deficiency.

Gypsum is used to supply calcium in areas where adding lime is not recommended because the pH is high enough. It is also used to help remove sodium from heavy "gumbo" soils in Texas. The calcium binds chemically with the sodium, then washes from the soil.

Magnesium sulfate or Epsom salts are used to correct a magnesium deficiency, such as may be found in the sandy soils in Florida. These materials are useful when the soil pH prohibits the use of dolomitic limestone.

Iron is often sold in a liquid form to apply to deficient soils. Chelated iron is a special form that does not bind with other elements in the soil, and therefore remains available to plants.

Borax, the laundry detergent, may be used to supply boron if the soil is deficient. A possible indication of boron deficiency is brown or hollow cores in turnips. Dissolve borax in water and apply it over the soil, using ⅛ pound in 5 gallons of water per 1000 square feet. Use your watering can or a sprayer to apply. Be extremely careful not to apply too much borax, because the range between deficiency and toxicity is quite narrow. Prepare the whole solution at one time in a large container to assure the proper dilution.

Organic Fertilizers

Unlike commercial fertilizers, which are chemical formulations, organic fertilizers are natural substances such as bone meal and manure. They release nutrients slowly; cow manure also provides enough organic matter to improve soil structure. Since many organic fertilizers are significantly lower in plant nutrients than commercial fertilizers, you must apply larger quantities.

The table below lists six common organic fertilizer sources and their approximate nutrient content. Remember that wood ashes are alkaline, so you will need to reduce the amount of lime you add to the soil by ¼ to ½.

Common Organic Fertilizers	Percent of Nitrogen	Percent of Phosphorus	Percent of Potassium
Blood meal	13-15	1.3-2	.7
Bone meal	1-4	15-22	.2
Cottonseed meal	6-7	2.5-3	.5-1.5
Cow manure	0.6-2	.2-1.1	.35
Dry poultry manure	2-4	4.5-6	1.2-2.4
Wood ashes	—	1-2	3-10

How to Apply Fertilizer

Work organic fertilizers into the soil at least two weeks before planting. To make later applications during the season, top-dress with the material, spreading it on top of the soil around the plants like a mulch. If you have room to work, you can scratch it into the soil lightly.

Make the first application of a chemical fertilizer at planting time, working it into the soil. Later in the season, apply the fertilizer as a side-dressing, spreading it close enough to plants so that roots can take it up, but not close enough to burn them. (*See Figs. 1,2.*) For large plants, place the fertilizer out as far as the outer leaves, or drip line, of the plant. If you apply the fertilizer to the surface of the soil, be sure to water the fertilizer into the ground after applying. Or make a furrow along the row, sprinkle in the fertilizer, and cover with soil.

In wide rows solidly covered with growth, the practical method is to broadcast the fertilizer across the row. It is impossible to keep the fertilizer from falling on the plants, so be sure to water until the particles are washed to the ground. Otherwise the foliage may be burned.

One way to apply a side-dressing of fertilizer is to dig a furrow along the row just beyond the drip line of the plants. This puts the fertilizer at the root zone.

Fig. 1. *To side-dress a row, spread fertilizer about 6 inches away from the base of the plants. Scratch it into the soil, being careful not to go too deep. If fertilizer containing urea stays on the surface, the nitrogen can be lost through evaporation.*

Fig. 2. *To side-dress individual plants, make a shallow depression around the plant under the drip line of the leaves. Sprinkle the fertilizer in the depression at the recommended rate and water into the soil.*

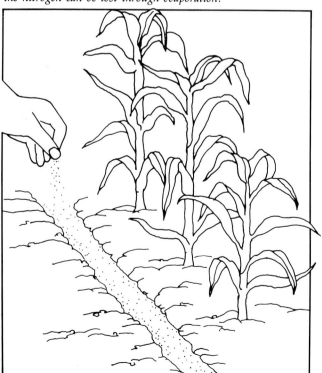

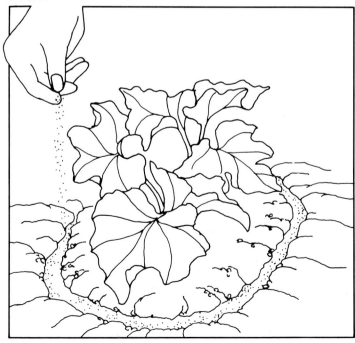

Watering the Garden

Regular watering is important. But how much and how often to water depend on the vegetable or herb, soil type, weather, temperature, whether mulch is used, and other factors.

As a general rule, the garden should receive 1 inch of water per week, either by rain or irrigation. In hot weather, plants need more water. (An additional ½ inch is usually required for each 10 degrees that the temperature averages above 60. The average temperature is the sum of the daytime high and nighttime low divided by 2.) Sandy soil requires watering more often than clay soil. And newly seeded rows or beds may need about ½ inch every one or two days until the seeds germinate and the seedlings sink their roots. The best way to determine when to water is by feeling the soil about 2 inches deep; it should be cool and moist. Also, observe the plants in your garden. Tomatoes and squash, for example, may wilt at midday in summer because they lose moisture faster than their roots can take it up. If they do not recover by late afternoon, they need water.

The most important point to remember about watering is that one thorough watering is better than several light sprinklings. Shallow watering encourages shallow rooting, because roots remain near the surface where the water is. Deep watering encourages downward root growth, and the deeper soil stays moist longer.

Watering is critical at certain times in the development of most vegetables and some herbs. If they are subjected to drought at these times, their production will be hurt.

Critical Times for Watering	
Asparagus	After harvest is over, when ferny growth is developing
Beans	Flowering, pod enlargement
English peas	Flowering, pod enlargement
Broccoli	Head development
Cabbage	Head development
Cauliflower	Head development
Carrot	Root enlargement
Salsify	Root enlargement
Turnip	Root enlargement
Potatoes, Sweet	Root enlargement
Garlic	Bulb enlargement
Onion	Bulb enlargement
Potatoes, Irish	Tuber enlargement
Corn	Silking, tasselling, ear development
Cucumber	Flowering and fruit development
Squash	Flowering and fruit development
Melon	Fruit set and early development
Eggplant	From flowering until harvest
Peppers	From flowering until harvest
Tomatoes	From flowering until harvest
Basil	Through all stages
Celery	Through all stages
Leeks	Through all stages
Parsley	Through all stages
Spinach	Through all stages

Weeding

Weeds can ruin a garden, robbing plants of moisture and nutrients. They also crowd plants, sometimes to the point of choking them out. Young plants of some vegetables, such as onions and carrots, cannot compete.

The best way to control weeds is to eliminate them as they appear. If you wait until they are large, removing them is more difficult and can disturb the roots of vegetables and herbs.

Pull weeds by hand when they are in tight places and close to plants. In open areas, you can use a small hand cultivator, bow rake, or scuffle hoe (a stirruplike tool that cuts through the soil beneath the weed) to uproot them. Do

To determine how long to run the sprinkler to supply 1 inch of water, place cans or other waterproof containers at equal distances within the sprinkler's area of coverage. Turn the water on at the pressure normally used, and note how much time is needed to fill the containers with 1 inch of water.

not cultivate deeper than 1 inch to avoid disturbing plant roots and turning up more weed seeds.

In large gardens, a tiller may be used between beds or rows occasionally. Do not till every time weeds appear, however, or you may eventually break down the soil's structure.

One of the best ways to prevent weeds from coming up is by mulching. Mulch blocks sunlight from the soil so that weed seeds do not germinate. To be effective, most mulches should be at least 3 inches thick.

Mulch Reduces Maintenance

Mulching is probably the greatest laborsaving technique available to gardeners. The benefits provided by a 3-inch layer of organic mulch include:

—conserving moisture by reducing the drying effects of the sun on bare soil

—discouraging weed growth and minimizing soil erosion

—insulating the soil against temperature extremes, keeping it cooler in summer and warmer in winter; root crops stored in the ground are protected from alternate freezing and thawing with a layer of mulch

—helping keep plants clean by preventing soil from spattering them during rain or irrigation. This is important in helping to prevent many soilborne diseases.

An organic mulch discourages weeds and slows the loss of moisture from the soil by evaporation. It also protects the soil against temperature extremes.

How to Apply Mulch

Young plants should be about 6 inches tall before you mulch. Spread the materials around the plants, being careful not to bury them. For small plants such as lettuce and spinach, lay the mulch down first, then brush it aside to set out plants or sow seeds. As the plants grow, push the mulch back around them. Delay mulching warm season vegetables set out in early spring until the soil has warmed up (usually three to five weeks after planting). Otherwise the soil will stay cool longer and growth will be slowed.

Mulching Materials

Organic mulches are easy to find and may even be available free for the collecting. Here are a few materials commonly available.

Compost: In addition to its use as a soil amendment, compost is also an excellent mulch. As the compost continues to break down, it improves soil texture, adds nutrients to the soil, and encourages earthworms, whose tunneling improves soil aeration.

Leaves: Shredded leaves are a good mulch. Chopped leaves are better than whole leaves because they do not wash or blow away or mat down as easily. Whole leaves of oak, birch, and sycamore do not mat as badly as maple, beech, poplar, and elm leaves. Leaf mold is also an excellent mulching material.

Pine straw: This is one of the best garden mulches. Pine needles are usually weed free, do not wash or blow away easily, and decompose slowly. If you do not have access to pines for raking the needles, you can buy bales of pine straw. One bale will mulch about 50 square feet when applied 3 inches thick.

Straw: Wheat, rye, and oat straw are readily available over much of the Upper South. Presprout weed seeds as described under hay.

Seaweed: Provided you wash it to remove some of the salt and chop it so it will lie smoothly, you can use seaweed as a mulch.

Sawdust: A layer of fresh or rotted sawdust, 1 to 2 inches deep, is an effective mulch. You will need about 8 bushels to cover a 100-square-foot area 1 inch deep. Do not use sawdust from lumber that has been chemically treated. Because sawdust requires a lot of nitrogen as it decomposes, double the amount of fertilizer you apply to vegetables through the seasons.

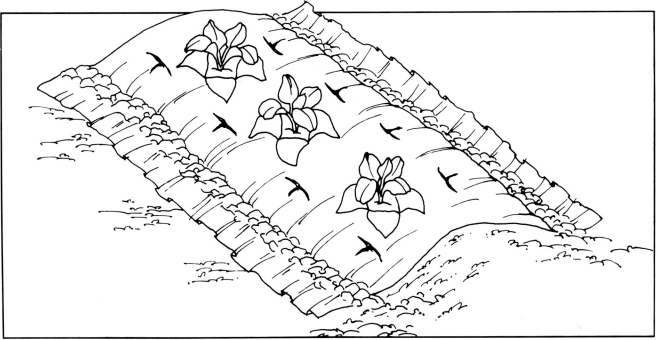

Black plastic mulch allows you to plant warm-weather vegetables a little earlier in spring because the soil underneath warms faster. Anchor the sides of plastic with soil and cut slits to set plants in place. Cut T-shaped slits to let water penetrate.

Hay: Spoiled hay (not rotting but no longer good for feed) may be available from farms, or small bales of hay may be purchased from a local farm supply store. Hay may introduce unwanted grass or weed seeds into the garden; to prevent this, you can presprout the seeds by sprinkling the hay to keep it moist for 2 to 3 weeks before you put it in the garden. Because it is so loose and light, apply hay 4 to 6 inches deep. If it has been sitting in a field, check it for fire ants, as they sometimes nest under the bales.

Although inorganic mulches are not as desirable, they may also be used.

Newspaper: Mulching paths with several layers of newsprint helps prevent weeds. Use only black and white pages, not those with colored ink. Cover the paper with the same materials with which you mulch the vegetables or herbs to keep the garden looking neat. Mulching the herbs or vegetables themselves with newspaper is not recommended. It does not allow water and fertilizer to penetrate easily and letting it decay into the soil consumes nitrogen.

Black plastic: Black plastic sheets can be used in early spring to mulch the soil around squash and other vegetables that require warm soil. The temperature under the plastic is 5 to 10 degrees warmer than exposed soil. Remove the plastic or cover it with another mulch as the weather warms; otherwise the soil underneath could get too hot as the sun shines directly on the plastic. Black plastic is available in sheets, or you can cut and unfold garbage bags. Shovel soil over the edges of the plastic to hold it in place. Sow seeds or set plants through holes cut into the sheets, and be sure the ground is watered before you cover it with the plastic. To let water penetrate during the season, cut T-shaped slits.

Structures

Your trellises, compost bin, and cold frame can be simple and temporary or they can be permanent structures in the garden. In either case, there are certain basic requirements the structures should meet to make sure they do the job you intend them to do.

Supports

Every gardener has his own method of trellising or staking vegetables such as tomatoes, beans, cucumbers, and English peas. The examples on these pages show some of the materials and methods you can use. Adapt them to your own garden or let them inspire you to devise your own way of training vegetables to grow vertically. Remember that the structure must be sturdy so that it does not fall over under the weight of the plants. Here are some types:

A-frame

An A-frame trellis is often used for beans and English peas. Cucumbers and tomatoes may be trained on them as well. The legs of the A should be about 8 feet long so the frame will be tall enough for long vines. A base 2 to 3 feet wide is adequately sturdy; making the base much wider than this wastes garden space.

Build the A-frame from 1 × 2 lumber or strong bamboo poles. Sink the legs 12 inches into the soil for a steady footing and space the A's 6 feet apart to keep the top crossbar from sagging. For extra support, place crossbars a few inches from the ground and along the middle of the frame as

well as at the apex of the A. Bolt them together, or tie securely with nylon cord. (Jute or cotton twine can stretch or eventually rot, gradually weakening the support.) Guy wires running from the apex of the A to the ground at both ends of the trellis will keep the frame from falling to the side. When tripods are used as the base, guy wires are not necessary.

Heavy bamboo poles create the frame of this vertical trellis. Lighter canes poked into the ground and wired to the top of the frame will support pole beans.

Vertical frames

Vertical frames require less space than A-frames and can be used to support cucumbers, beans, English peas, and tomatoes. For the frame, use 4 × 4 lumber, sturdy treated posts, or even iron pipes, spaced 6 to 8 feet apart. Use a posthole digger to sink the posts at least 18 to 24 inches into the ground. Depending on the vegetable to be grown on the support, staple chicken wire or fencing wire to the frame; or you can use nylon mesh netting. If possible, orient the frame so that it is parallel to the prevailing wind.

Tripods

Tripods are 3-legged teepees whose design is inherently stable. Under normal use, they will not topple. Quadripods (4-legged teepees) are equally sturdy and make more efficient use of space, providing another leg for plants to climb on. Tripods and quadripods work best for beans as the vines can run up the support and cascade down when they reach the top. Allow two to three vines to climb each leg.

Construct this type of support with lengths of lumber, bamboo, or other poles at least 8 feet long. Tie them together at the top with strong nylon cord, and sink legs into the ground a few inches for added sturdiness.

A vertical trellis makes the most efficient use of garden space. Even cucumbers can be trained to such a trellis if it is sturdy enough. This one is made of metal posts with wire mesh; a bamboo pole provides support for the mesh at the top.

An A-frame trellis is used for English peas, pole beans, cucumbers, and tomatoes. Guy wires and crossbars will help hold it steady.

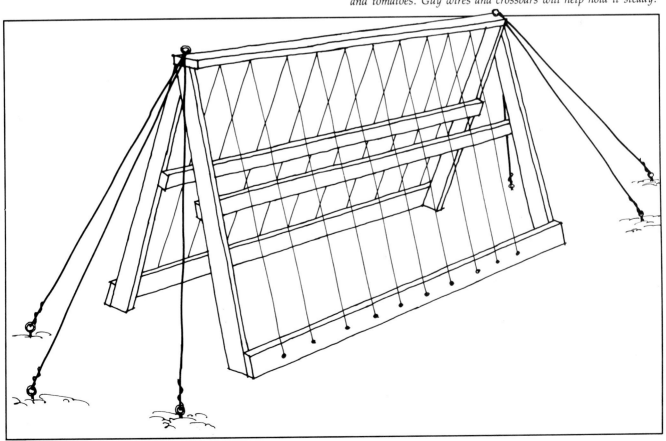

Peppers often need staking, because they can fall over under the weight of the fruit, wet foliage, and wind in a summer thunderstorm. Lightweight plastic pipe firmly anchored into the soil should provide enough support.

Use small cages to support bush-type tomato selections.

Stakes

Tomatoes are often supported by a single stake to which you tie the plant as it grows. This requires pruning the plant to a single or double stem. (*See page 203.*) Peppers and eggplants should also be staked as they can fall over when loaded with fruit.

Stakes can be made of 1 × 2 or 2 × 2 lumber, but even pieces of PVC pipe or steel rods work well for low-growing plants such as peppers. There are also commercially available plastic-coated metal stakes that are especially designed for staking vegetables. For vining tomato selections which grow 6 feet tall or more, use stakes 8 feet long.

Drive the stakes in at planting time or shortly after to avoid disturbing established roots. Place the stake about 3 inches from the plant and use a mallet or heavy hammer to drive it one-quarter of its length into the ground.

Cages

Tomatoes and cucumbers are easy to grow in cages. You do not need to prune or train caged tomatoes, and cucumbers are easy to harvest because the fruit hangs down in full view. Just be sure to buy a cage that is tall enough to accommodate the vegetable selection you are growing.

You can make your own cage from wire the same way you construct a compost bin from wire. (*See next page.*) Be sure to use 4 × 6 wire mesh or larger so that you reach into the cage to harvest. The cage should be 4 to 6 feet tall and 2 to 2½ feet in diameter to support tall-growing tomato selections. To anchor the cage, wire it to a stake; or weave a stake through the mesh and drive the stake into the ground. You can also bury the base of the cage about 6 inches deep.

Compost Bins

For a garden that is in open view, you will want an attractive compost bin. If the bin is out of sight, however, a simple wire structure may be all you need.

The compost bin should be 3 to 6 feet tall and at least 3 to 5 feet in diameter. The 2-section bin shown here allows for the air circulation needed to speed the decay process. As you use the compost in one section, fill the other to maintain a continuous supply. When the first bin is empty and you are ready to use materials in the second bin, begin dumping undecomposed matter into the empty bin and start the cycle over again.

Some gardeners prefer a 3-section bin; one section is filled with the freshest, undecomposed materials, one with compost in the process of decomposing, and a third with compost ready to use. In this case, adapt the 2-section bin to build 3 bins.

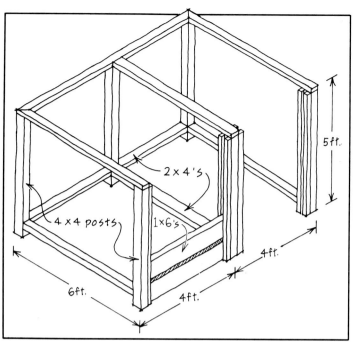

Plan for 2-section compost bin.

Staple 2- x 4-inch welded wire fencing to the frame and inner divider. This provides the air circulation organic materials need to decompose.

Building a 2-section bin

Set 4 × 4 posts in two rows, with three posts in each row. Space the rows 6 feet apart, squarely in line with each other. In each row, space the posts 4 feet apart. Dig postholes about 30 inches deep and pour a few inches of gravel into each hole. Set the post at least 24 inches deep in the hole, then fill in with more gravel and soil. Be sure the post is vertical while you compact this footing. After the posts are in place, cut them to a uniform height of 5 feet.

Next attach 2 × 4s on top of the posts and about 4 inches above the ground. Join the top corner boards with miter joints. Butt and toenail all others in place, using twelvepenny galvanized nails. Leave the front of the bin open. (*See sketch.*)

Wrap the frame with 5-foot-high 2 × 4-inch welded wire fencing. Fasten the fencing tightly in place with galvanized wire staples. Also fence the inner divider. For added support and a neater appearance, attach 1 × 6s around the entire top of the bin, including the front. Also center 1 × 6s across the back and sides.

Your compost bin can be a simple and inexpensive cage made from a 12½-foot section of welded wire fencing. You need 2 x 4 mesh 5 feet high. Simply join at the ends to form a cylinder.

At the front openings, attach 2 × 2s to facing sides of the posts to create a groove for 1 × 6s to slide into and stack. The inner 2 × 2 may have to overhang the inside edge of the post slightly to create a groove at least ¾ inch wide so that the 1 × 6s can slide freely in the track. Cut the 1 × 6s to fit between the posts. You will need about nine panels per section.

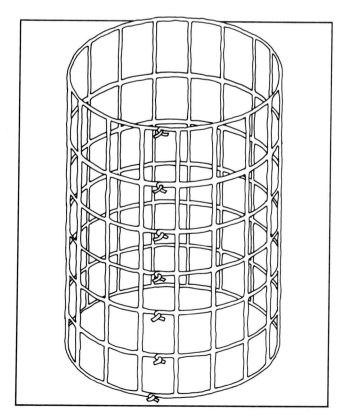

Cold Frames

One of the most useful items a gardener can have is a cold frame. A bottomless box covered with plastic, glass, or other transparent material, a cold frame functions like a minigreenhouse. It is particularly useful for hardening off transplants started indoors, or for starting transplants in late winter and early spring. You can also extend the season by growing the less hardy cool weather crops during the winter in the cold frame. And in areas where winters are severe, you can overwinter tender herbs such as bay, pineapple sage, and rosemary.

You can purchase a ready-made cold frame, or design and build your own. If you build a cold frame, be sure to use wood that is pressure-treated for ground contact or that is rot resistant.

Cold frames are usually about 3 × 5 feet, but you can make yours smaller or larger, depending on the space you have available. It should be about 10 inches deep at the front to allow room for transplants under the closed lid, and 20 inches deep at the back; this angles the lid properly to let in the most sunlight and let rain run off. One way to build your own is to use 2 × 10s for the sides, front, and back. (*See sketch.*) The lid

should be lightweight, built with 1 × 2s or 1 × 4s. Choose hinges large enough to support the weight of the lid. If you use clear, 4-mil or 6-mil polyethylene for the cover, you can staple it to the wood, but be sure to leave some slack. Cold weather causes shrinkage and if the plastic is fastened too tightly, it will tear. You may need to run one or two thin wooden slats or strands of wire across the lid under the plastic to keep it from sagging and collecting water.

Place the cold frame facing south so that it receives the most sunlight. On mild, sunny

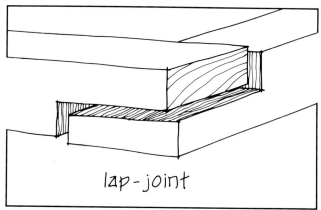

Cold frame top detail.

Cold frame.

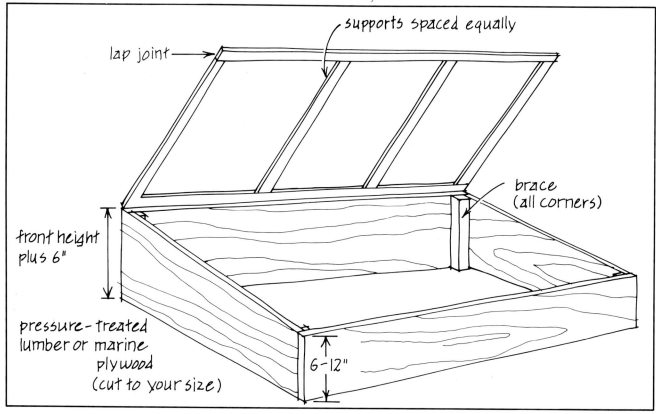

Be sure to water plants in the cold frame regularly, because they are shielded from rain.

days, you will need to open the lid for ventilation. Otherwise the temperature inside can quickly become hot enough to damage or even kill the plants. Late in the afternoon, lower the lid to trap heat and protect the plants from low nighttime temperatures.

Having to open and close the lid requires trips to the cold frame in the morning and afternoon. You can eliminate this chore, however, by using an automatic ventilator. It operates on a thermal principle, raising the lid when the temperature in the cold frame reaches 72 degrees and lowering it when the temperature falls to 68 degrees. The ventilator adjusts the lid constantly, opening it from a fraction of an inch to several inches. On cold days the frame lid usually remains closed. These ventilators are offered in catalogs of some of the major seed companies, or you can order them from the manufacturers listed on pages 264-265.

If you install an automatic ventilator on a cold frame you build yourself, be sure to check its specifications for the weight it can lift before you build the frame lid.

Automatic ventilators work on a thermal principle, making constant adjustments in the opening of the cold frame lid according to the temperature inside. Ventilators may be installed on a cold frame you build yourself; they are also available as part of a ready-to-assemble clear acrylic cold frame like the one shown.

Pests and Diseases

Once you recognize an insect or disease, you have won half the battle in controlling it. The photos on the following pages will help you identify the most common insect and disease problems in Southern vegetable gardens. Although pesticides are often necessary to control insects and diseases already present, it is best to prevent or reduce problems before they get started. Some pests, once established, are extremely difficult to control.

What You Can Do to Reduce Insect Problems

Remove plants as soon as the crop is harvested. Otherwise, they provide a place for squash bugs, Mexican bean beetles, European corn borers, and many other insects to spend the winter. The plant debris can be a source of reinfestation in the spring when the pests emerge and begin breeding.

Another good practice is turning the soil several times in late winter, using a fork or tiller. This exposes to freezing weather insects that live in the soil over the winter, such as corn earworm and cutworm.

Some insect problems, such as sweet potato weevil and cowpea curculio, begin with the seeds or plants you use. To prevent such problems, use only certified plants or seeds.

What You Can Do to Reduce Disease Problems

The most effective disease control is also prevention. Once diseases get started, they are hard to stop. The best way to control many common diseases is to plant selections bred to be resistant to them. The second best choice is a tolerant selection; the plant may be mildly affected by the disease, but it will continue to produce.

To avoid introducing disease into the garden, buy only healthy transplants. Spotted, mottled, or blighted leaves, soft stems, or a generally sickly appearance are signs of disease.

Because viruses and certain other diseases may be transmitted in seeds, always buy seeds from a reputable source. Never save seeds from your garden if any of the plants displayed symptoms of a virus.

Rotate vegetables that are susceptible to the same diseases to a different location in the garden every season. This helps reduce the incidence of disease by keeping it from building up. For example, black rot attacks cabbage and its relatives, collards, kale, broccoli, and brussels sprouts. To control it, do not grow any of these plants on the same spot more often than every three years. The chart on pages 101-103 shows which vegetables share common diseases.

Thinning seedlings and setting transplants at the proper spacing also helps prevent disease by allowing good air circulation. This helps to keep the foliage dry. Crowded plants may remain wet from dew, rain, or irrigation long enough to allow certain diseases to develop.

If applying a fungicide at the first sign of

disease does not help control the infection, destroy the infected plants. Leaving them in the garden ensures reinfection later. Viruses cannot be treated with pesticides; remove and destroy infected plants immediately to prevent the spread of disease. Also, be sure to replace old mulch with fresh mulch every year to remove this source of reinfection.

What You Can Do to Control Nematodes

Nematodes are microscopic worms found in soils throughout the South. Signs of their presence include poor growth, wilting, and yellowing foliage. Plant roots may be stubby, galled, rough, black or discolored, or decayed. Root-knot nematodes, which are among the most common types, produce characteristic knots in the roots of plants.

Nematodes are difficult to control. If the soil is not badly infested, however, you may be able to keep them from multiplying to a serious level. Use resistant tomato selections when possible. Planting a cover crop of French marigold selections Tangerine, Petite Gold, Petite Harmony, Goldie, or Nemagold every other year can also help reduce the root-knot nematode population. Space the marigold plants 7 inches apart each way, and keep the area free of any other plant or weed that can be a host for the nematodes. Leave the marigolds in the garden for at least 90 days, then discard the plants. The area should be safe for planting the following season.

For severe infestations, you will need to sterilize the soil with a fumigant such as Vapam® several weeks before planting. Be sure to follow label directions carefully. After sterilizing the soil, take care not to bring contaminated soil into the garden from other parts of the yard. Nematodes can be spread from one area to another by infested soil that clings to pets, shoes, clothing, or tools.

Use Pesticides Wisely

Pesticides that control fungus diseases are categorically called fungicides. Those that control insects are called insecticides. It is important to know the difference because you cannot control a fungus with an insecticide or an insect with a fungicide.

Remember that pesticides are poisons. For safe and effective use, *ALWAYS FOLLOW DIRECTIONS ON THE LABEL*. It is the most authoritative source of information on using a pesticide correctly. Using the pesticide in a way other than that directed on the label is against Federal law.

Pesticides are available in various forms, including dusts, sprays, baits, and granules. Sprays provide the best coverage. And once dry, sprays are more weather resistant than dusts, which are easily washed away.

Protect Bees from Pesticides

Many pesticides kill bees as well as the insects you wish to control. And without bees to pollinate blossoms, crops such as squash, melons, and cucumbers will not set fruit. By taking the following precautions, you can reduce the danger to bees working in your garden.

When you have a choice, choose the pesticide least hazardous to bees. If you have to apply a pesticide that is toxic to bees, try to avoid using it when a vegetable is in bloom. For example, pesticides applied to corn when it is tasseling can kill bees. If you must apply to control corn earworm, avoid spraying or dusting the tassels. Also try to apply pesticides in early evening after bees have completed their daily visits.

Dusts and wettable powder sprays are more toxic than other sprays because they leave a residue that is easily picked up on the bee's hairy body. Bees carry the pesticide back to their hive, where additional bees may be killed. Liquid concentrate-type formulas are generally safer to use:

Misshapen cucumbers are the result of poor pollination. Since proper pollination depends on bees, avoid dusting or spraying cucumber plants with pesticides known to kill bees.

The following chemicals are most hazardous (will kill bees if they are present when pesticide is applied or within a day after): diazinon, malathion, Sevin®.

Thiodan® is a moderately hazardous chemical (can be used where bees work, but apply in evening to avoid direct contact with the bee).

Relatively nonhazardous chemicals which can be used around bees with a minimum of injury include *Bacillus thuringiensis*, Kelthane® miticide, methoxychlor, rotenone, and most fungicides.

Tips for Control of Insects and Related Pests
APHIDS: Control early. Serious infestations can build up in a few days.
ASPARAGUS BEETLE: During harvest season, remove volunteer plants and cut shoots just below the soil surface so adults do not have a place to lay eggs. Control early on ferns.
CORN EARWORM: Eggs are laid on silks. Apply pesticides when the silks first appear, and continue application until they dry.
CUTWORM: Treat soil with recommended insecticide before sowing seeds or transplanting. Or use cutworm collars. Wrap the stem with newspaper or make a collar of toilet tissue or paper towel rolls cut into 2 inch sections. Or use a plastic foam or paper cup with the bottom removed. Sink the collar 1 inch into the soil to secure it and leave 1 to 2 inches above the ground.
EUROPEAN CORN BORER: Look for young caterpillars in a leaf whorl, in the tassel, beneath the husks, or between the ear and the stalk. Control at first sign of infestation before they enter the stalks and ears. Crush white egg masses found on the underside of corn leaves.
HORNWORM: Control while small.
LEAF MINERS: Apply pesticide regularly to kill the adult as it emerges from the mine. Inside the leaf, miners are protected. Tomatoes can withstand infestation of ¼ to ⅓ of the foliage without a significant decrease in yield.
MEXICAN BEAN BEETLE: Thoroughly cover the underside of the foliage with pesticide. Control at the first sign of infestation. Crush egg clusters.
SPIDER MITES: Worse during dry weather. Spray underside of foliage thoroughly.
ONION THRIPS: First signs of infestation are white blotches and dashes on the leaves. Be sure to apply pesticide at the neck between leaves. Add a few drops of dishwashing detergent to spray to help wet the waxy foliage.
SLUGS: Tend to be worse in moist soils covered with mulch. As an alternative to poison bait, you can try trapping slugs with containers of beer. Use a container with a fitted lid, such as a coffee can or margarine tub. Sink the container into the soil so that the lip is flush with the ground and pour an inch or more of beer into the container. Cut a 2- to 3-inch hole in the lid and put the lid in place to keep slugs from crawling back out. This also prevents pets from finding the beer before the slugs do. Check the containers every morning to dispose of the drowned slugs. Replace beer every 3 days or when diluted by rain or irrigation water.
SOUTHERN CORNSTALK BORER: Destroy corn plants after harvest, because the insects overwinter in old stalks.
SQUASH BUG: Control early, because serious infestations can quickly kill a plant.
SQUASH VINE BORER: Plant squash as soon as weather allows so that plants will be producing by the time borers become numerous. Borers must be killed before they enter the stem; inside, they are protected from pesticides. Begin applying pesticides when plants are small. Cover thoroughly, especially the base and stems, because this is where most of the eggs are laid. A yellow excrement on the stems indicates where borers have entered. Split infested stems open lengthwise to remove them.
TOMATO FRUITWORM: Same pest as corn earworm. Apply pesticides regularly so that caterpillars come in contact with the poison as they move from one tomato to another. Inside the fruit, they are protected from pesticide.
WHITE GRUB AND WIREWORM: Usually limited to former farmland, grassy pasture or previous lawn area. Control before planting.

Other Problems
Certain vegetables may develop problems that look like diseases but are actually caused by environmental factors.
Squash: Blossom Drop, Poor Fruit Set
It is normal for the first blossoms to drop. These are the male flowers, which produce pollen but do not set fruit.

The female flowers have a tiny fruit at their base which develops into squash when the flower is pollinated. If female flowers are not fertilized, the miniature fruit rots, sometimes growing slightly before rotting begins. Poor fertilization may be the result of few bees working in your garden. Try planting colorful flowers in the garden to attract bees; in the meantime, pollinate by hand with an artist's paintbrush. Or pinch off the male flower and dust the anthers across the curved pistil in the center of the female flower. You will need to do this in the morning, because male blossoms stay open only a few hours.

Poor fruit set also results from drought stress, unseasonably low temperatures, or crowding of plants in the row.

Tomatoes and Peppers: Blossom-End Rot

Blossom-end rot is a common problem of tomatoes and peppers. Affected fruit develop a round, sunken brown area on the blossom end; on ripe tomatoes, the area usually turns black.

Fluctuations in soil moisture are likely to bring on the condition. Keep the soil evenly moist rather than letting it dry out between waterings.

Liming the soil in the fall according to soil test recommendations will add the calcium necessary to help prevent blossom-end rot. As an immediate treatment, spray plants with calcium chloride, applied according to label directions. This will not "cure" affected fruit but can help prevent blossom-end rot on developing ones.

Also avoid overfertilizing. Follow recommendations carefully for preplant fertilization and side dressings.

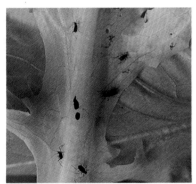
APHID: General pest, attacks most vegetables; Control: diazinon, malathion, methoxychlor, Thiodan®

ARMYWORM: General pest, attacks most vegetables; Control: diazinon, carbaryl, Thiodan®

ASPARAGUS BEETLE: Asparagus; Control: rotenone, carbaryl

CABBAGE LOOPER: Broccoli, Brussels sprouts, cabbage, cauliflower, celery, collards, kale, mustard, kohlrabi, turnip, rutabaga; Control: carbaryl, Bacillus thuringiensis*, Thiodan®, rotenone

COLORADO POTATO BEETLE: Eggplant, Irish potato; Control: diazinon, carbaryl, methoxychlor, Thiodan®, rotenone

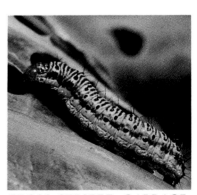
CROSS-STRIPED CABBAGE-WORM: Cabbage; Control: Thiodan®

SPOTTED CUCUMBER BEETLE:
Beans, beet, corn, cucumber, squash,
melons; Control: diazinon, carbaryl,
methoxychlor, Thiodan®, rotenone

CUTWORM: General pest, attacks
most vegetables; Control: cutworm
collar, diazinon granules

EUROPEAN CORN BORER: Corn;
Control: diazinon granules, carbaryl,
Thiodan®

GREENHOUSE WHITEFLY: Cucumber, eggplant, English peas, pepper,
squash, tomato, melons; Control: diazinon, malathion

TOBACCO HORNWORM: Tomato,
pepper; Control: carbaryl, Bacillus
thuringiensis*, Thiodan®; handpick

MEXICAN BEAN BEETLE: Beans;
Control: diazinon, carbaryl, methoxychlor, Thiodan®, rotenone

SPIDER MITES: General pest, attacks
most vegetables; Control: diazinon,
malathion, Kelthane® miticide

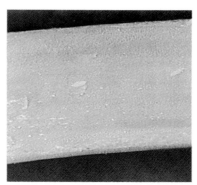

ONION THRIPS: Onions, leeks; Control: diazinon, malathion

SOUTHERN CORNSTALK BORER:
Corn; Control: diazinon granules

SQUASH BUG: Cucumber, pumpkin,
squash; Control: methoxychlor,
Thiodan®

SQUASH VINE BORER: Cantaloupe,
cucumber, pumpkin, squash; Control:
methoxychlor, Thiodan®

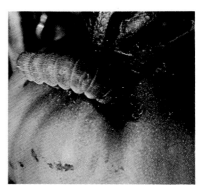

TOMATO FRUITWORM: Tomato,
Corn; Control: carbaryl, Thiodan®.

*Preferred control. Bacillus thuringiensis is a biological, not chemical, control.

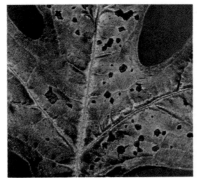

Anthracnose on Watermelon Leaf.

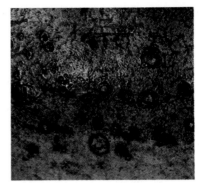

Anthracnose on Watermelon Fruit.

Bacterial Spot on Pepper Leaf.

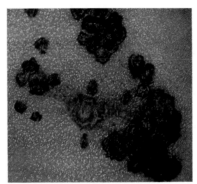

Bacterial Spot on Tomato Fruit.

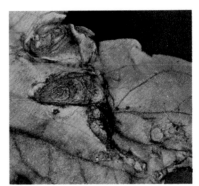

Early Blight on Tomato Foliage.

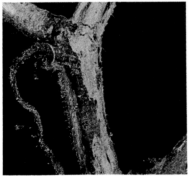

Gummy Stem Blight on Cucumber Stem.

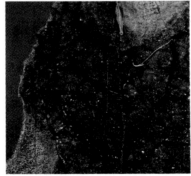

Gummy Stem Blight on Cucumber Leaf.

Southern Stem Blight on Tomato.

Alternaria Leaf Spot on Cantaloupe.

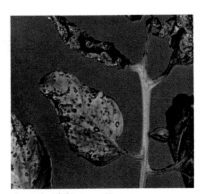

Gray Leaf Spot on Tomato.

Fusarium Wilt on Tomato.

Downy Mildew on Upperside of Cantaloupe Foliage.

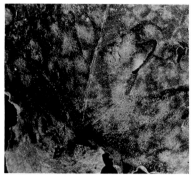

Powdery Mildew on Cantaloupe.

Rust on Snapbean Leaf.

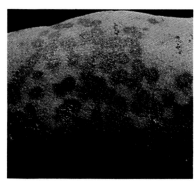

Scurf on Sweet Potato.

Corn Smut.

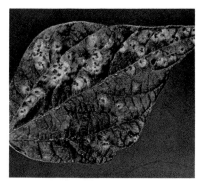

Angular Leaf Spot on Cucumber.

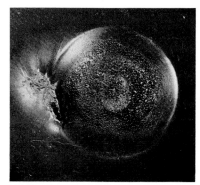

Anthracnose on Tomato Fruit.

Anthracnose on Snapbean Pod.

Anthracnose on Cucumber Leaf.

100

Common Vegetable Controls

Vegetable & Disease	Description	Control*
Asparagus Rust	Reddish spots appear on new shoots, ferns.	Resistant selection: Mary Washington. Spray with maneb.
Beans, (Snap and Lima) Anthracnose	See photo, page 100.	Purchase clean seeds. Rotate crops. Spray with zineb.
Rust	See photo, page 100.	Resistant selections: Kentucky 191, Dade. Spray with chlorothalonil, zineb.
Common bean mosaic virus	Light-green patches appear on foliage; leaves pucker, especially along mid-rib; leaf edges curl.	Resistant selections: Contender, Topcrop, Provider, Dade, Astro, Harvester.
Powdery mildew	See General Diseases.	Resistant selection: Contender.
Downy mildew	See General Diseases.	
Beets	No serious diseases.	
Broccoli	Same as Cabbage.	
Brussels Sprouts	Same as Cabbage.	
Cabbage Black rot	Leaf edges turn yellow; veins darken.	Use disease-free plants; rotate crops.
Blackleg	Light-gray spots speckled with black appear on leaves; stem is girdled and turns black.	Use disease-free plants; rotate crops.
Downy mildew	See General Diseases.	Spray with maneb, zineb, chlorothalonil.
Yellows	Leaves yellow and curl, then turn brown and brittle.	Resistant selections: Stonehead, Golden Acre.
Carrots Leaf blight (Late blight)	Leaves are spotted, turn yellow and brown.	Spray with zineb, maneb, chlorothalonil.
Cauliflower	Same as Cabbage.	
Celery Early blight	Foliage develops ash-gray spots covered with velvety spores in warm, humid weather. Long sunken tan spots appear on stalks.	Spray with maneb.
Late blight	Leaves are yellow spotted; in severe cases, spots fuse and leaves turn brown and rot.	Spray with maneb.
Swiss Chard Cercospora leaf spot	Ash-gray spots with purple edges appear; centers may drop out.	Spray with zineb.
Downy mildew	See General Diseases.	Spray with zineb.
Collards & Kale	Same as Cabbage.	
Sweet Corn Southern leaf blight (Helminthosporium)	Tan spots with parallel sides fuse to cover leaf.	Resistant or tolerant selections: Florida Staysweet, Silver Queen.
Northern leaf blight (Helminthosporium)	Greenish tan, spindle-shaped water-soaked spots ½-2 inches wide, 2-6 inches long appear on lower leaves first and move up.	Resistant or tolerant selections: Florida Staysweet, Silver Queen. Spray with zineb, chlorothalonil.
Smut	See photo, page 100.	Resistant or tolerant selections: Bi-Queen, Merit. No pesticide registered.
Maize dwarf mosaic	Leaves are streaked yellow and green.	Resistant or tolerant selection: Merit.
Cucumbers Anthracnose	See photo, page 100.	Resistant or tolerant selections: Gemini 7, Carolina, Poinsett 76. Spray with maneb, captan, chlorothalonil, zineb.
Angular leaf spot	See photo, page 100. Spots on fruit turn white and may crack.	Resistant or tolerant selections: same as above. Spray with captan. Use disease-free seed. Rotate crops.
Gummy stem blight	See photos, page 99.	Spray with maneb, chlorothalonil, zineb.
Downy mildew	See General Diseases.	Resistant or tolerant selections: Ashley, Sweet Success, Poinsett 76, Gemini 7, Victory, Patio Pik, Carolina. Spray with maneb, captan, chlorothalonil, zineb.
Powdery mildew	See General Diseases.	Resistant or tolerant selections: Ashley, Sweet Success, Poinsett 76, Saladin, Gemini 7, Victory, Patio Pik, Carolina. Spray with chlorothalonil.
Scab	Gray, sunken spots appear on fruit.	Resistant or tolerant selections: Patio Pik, Comanche Carolina, Sweet Success, Sweet Slice, Poinsett 76, Gemini 7.
Viruses	Leaves are small, mottled, curled; fruit is mottled and deformed.	Resistant or tolerant selections: Spacemaster, Gemini 7, Victory, Comanche, Carolina, Bush Champion.
Eggplant Phomopsis blight (Fruit rot)	Brown spots on leaves and stems enlarge, become gray with black specks. Pale, sunken spots appear on fruit.	Spray with maneb.
Verticillium wilt	Lower leaves turn yellow; plant growth is stunted.	Rotate crops; do not plant where tomatoes or okra grew.

* In addition to resistant selections listed here, check seed catalogs for other, newer ones.

Common Vegetable Controls		
Vegetable & Disease	**Description**	**Control***
Greens, Unusual Endive, Escarole	Same as Lettuce but less susceptible.	
Celtuce, Nasturtiums, Cress	No serious problems.	
Jerusalem Artichoke	No serious problems.	
Kohlrabi	Same as Cabbage.	
Lettuce Downy mildew	See General Diseases.	Spray with maneb, zineb.
Melons Anthracnose	See photo, page 99.	Resistant watermelon selections: Congo, Charleston Gray. Spray with chlorothalonil, maneb, captan, zineb.
Downy mildew	See photo, page 100.	Resistant or tolerant cantaloupe selections: Planters Jumbo, Edisto 47. Spray with maneb, captan, chlorothalonil, zineb.
Powdery mildew	See photo, page 100.	Resistant or tolerant cantaloupe selections: Ambrosia, Planters Jumbo, Saticoy, Burpee Hybrid, Edisto 47. Spray with chlorothalonil.
Gummy stem blight	See photo, page 99.	Spray with chlorothalonil, maneb, zineb.
Leaf spot	Leaves have round or irregular dark spots, which may have concentric rings or halo appearance.	Resistant cantaloupe selection to Alternaria leaf spot: Edisto 47. Spray with captan, chlorothalonil.
Fusarium wilt	See General Diseases.	Resistant or tolerant watermelon selections: Charleston Gray, Calhoun, Smokylee, Sugar Doll, Crimson Sweet; cantaloupe: Saticoy, Burpee Hybrid; honeydew: Earli-Dew.
Mustard Downy mildew	See General diseases.	Spray with zineb, maneb.
Leaf spot	Leaves have gray spots with tan edges.	Spray with zineb.
Okra Fusarium wilt	See General Diseases.	Rotate crops.
Verticillium wilt	Leaves turn yellow; plants are stunted.	Rotate crops.
Onions & Leeks Purple blotch	Leaves develop purplish spots with yellow haloes that extend up or down leaf; leaves fall over.	Spray with maneb.
Downy mildew	Purplish mold on leaf surfaces is visible while leaves are still wet with dew. Leaves turn yellow and collapse.	Spray with maneb.
Peas, English Powdery mildew	See General Diseases.	Spray with sulfur.
Peas, Southern Fusarium wilt	See General Diseases.	Resistant or tolerant selections: Mississippi Silver, Mississippi Cream, Magnolia Black-eye.
Mosaics	Leaves are mottled; plants may be stunted; pods may not develop normally.	Resistant or tolerant selections: same as above. No pesticide registered.
Peppers Anthracnose	See General Diseases.	Spray with maneb, zineb.
Cercospora leaf spot	Small water-soaked spots turn white with brown margins. Leaves turn yellow and drop; stem end of fruit rots.	Spray with zineb.
Bacterial leaf spot	Wartlike spots appear on leaves, turn dark brown. Leaves turn yellow and drop.	Spray with streptomycin, zineb, Kocide®.
Phytophthora blight (Fruit rot)	Leaves have large bleached spots; water-soaked patches on fruit are covered with white fungus; stems are girdled at soil line.	Spray with maneb, zineb.
Potatoes, Irish Early blight	Dark spots like bull's-eyes appear on lower leaves.	Spray with maneb, captan, chlorothalonil.
Late blight	Water-soaked spots on leaves enlarge, become dry and brown in center, and white mold appears on underside of leaves. Disease occurs in cool, wet weather.	Spray with maneb, captan, chlorothalonil.
Scurf & stem rot (Rhizoctonia)	Emerging sprouts die. On older plants, tubers may be small and spotted with black; or stems may decay just below soil line and small green or reddish tubers form aboveground.	Use disease-free seed potatoes. Dust seed pieces with captan.
Seed piece decay	Seed pieces rot in ground.	Start with disease-free certified seed potatoes. Do not plant in cold, wet soil; see page 184.
Potatoes, Sweet Scurf	See photo, page 100. Harvested roots shrink in storage because of water loss.	Use certified plants. Rotate crops. Avoid planting. where organic matter is not well decomposed.
Black rot	Foliage yellows, underground portion of stem develops black cankers; dark, circular, sunken spots appear on potato; flesh tastes bitter.	Same as for scurf.

* In addition to resistant selections listed here, check seed catalogs for other, newer ones.

Common Vegetable Controls

Vegetable & Disease	Description	Control*
Pumpkins	Same as Cucumbers.	
Radishes	No serious diseases.	
Rhubarb Crown rot	Stalks rot at base.	Plant in well-drained soil. Remove infected plants.
Salsify	No serious diseases.	
Spinach Downy mildew	See General Diseases. Bloomsdale selections are especially susceptible.	Resistant or tolerant selections: Early Hybrid 7, Chesapeake, Avon. Spray with maneb, zineb.
White rust	White blisterlike spots appear on underside of leaves; upper surfaces turn yellowish, developing white spots in severe cases.	Spray with maneb, zineb.
Squash	Same as Cucumbers.	
Tomatoes Bacterial spot	Small, dark water-soaked spots are scattered over leaves. Spots are often elongated on leaf margins. On fruit, see photo, page 99.	Spray with Kocide® or streptomycin; disease difficult to control once established.
Early blight	See photo, page 99.	Resistant selection: Floramerica. Spray with maneb, zineb, captan, chlorothalonil.
Late blight	Irregular, greenish black water-soaked spots on leaves enlarge and turn brown. White moldy growth appears on underside of leaves. Dark water-soaked spots are on stems and fruit.	Spray with maneb, zineb, chlorothalonil, captan. Apply preventative sprays in spring and fall.
Southern blight	Plants wilt and die rapidly. Fungus forms white mass over diseased stem at soil line and surrounding soil.	Water transplants with solution of Terracolor®. Remove and destroy diseased plants; turn soil deeply.
Tobacco mosaic	Leaves have yellow mottling.	Resistant selection: Tropic VF. Sanitation is important. Do not smoke or chew tobacco when working with plants. Wash hands with soapy water before handling plants if you use tobacco.
Fusarium wilt	See photo, page 100.	For resistant selections, see page 204.
Verticillium wilt	Older leaves turn yellow, tips of shoots wilt. Whole plant affected rather than one side as with fusarium wilt.	For resistant selections, see page 204. Rotate crops.
Septoria leaf spot	Small water-soaked spots on lower leaves turn light gray with dark edges. Disease occurs in cool, wet weather.	Spray with maneb, zineb, captan. Rotate crops.
Gray leaf spot	See photo, page 99.	Resistant or tolerant selections: Tropic, Floradade, Floramerica, Walter, Manalucie, Early Cascade. Spray with maneb, zineb, captan, chlorothalonil.
Anthracnose	See photo, page 100.	Spray with maneb, zineb, captan, chlorothalonil. Rotate crops.
Turnips & Rutabagas Downy mildew	See General Diseases.	Spray with zineb.
Leaf spot	Gray-brown or yellow circular spots on leaves.	Spray with zineb.

* In addition to resistant selections listed here, check seed catalogs for other, newer ones.

General Diseases	Description	Control
Anthracnose	Small, dry, gray to tan spots appear on foliage; dead tissue may crack and fall out. Sunken, dark, water-soaked spots with sticky, pink spores appear on fruit.	See specific vegetables.
Downy mildew	Yellow areas or angular spots appear on upper surface of leaf, with downy patches of white, gray, or violet-gray mold on underside. Disease occurs in cool humid weather.	See specific vegetables for chemical controls.
Fusarium wilt	Lower leaves yellow and wilt, progressing up the plant. It often appears on only one side of plant.	See specific vegetables. Use resistant selections.
Powdery mildew	White powdery mold appears on underside of leaves in spots which enlarge, fuse, and appear on upper surface. On English peas, disease may cover whole plant.	See specific vegetables.
Damping off	Seedlings rot or wilt soon after emerging; usually occurs in warm, humid weather.	Use sterile soil when starting seed indoors. Treat seed with captan or thiram.
Seed rot	Sprouting seeds rot before emerging; usually occurs in cold, wet soils.	Buy treated seed or treat with captan or thiram.

Tools and Equipment

Having the right tools and equipment makes gardening easier and more efficient. Remember to look for quality when you shop. Buying good tools and equipment is an investment that will pay off in the long run.

The Five Basic Tools

Although your tool collection can become quite elaborate, these five basic ones will do most jobs: bow rake, hoe, round-point shovel, spading fork, and trowel.

Your best bet is to buy recognized brand-name tools. Most manufacturers offer different levels of quality for each type of tool, with prices varying accordingly. Tool quality and price are based on the gauge of the steel (heaviness and durability) and solid construction (lack of welded parts). Every weld on a tool provides a potential breaking point, so the fewer welds, the better. Wooden handles are also characteristic of good-quality tools, and ash or hickory is best. Wood provides the elasticity that keeps handles from breaking easily, as well as a more comfortable grip than either plastic or steel.

Bow rake—Especially useful early in the season for soil preparation, a bow rake is just what you

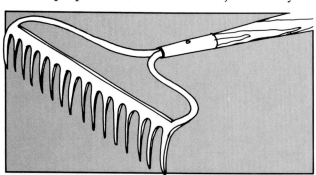

need for pulling out stones and smoothing the soil. In addition, its flat back can level the surface of planting beds and tamp down soil over newly planted seeds. A medium-quality product is adequate, but be sure to get one with the tines and bow forged from one piece of steel.

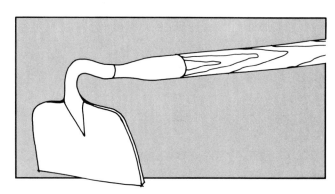

Hoe—A hoe is essential for laying off rows or building raised ones. One variation, the Warren hoe, has a small triangular blade and is handy for opening furrows and cultivating in tight spots. A medium-quality hoe is generally adequate; it will feature a sharp blade, with the blade and shank forged from one piece of steel. Avoid a lower-quality hoe with shank and blade welded together.

The standard hoe has a 48-inch handle, but select a length that is comfortable. You should be able to stand nearly upright and grip the handle almost at its end when the hoe is in a comfortable working position.

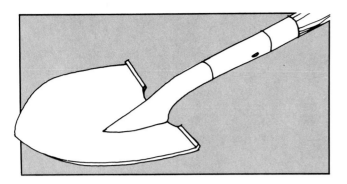

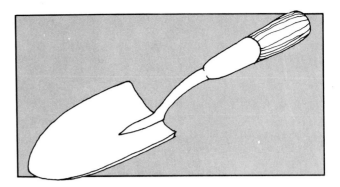

Round-point shovel—You will need a round-point shovel for digging holes and moving soil when preparing planting beds. The highest-quality shovels have the blade, shank, and socket forged from one bar of steel; the least expensive ones have a hollow back in which dirt and mud can cake. For normal home garden use, you may want to select a medium-quality shovel; while not of solid construction, the back of the shovel is sealed with a piece of steel to prevent dirt and mud from collecting and causing rust.

When buying a shovel, also look for a turned step. This means that the metal is rolled over on the upper edge of the blade, making a more comfortable place for stepping.

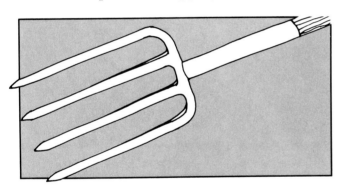

Spading fork—A manual substitute for the rotary tiller, this tool can be used to loosen and turn soil, mix in manure and lime, turn a compost pile, and harvest root crops. Since this is a prying tool that takes a lot of stress, especially in areas with heavy soils, buy one of top quality. It should have heavy-gauge tines that are forged rather than welded so they will not bend or break the first time you try to lift a rock or break heavy soil. Also look at the ferrule (collar that attaches the handle to the prongs). The longer the ferrule, the stronger the tool will be. The best forks are called weldless; that is, the fork has a solid shank rather than being inserted into the end of the handle and wrapped with metal. (*See page 264 for a source of unwelded forks.*)

Trowel—A trowel is a versatile hand tool for setting out transplants and digging tough weeds. Look for a heavy-gauge steel, because cheap trowels bend easily. Be sure its grip feels comfortable.

Other Useful Tools

A *D-handle spade* makes breaking ground and digging easier. It is designed so that you can dig using your body weight efficiently without straining your back. The straight sides and flat blade are helpful when you are removing sod to start a garden, and for prying up rocks.

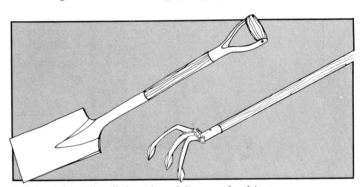

Left to right: D-handled spade and 3-pronged cultivator.

A *pronged cultivator* is good for weeding, especially in stony soil. It is available with a 4-foot handle or a 1- to 1½-foot handle. Choose one that is lightweight, because it will be easier to use close to plants without cultivating too deeply and damaging roots.

A *leaf rake* is useful for collecting and removing mulch, and for the final smoothing of a seedbed.

Equipment for the Garden

A wheelbarrow is indispensable for transporting compost and mulch, and makes it easier to haul tools and fertilizer to the garden. A well-designed wheelbarrow should support 80 to 85 percent of the load. Look for rigid construction and heavy-gauge metal. Thick steel will last longer than thin, and one of the first places a wheelbarrow gives out is in the tray, where the metal rusts through.

Wooden handles are more comfortable to most gardeners, and long ones offer more leverage and control than short. Look for a sturdy wheel with a good tire. Pneumatic (air-filled) tires cushion the load for better balance and control, especially on rough ground. Wide tires also provide better balance.

Choose one large enough to carry a bale of pine straw or a bushel of compost. A contractor's wheelbarrow is a good size for typical gardening jobs.

Before you buy a wheelbarrow, get a feel for it by putting a few bags of fertilizer in the tray and wheeling it around. Be sure it feels sturdy, balanced, and has a comfortable grip.

Garden carts can carry more than a wheelbarrow and are easier to use.

A garden cart may be better than a wheelbarrow for big jobs such as hauling large loads of pine straw or manure. The flatbed design of some carts is also particularly useful for carrying flats of transplants. As for a wheelbarrow, look for rigid construction from durable materials.

Because garden carts have two wheels, they are more stable than a wheelbarrow; therefore, they are easier to maneuver on rough ground. Look for a design that allows easy dumping so the contents will not have to be shoveled out. Also bicycle-type wheels are best.

Tillers save time in a large garden, but they can be expensive. Before you buy, try renting one a few times to see if owning a tiller might be worthwhile.

There are many models available, from small minitillers to large heavy ones that require their own trailer for transporting them. All tillers, however, are of two basic types: front tine and rear tine. Front-tine tillers are moved forward by the digging action of the tines. They may be more maneuverable, but they also require more effort to control them.

Rear-tine tillers have the engine mounted up front for better balance and handling. The wheels move the machine forward, so the tines can move faster and break up the soil more efficiently.

Also consider these points:

• A model with interchangeable tines can be used for working manure and other materials into the soil as well as cutting through new ground and breaking up clods of soil. Some models also have attachments for laying off rows, building raised beds, cultivating, and plowing under plant debris or cover crops.

• Be sure the throttle is conveniently located and easy to control.

• Make sure the tiller has a clutch or some other safety device to ensure that tines stop rotating if you should fall.

• Look for adjustable tilling depth.

• Ask a knowledgeable dealer about the machine's capacity. It is better to purchase a machine with a little too much capacity than one not powerful enough to perform satisfactorily.

• The machine should be well balanced and of a weight that is easy for you to handle. Be sure replacement or repair parts are available, especially belts for belt-driven types.

One final piece of equipment you may need is a sprayer to apply liquid pesticides to control insects and diseases. Compressed air sprayers provide the best coverage. They are powered by air that you pressurize by hand pumping much the same way you operate a bicycle pump. The sprayers are available in 1- to 4-gallon capacity; but for most gardens, a 1-gallon capacity is adequate and is easier to carry around. A large sprayer full of water is quite heavy, as a gallon of water weighs 8⅓ pounds.

Compressed-air sprayers are the most versatile for the vegetable garden. They are available in tank capacities of 1 to 4 gallons.

An emitter drip system has emitters installed at desired intervals along the tube to deliver water slowly and steadily to plants. Little water is lost to evaporation with trickle systems like this one.

Stainless steel sprayers are the most expensive but also the most durable. Other good sprayers are made of plastic, brass, or aluminum.

Spray nozzles should adjust from a fine mist to a single stream. Also look for a long hose (2 to 3 feet) that allows freedom of movement to reach into the plants. An on/off valve or handle lock keeps the spray going without your having to maintain a hand-cramping, constant grip.

Irrigation Equipment

Sprinklers are the most common type of irrigation system used. Oscillating sprinklers deliver water in a square or rectangular pattern. Depending on the model, this type may water an area up to 3000 square feet. Those with timers for automatic shutoff are convenient and help prevent overwatering.

Stationary sprinklers deliver a gentle spray, usually over a small area. These are particularly good for low-growing vegetables.

Impact or pulsating sprinklers are nozzle types that rotate in a full circle to deliver water to an area up to 5000 square feet. Many models have a deflector that adjusts to limit delivery to any part of the circle, and some have a distance control dial to limit the diameter of the circle that is watered. When set on risers 4 to 5 feet high, impact or pulsating sprinklers provide the best method of irrigating a large garden.

When you shop for any type of sprinkler, look for one made of brass, high impact plastic, or a long-lasting, noncorrosive material, such as stainless steel. Zinc is not durable enough for movable parts that receive a lot of wear.

A trickle or drip irrigation system is the most efficient watering system you can use. It delivers small amounts of water directly to the plants at a steady rate, and reduces the amount of water used for irrigation by up to 50 percent.

A basic trickle system consists of tubing that is laid down in the row, a device to control water pressure, a filter to prevent clogging, and a distribution system to deliver water to the plants. There are three types of distribution systems. One type has double, perforated tubing; water runs through the inner hose at high pressure and sprays into the outer, surrounding hose. This tube also has holes in it, through which water drips slowly.

A second type has emitters (tubular sections with openings) installed at intervals along the tube to deliver water to the plants. The third type has smaller, spaghetti-size distribution tubing that connects to the emitter or to the tubing itself to deliver water to plants several inches away from the main line of tubing.

Another system, the soaker hose, consists of porous canvas tubing. It attaches to a garden hose and allows water to seep through the walls.

The best garden hoses are 100 percent high-quality reinforced rubber. They are flexible even in cold weather and withstand a high water pressure, such as when a hose-end nozzle is shut off. Hoses made from reinforced vinyl or rubber and vinyl have the good qualities of a rubber hose but are not as heavy.

The inside diameter of the hose should be at least ½ inch. With normal water pressure, this size hose should deliver 1 inch of water to an area 5000 square feet in about 5 hours. A hose ⅝ inch in diameter delivers the same amount in about 3 hours.

Harvest and Storage

Perhaps the greatest rewards of vegetable gardening come at harvest, when you can pick your own vine-ripened tomatoes, crisp snap beans, and juicy sweet corn. It takes practice to judge the best time to harvest each vegetable for peak flavor and quality. The information under the individual vegetables (*starting on page 125*) will guide you.

Remember that "biggest" is not necessarily best. If you let vegetables grow until they are oversize or overmature, you will probably harvest vegetables that are seedy, tough, stringy, flavorless, or bitter. And leaving mature fruit on the plants often lowers yields. When seeds inside the fruit mature, the plant stops producing.

For many vegetables, the more you pick, the more the plants bear. This is true for okra, summer squash, eggplant, beans, and cucumbers, as well as for all types of greens. If you are away for more than two days during harvesttime, ask a neighbor to harvest for you. That way, plants may still be producing when you return.

In spring and summer, it is usually best to harvest in the morning, after the dew has dried. Some vegetables, especially leafy greens, wilt quickly if harvested in the middle of the day. Keep all harvested vegetables shaded so they do not lose moisture before you get them to the kitchen.

Heavy rains just before harvest can swell some vegetables with extra water. This makes them split or bruise easily. If you must harvest after a period of wet weather, handle vegetables carefully to avoid bruising them. Be sure to cure sweet potatoes, pumpkins, winter squash, and onions properly and handle Irish potatoes carefully. Use split tomatoes and cabbages as soon as possible.

Avoid harvesting vegetables when foliage is wet, because you may spread diseases from plant to plant. Also be careful not to break stems or vines; the wounds provide entry for disease.

Pick the outer leaves of turnip greens often, and the plant will keep producing foliage from the center for continued harvest.

A bounty of fresh tomatoes and a well-stocked pantry.

Spring radishes.

Harvest of early-spring vegetables.

An abundant harvest from the summer garden.

Eggplant and peppers.

Storing Vegetables for Fresh Use

Once harvested, most vegetables should be placed in perforated plastic bags and refrigerated immediately to keep them fresh. Cold temperatures slow aging, and high humidity prevents moisture loss.

In fall, vegetables such as collards, kale, brussels sprouts, cabbage, root crops, leeks, and spinach can remain in the garden. This is the most common way to store them for winter use in the Middle and Lower South. (If your soil drains poorly, however, root crops will rot if left in the ground; so you will need to store them indoors.)

In areas where the soil rarely freezes, such as along the Southeastern and Gulf Coasts, no protective mulch is necessary. If your soil usually freezes, even temporarily, as in the Upper and Middle South, cover vegetables with a layer of straw, hay, or similar mulch before the first hard freeze. Pile the mulch 10 to 12 inches deep and cover the row to a width of 18 inches. This prevents alternate freezing and thawing, which can heave vegetables out of the ground and damage the quality of root crops. It also keeps the ground from freezing so that you can dig root crops easily.

If mice tunnel under the mulch and eat your root crops, lay hardware cloth over the ground before mulching. Also keep the area around the garden free of weeds and brush that provide cover for rodents. Be sure to mark the rows with stakes so that you know where to begin harvesting roots each time; top growth has often died back by this time.

In the coldest parts of the Upper and Middle South, a root cellar is the best place to store most vegetables for winter use. Over much of the South, however, the soil does not get cold enough for a sufficiently long time to make a root cellar practical. But you can use an unheated room, closet, basement, or crawl space under the house for storage.

Make sure the area has good air circulation to help prevent the development of mold. Build shelves slightly away from the walls, and set boxes of produce on benches or slatted shelves rather than directly on the floor. This allows air to move all around the vegetables.

For root crops, Irish potatoes, and cabbage, choose an unheated room or corner of the basement on the northeast or northwest side of the house. The ideal conditions for these crops are low temperatures (32 to 40 degrees) and high humidity (90 percent relative humidity). You can keep them at warmer temperatures, but their storage life will be shorter.

Onions, hot peppers, pumpkins, winter squash, and green tomatoes keep well where the temperature is about 55 degrees and relative humidity is 60 percent. Onions and hot peppers can also be stored at cooler temperatures, to 45 degrees. Pumpkins, winter squash, and green tomatoes tolerate warmer temperatures, to 60 degrees. Sweet potatoes store longest at 55 to 60 degrees and 85 percent relative humidity.

To check conditions in the storage area, use both a thermometer and a hygrometer, which measures relative humidity. You may need to open or close windows to keep conditions constant. A basement with a dirt floor is best for providing high humidity. If you have concrete or stone floors, you can raise the humidity to the recommended level by placing shallow pans of water on the floor. Or cover boxes of vegetables with damp burlap bags. Remember to dampen the bags regularly. Check vegetables often and discard or use any that are beginning to spoil.

One way to store root crops such as turnips is to pack them in damp sand. Trim tops and part of the taproot first. Be sure roots do not touch and are completely covered with sand. Store in a cold, humid location, such as an unheated basement or root cellar.

Red potatoes and Vidalia onions.

Storing Vegetables in the Refrigerator Place in perforated plastic bags and seal or tie with twist tie.		
Vegetable	**Preparation/Storage Tips**	**Storage Life**
Asparagus	Can also stand cut ends in water in refrigerator. Use as soon as possible; stalks toughen with time.	1 week
Beans, Lima	Shell before refrigerating.	1 week
Beans, Snap	No preparation necessary.	2-3 weeks
Beets	Trim tops to within 2-3 inches of root.	2-4 months
Broccoli	Do not wash florets.	1 week
Brussels Sprouts	No preparation necessary.	3 weeks
Cabbage	Remove outer leaves; wash heads, pat dry	2-3 months
Cabbage, Chinese	No preparation necessary.	3-4 weeks
Carrots	Trim tops to within 1 inch or less of root	2-4 months
Cauliflower	Remove leaves.	2 weeks
Celery	Can also wrap bunches tightly in foil before refrigerating.	1 month
Chard, Swiss	No preparation necessary.	2 weeks
Collards & Kale	No preparation necessary.	2-3 weeks
Corn, Sweet	Shuck & clean before refrigerating, or leave unshucked.	2 days; extra-sweet selections keep several days
Cucumbers	No preparation necessary.	1-2 weeks
Eggplant	No preparation necessary.	1-2 weeks
Greens, Unusual	No preparation necessary.	2-3 weeks
Jerusalem Artichokes	Wash and dry.	3 months
Kohlrabi	Trim leaves.	1 month
Leeks	Store unwashed with roots attached.	1-3 months
Lettuce	Wash and pat thoroughly dry before refrigerating.	2-3 weeks
Melons:		
Cantaloupe	No preparation necessary.	1-2 weeks
Honeydew	No preparation necessary.	3-4 weeks
Watermelon	No preparation necessary.	2 weeks
Mustard	No preparation necessary.	2 weeks
Okra	No preparation necessary.	1 week
Onions, Green	Wash; trim roots and part of top; pat dry	1 month
Onions, Dry	Cure; place in mesh bag in crisper drawer or cool, dry place.	3-6 months
Peas, English	Refrigerate unshelled.	1 week
Peas, Southern	Shell or leave unshelled.	1 week
Peppers, Sweet	No preparation necessary.	2-3 weeks
Potatoes, Irish	Place in mesh bag in crisper drawer or cool, humid place (50 degrees). Will taste sweet if refrigerated.	2-3 months
Radishes, Spring	Trim tops close to root.	1 month
Radishes, Winter	Trim tops close to root.	2-4 months
Rhubarb	Discard leaves.	2 weeks
Salsify	Trim tops to within 1 inch or less of root; wash and pat thoroughly dry.	2-4 months
Spinach	Do not wash until ready to use.	2 weeks
Squash, Summer	No preparation necessary.	1-2 weeks
Turnip & Rutabaga Roots	Trim tops to within 1 inch or less of root.	2-4 months; rutabagas, to 5 months
Turnip Greens	No preparation necessary.	2 weeks

Storing Vegetables in the Garden for Winter*		
Vegetable	**Storage Tip/Alternate Storage**	**Storage Life**
Beets	Can also trim tops, pack in boxes of damp sand or sawdust. Do not let roots touch each other or sides of box, and cover completely with packing material. Keep box in cold, humid place.	2-4 months
Broccoli	Leave in garden until hard freeze is predicted.	
Brussels Sprouts	Treat same as Broccoli.	
Cabbage	Can also pull, wash soil from roots, and hang upside down in cold, damp basement. Or harvest, remove outer leaves, wrap heads in newspaper, and store in cold, humid place.	2-3 months
Carrots	Can also dig, and treat like beets.	2-4 months
Celery	Leave in garden until first hard freeze.	
Collards & Kale	Leave in garden all winter.	
Jerusalem Artichokes	Leave in garden all winter.	
Radishes, Winter	Can also dig and treat like beets.	2 months
Salsify	Leave in garden all winter.	
Spinach	Leave in garden all winter.	
Turnips & Rutabagas (roots)	Can also pack in damp sand as for beets. Or dip in paraffin; melt wax in water and quickly dip root through wax into water and remove; let dry (prevents shriveling).	2-4 months; rutabagas, up to 5 months

*In Upper and Middle South, mulch as directed on page 113.

Storing Warm Season Vegetables for the Long Term		
Vegetable	**Preparation/Storage Tips**	**Storage Life**
Peppers, Hot	Dry peppers by hanging plants upside down in warm, well-ventilated place. Or string peppers on strong thread and hang to dry. Store in cool, dry place (45 to 55 degrees), such as a closed pantry.	2 years
Potatoes, Sweet	Cure (*see page 187*), pack in crates; store in warm, humid location (55 to 60 degrees and 85 percent humidity).	2-3 months
Pumpkins	Cure (*see page 188*), place in single layers on shelf in cool, dry location (55 to 60 degrees).	2-3 months
Squash, Winter	Same as for Pumpkins.	1-3 months, depending on selection
Tomatoes*	Green: place in single or double layers in cool, dark, dry place; may also wrap in newspaper; or hang plants upside down in pantry or dry basement. Avoid temperatures below 45 to 50 degrees.	3-5 weeks

*Store ripe tomatoes at room temperature, above 60 degrees. Do not refrigerate; it causes rapid deterioration.

Be sure to use firm, ripe fruit for canning.

Canning the Harvest

In canning, the important thing to remember is that food must be heated to a specific temperature for a certain length of time to destroy organisms that might cause food spoilage. The process also stops the enzyme activity at the peak of the vegetable's maturity, preserving flavor and nutritional value.

The boiling-water-bath method is used for processing acid foods such as tomatoes, pickled vegetables, and sauerkraut. Most vegetables, however, are low in acid and should be canned by the steam-pressure method, which provides a temperature higher than boiling necessary to can these safely. By this method, food is processed in a steam-pressure canner at 10 pounds of pressure or 240 degrees to make sure that all spoilage organisms are destroyed.

Note: Canning vegetables of any sort in the microwave oven is NOT recommended.

General Canning Procedure

For both canning methods, be sure to use jars made especially for home canning. They have specially designed lids that ensure a complete seal. One type consists of a flat metal lid with a rubbery sealing compound around the edge and a threaded metal band that screws over it. The threaded bands may be reused, but use new flat lids each time to ensure a perfect seal.

Another type of lid is the porcelain-lined zinc cap with shoulder rubber ring. The caps may be reused as long as they are in good condition, but use clean, new rubber rings every year. Ones saved from last year may have deteriorated; do not test rings by stretching them.

Do not use containers with chips, cracks, rust, or dents, since defects prevent an airtight seal. Wash jars and lids in hot soapy water and rinse well. Keep the jars in hot water until you are ready to fill them. Follow manufacturer's directions for boiling metal lids.

Choose only fresh, firm vegetables that are fully ripe but not overripe. Process as soon after harvesting as possible. Sort them according to size and ripeness for more even cooking.

Wash vegetables thoroughly under cold running water to remove dirt and bacteria. Avoid letting vegetables soak in water, because they may lose flavor and food value.

Before processing, pack vegetables into jars, using either the cold-pack (raw-pack) method or the hot-pack method. For the cold-pack method, fill jars with unheated or raw vegetables, then cover with boiling water or other liquid to within ½ inch of the top of the jar. Pack the vegetables tightly in the containers, because shrinkage will occur during processing.

For the hot-pack method, fill jars with hot or cooked vegetables. Pack vegetables loosely, within ½ to 1 inch of the top, and fill the jar with boiling liquid to within ½ inch of the top.

The headspace you leave at the top of each jar lets the vegetables expand during processing. The amount to leave varies with the type of vegetable and jar size. In general, leave ½ inch for nonstarchy vegetables and 1 inch for starchy vegetables.

Remove all air bubbles before sealing jars. For loose packs, run a rubber spatula or knife gently between the jar and the vegetables. For solid packs (corn, greens, mashed pumpkin), cut through the center several times. Add more liquid if necessary to cover packed food. If not completely covered, the food at the top of the jar may darken.

After packing the jar, wipe the rim and put on the cap. When using jars with metal screw bands and flat lids, put the flat lid on with the sealing compound next to the jar top. Screw the metal band as tight as you can by hand. Never tighten bands after removing jars from the canner because this breaks the seal. Remove screw bands after jars cool, since they often rust and become difficult to loosen.

If you use a porcelain-lined zinc cap, fit the wet rubber ring down on the jar shoulder, stretching the ring as little as possible. Screw the cap on firmly, then turn back ¼ inch. As soon as you remove the jar from the canner, screw the cap on tightly to complete the seal.

To prevent overcooking after processing, remove jars from the water-bath canner immediately. Wait until pressure is zero in steam-pressure canners before removing jars. Place jars upright on a rack, folded cloth, or wooden cutting board, leaving space between the jars for air circulation.

A popping sound as jars with metal lids cool means that the flat lid is settling onto the top of the jar and that you have a good seal. When jars are cool, test the seal by running your fingertip over the top of the lid. If the lid curves downward, the seal is good.

To test the seal on jars with porcelain-lined zinc caps, turn each jar partly over in your hands and look for leakage. If any jar fails to seal, either repack and reprocess the contents or refrigerate the jars and use the contents as soon as possible.

Store canned vegetables in a cool, dry, dark place. If the jars have a good seal, vegetables should retain flavor and color for a year.

Boiling-Water-Bath Canning: Specific Tips

A water-bath canner is simply a large metal container with a tight-fitting lid. It must be deep enough to allow water to boil freely over and around each jar. Allow 2 to 4 inches above jar tops for brisk boiling. The canner must also have a wire or wooden rack on which to place the jars so that they do not sit directly on the bottom of the canner. Water must circulate freely under jars during processing.

To process, fill the canner half-full with water, cover, and heat over high heat. Water should be hot but not boiling for cold pack and boiling for hot pack.

Canned tomato stock will retain good flavor and color for at least a year if the jar was sealed properly.

Arrange jars on the rack so they do not touch the canner or each other. Add enough boiling water to cover the tops of the jars with 1 or 2 inches of water, but be careful not to pour the water directly on the jars.

Cover the canner and begin counting the processing time when water comes to a full, rolling boil. Lower heat, but maintain a steady gentle boil for the recommended length of time (given with each recipe). Be sure the water covers jars at all times.

Steam-Pressure Canning: Specific Tips

A steam-pressure canner is a heavy metal kettle with a cover that can be clamped or locked down to make the kettle airtight. Controls include a petcock to allow air to be driven out as the canner fills with steam, a safety valve to let steam escape if pressure becomes too high, and a gauge to measure pressure in the canner. *Note*: A steam-pressure canner is not the same as a pressure cooker, and they cannot be used interchangeably. Follow the manufacturer's directions carefully to use the steam canner.

Freezing the Harvest

The best way to retain the natural flavor of vegetables is through freezing. It also maintains nutritional value and is one of the easiest and fastest methods of food preservation.

Remember that freezing does not improve overripe, underripe, or otherwise inferior vegetables. So choose only high-quality produce.

Be sure to use moisture-proof, vapor-proof packaging to keep the vegetable's natural moisture from escaping. In addition to special freezer bags and cartons, you can use glass, metal, or rigid plastic containers. Suitable wrapping materials include heavy-duty aluminum foil and laminated freezer paper.

Before freezing, blanch vegetables to stop enzyme action so that food retains good color, flavor, texture, and nutritive value. Wash vegetables in cold water. Then place 1 pound of vegetables in the basket of a blancher or in a wire-mesh basket, colander, or cheesecloth bag. Immerse in 1 gallon of boiling water (2 gallons for leafy greens). Cover and boil for the time indicated in the chart. Start timing immediately, allowing 1 minute longer in areas over 5,000 feet above sea level.

Cool vegetables quickly after removing from boiling water by immersing in ice water for a few minutes. Drain well before packaging.

You can also blanch vegetables in a microwave oven. Work with small amounts of vegetables at a time. If you chop vegetables before freezing, make the pieces a uniform size. Wash the vegetables in cold water, place in a microwave-safe dish, and add ¼ to ½ cup of water (leafy vegetables need no water). Cover the dish with a lid or heavy-duty plastic wrap.

Blanching time will vary from as little as 2 to 3 minutes for yellow squash and spinach to 4 to 5 minutes for broccoli and carrots. Stir the vegetables halfway through blanching, and check at the lower end of the range. Blanching is complete when the vegetable is evenly heated and has a uniformly bright color.

After blanching, immediately plunge the vegetables into ice water to stop the cooking process. When thoroughly cooled, drain well on paper towels and pat dry.

When you fill containers, be sure to leave headspace for the vegetables to expand during freezing: ½ inch in wide-mouthed pint containers, 1 inch in wide-mouthed quart containers, ¾ inch in narrow-top pint containers, 1½ inches in narrow-top quart containers. If you use plastic bags, be sure to press out all excess air before fastening them. Wrapping should be tightly molded to vegetables to prevent air pockets; tape securely with freezer tape. Frozen vegetables keep well for 8 to 12 months.

Blanching Times—Conventional Method	
Vegetable	**Blanching Time (in minutes)**
Asparagus	2-4
Beans, Green (pieces)	3
Broccoli (spears)	3
Brussels Sprouts	3-5
Cauliflower (florets)	3
Corn (off cob)	4
Corn (on cob)	7-11
Greens	2-3
Okra (whole)	3-4
Peas, English	1-2
Squash, Summer	3
Squash, Winter	cook until tender
Tomatoes, Stewed	cook until tender

After blanching and cooling vegetables, drain them well by spreading them on a clean towel before packing.

Pickling

Pickles are usually made by two general methods: brined and fresh-pack. Brined pickles, also called fermented or long-process pickles, are soaked in brine for at least two weeks. After removing the salt from the cured product, vinegar, sugar, and spices are added.

Fresh-pack or quick-process pickles are soaked in a brine overnight or in ice water for a few hours.

General Instructions

Use only fresh, firm, unbruised vegetables. Immature or slightly underripe produce makes the best pickles. Use a high-grade cider or white distilled vinegar of 4 to 6 percent acidity. Do not use vinegars of unknown acidity, and do not dilute vinegar unless instructed to do so. When color is important, such as in pickled onions and cauliflower, use white distilled vinegar.

Use pure granulated pickling salt rather than iodized table salt, which could cause the pickles to turn dark. Noniodized table salt may be used, but it may make the brine dark and cloudy.

Make sure spices are fresh; if they have been stored several years, they have probably lost their flavor.

To make brine, use soft water. If your water is hard, boil it 15 minutes, then let it stand 24 hours. Remove any scum on the top and ladle water out without disturbing sediment on the bottom. Before using, add 1 tablespoon of vinegar to each gallon.

Heat pickling liquids in enamel, stainless steel, aluminum, or glass containers. Iron, copper, brass, or zinc containers or utensils may cause an undesirable taste and color and should not be used.

To soak pickles in brine, use glass or stoneware containers. For canning, use standard canning jars and lids that have been sterilized. As for canning vegetables, use new lids every year.

Pack pickles and relishes according to the recipe you are using. Can and process as directed under "General Canning Procedure" for boiling-water-bath canning. Make sure the water is boiling when you place the jars on the rack.

When processing is completed, remove jars from the canner and cool as directed in "General Canning Procedure."

Pickled vegetables and fruits are best if you use slightly underripe or immature produce.

Causes of Pickling Problems

Shriveled pickles may be caused by too strong a vinegar, sugar, or salt solution at the start of the process. If you are making very sweet or very sour pickles, start with a diluted solution and increase strength gradually. Overcooking or overprocessing may also cause shriveling.

Hollow pickles usually result from using poorly developed cucumbers or cucumbers which have been stored too long; pickles fermenting too rapidly (caused by high temperatures), or using too strong or too weak a brine during fermentation.

Soft or slippery pickles result from spoilage caused by having too weak a brine, not covering pickles with brine, or not removing scum when it forms.

Dark pickles may be caused by overcooking or use of iron utensils, ground spices, too much spice, iodized salt, or minerals in the water.

Drying the Harvest

Drying vegetables can be as easy as stringing them on wire or strong thread and hanging them from rafters. All you need is a warm, insect-free area where air circulates freely. This works well for long-stemmed onions, beans, chile peppers, and corn on the cob. Other vegetables may take weeks to dry this way, however, and they lose color and flavor.

Home dehydrators make vegetable drying faster and easier and assure consistent results. The dehydrator circulates warm air over the vegetables so they dry quickly and evenly. Most vegetables take 4 to 24 hours to dry in a dehydrator; but many factors, such as size of the load and moisture content of the vegetables, affect drying time. Follow the manufacturer's directions when using a home dehydrator.

For best results, dry only those vegetables that are at their peak of maturity. Immature vegetables tend to have poor color and flavor when dried. Overmature ones tend to be tough. All vegetables may be dried together except onions and peppers; these tend to flavor milder vegetables. Do not dry thin vegetables such as greens with larger, moist vegetables.

Using Dried Vegetables

Before using dried vegetables, soak them so they can reabsorb most of the lost water. If you place them directly into a boiling soup without rehydrating them, they will be tough.

To rehydrate, cover the vegetables with cold or boiling water and let stand until vegetables are plump. Rehydrating may take 15 minutes to

To dry hot peppers for winter use, string them on strong thread or very fine cotton string. Hang them to dry in a warm, well-ventilated place until the peppers are dry. Then store in a cool, dry location.

2 hours, depending on the thickness of the vegetable and the temperature of the water used. When you cook rehydrated vegetables, remember that they are more tender if simmered than if cooked over high heat.

Cabbage.

Cherry pepper.

Asparagus.

Spinach.

Broccoli.

Vegetables

Every gardener has favorite vegetables he or she wants to grow. In this section, you will find information for growing the most popular vegetables. There are also some less familiar ones that can add variety and interest to menus or present a challenge to the adventurous.

An in-depth review gives the basics for growing each vegetable, as well as tips from experienced gardeners. The "At-A-Glance" is a special feature providing a quick reference and essential information.

"Garden Season" refers to the season or seasons during which the plants normally grow and produce harvests. Remember that a fall garden season for many cool weather vegetables requires planting in late summer. (You will find specific planting information in the in-depth review and in the planting charts in the chapter on "Getting Started.")

The phrase "Days Until Harvest" means from the time of sowing seeds, unless otherwise indicated by the words "after transplanting." The range of dates indicates the shortest time to harvest, using early-maturing selections; and the longest time, using later-maturing ones.

The "Amount to Plant per Person" is largely based on USDA data, with additional information from other sources, including the experience of the authors. Use the figures as a general guideline at first; then, based on your own experience and your family's preferences, you can adjust the amount you plant.

The item "Comments" highlights some of the most important cultural information for that particular vegetable.

You will also find a bonus in this chapter; recipes have been included for each vegetable. To ensure the quality of the recipes, each has been prepared and evaluated by the *Southern Living* Foods Staff in the *Southern Living* test kitchens. In choosing the recipes, they considered taste, appearance, ease of preparation, and cost of the dish. These recipes should allow you to enjoy the true flavor of the fresh vegetable.

So, if you have never grown leeks, Jerusalem artichokes, or salsify before, the recipes may tempt you to try. And if you have a bumper crop of tomatoes, squash, or beans, the recipes might give you ideas for some different ways to prepare them. We hope that the unique combination of cultural information and recipes will help you receive more enjoyment from growing vegetables and using the fresh harvests.

Pumpkins.

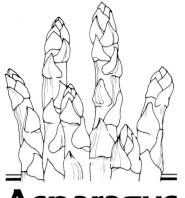

Asparagus

Starting an asparagus bed requires patience in the beginning: You must wait 2 full years from the time you plant until you can harvest the first spear. But then the bed rewards you with succulent spears spring after spring, with no replanting necessary.

Asparagus requires a dormant period in winter, so it grows best in the Upper and Middle South, where the ground often freezes. In the Lower South, spears are thinner and less numerous because of the mild winter and hotter growing season.

Soil Preparation

Being a perennial, asparagus remains in the same bed for years. Choose a location where the plants are undisturbed by gardening activities and will not shade other vegetables. The site must also drain well, or the asparagus will rot.

Because you cannot work the soil deeply once the asparagus is planted, proper bed preparation is a must. In North Florida and southeastern coastal areas, asparagus requires an extrarich soil, such as muck, for better growth and to compensate for the mild climate.

In late winter or early spring, just before planting time, dig a trench 18 inches deep and 18 to 24 inches wide. According to recommendations from your soil test, add lime to the soil from the trench. Work in 2 parts organic matter, such as leaf mold or compost, to 1 part soil. Use 3 parts organic matter when mixing soil in North Florida and southeastern coastal areas. To help improve drainage of heavy clay soils, also work in 1 part sand. In the bottom of the trench, spread 4 to 6 inches of amended soil and 2 inches of well-rotted manure and work in 10-10-10 at the rate of 1 cup per 50 square feet. Cover with 2 inches of amended soil. Now the bed is ready for planting.

Planting and Culture

The easiest way to start asparagus is from crowns in early spring. (The crown is the portion of the plant with an underground stem and attached roots.) Purchase disease-free 1- or 2-year-old crowns from a reputable nursery or mail-order source. They should be firm and moist; avoid crowns that look dry, shrivelled, or are soft and brown with rot.

AT A GLANCE

Garden Season: Perennial, comes up in early spring
Days until Harvest: 2 years after planting (3rd spring)
Amount to Plant Per Person: 10-15 crowns for fresh use, an additional 10-15 for storage
Serious Insects: Asparagus beetle
Serious Diseases: Rust
Comments: Be sure to amend soil well and prepare bed deeply before planting. Not recommended for Central and South Florida.

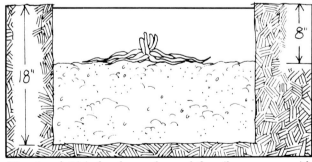

Dig a trench 18 inches deep and amend the soil you remove with organic matter. Refill the trench with amended soil, a layer of well-rotted manure, and more soil. Set crowns so that roots are spread out in their natural position.

Asparagus spears emerge every year in early spring. Do not harvest those that appear the first or second spring after planting. The plants need at least 2 years to become well established.

Plant crowns 18 to 24 inches apart in the trench, spreading roots out in their natural position. They will be 8 to 10 inches below ground level. Cover with 2 to 3 inches of amended soil. As the plants grow, add more amended soil, being careful not to cover the growing tips. By the end of the first growing season, the trench should be overfilled to form a 3-inch ridge. This ridge promotes good drainage and helps avoid root and crown rot.

Do not harvest spears that appear from newly planted crowns the first spring. The spears will grow into 4- to 6-foot-tall stalks with wispy foliage that supplies food to the plant. This food supply is critical to the plant's initial establishment and the next year's growth. Each fall, after frost kills the stalks, remove them and cover the bed with 2 to 3 inches of manure.

When shoots appear the second spring, again resist the temptation to harvest them. The bed needs this year to become better established. Apply ½ cup of 10-10-10 per 50 square feet in late winter and late spring the second year.

Beginning the third year, fertilize the asparagus bed in late winter before growth begins and after the season's harvest. Apply ¼ cup of 10-10-10 per 50 square feet. The third spring, you can harvest for 2 weeks, but do not overharvest or you will reduce future production. The next year, harvest for 4 weeks, and 8 weeks each spring thereafter.

Cooling the soil around the crowns can increase spear size during the harvesting season. To do this, mound soil over the row 2 to 3 weeks after the first cutting. After the harvest ends, rake the soil back to the 3-inch ridge.

Harvest

To harvest, cut or snap the spears barely below ground level when they are 6 to 7 inches long and less than 1 inch in diameter. Cut before the tip of the spear begins to open. Check the beds daily because spears emerge quickly as the weather warms. Stop harvesting if emerging spears are pencil-sized. In North Florida and southeastern coastal areas, asparagus spears are likely to be fibrous, so peel the spears before cooking.

Recommended Selection

Mary Washington is recommended.

EASY FRESH ASPARAGUS
1 pound fresh asparagus spears
2 tablespoons butter or margarine
1 teaspoon chicken-flavored bouillon granules
2 teaspoons lemon juice
  Dash of pepper
½ cup water

Wash asparagus; snap off tough ends. Remove scales with a knife or vegetable peeler.

Arrange asparagus in a large skillet. Dot with butter. Sprinkle with bouillon granules, lemon juice, and pepper. Pour ½ cup water into skillet; cover and steam 5 to 7 minutes or until asparagus is crisp-tender. Yield: 4 servings.

ASPARAGUS VINAIGRETTE
1 pound fresh asparagus spears
⅓ cup chopped sweet pickle
¼ cup olive oil
2 tablespoons sweet pickle juice
2 tablespoons vinegar
1 teaspoon chopped fresh chives
¼ teaspoon salt
  Dash of pepper

Wash asparagus; snap off tough ends. Remove scales with a knife or vegetable peeler.

Cook asparagus in a small amount of boiling water 6 to 8 minutes or until crisp-tender; drain. Arrange asparagus in a shallow serving dish.

Combine remaining ingredients; mix well, and pour over asparagus. Cover and chill until ready to serve. Yield: 4 servings.

Unharvested spears eventually grow into 4- to 6-foot stalks of feathery foliage. Frost kills them back in the fall.

Beans are one of the easiest vegetables to grow and are also among the most productive. The large seeds germinate quickly and the plants grow fast, sometimes producing the first harvest before spring officially ends.

The two most popular beans grown in the South are snap beans (also called green beans or string beans) and shell beans (such as limas). Snap beans are grown for their tender, immature pods, which are harvested before the seeds inside mature. The term string bean refers to the stringy fiber that was present in older selections. Today's improved selections generally do not develop strings until the pods are mature.

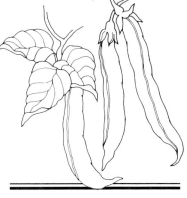

Beans

Shell beans are not grown for their pods but for the seeds (the beans) inside the pod. The beans are used fresh in the immature, "green shell" stage. Among these are the popular baby limas and horticultural beans. You can also let shell beans mature on the vine for easy storage as dried beans.

Bush and Vining Growth Habits

Snap and shell beans have two basic growth habits: bush and vining. Bush beans grow 1 to 2 feet tall and do not need support. Vining plants, called "pole beans," are twining vines 5 to 10 feet long; they must climb on a trellis or other support. (*See page 88 for supports.*)

Bush beans mature about 2 weeks sooner than pole beans, but they do not bear as much or as long. They usually give 2 to 3 good harvests over a 4-week period.

Pole beans continue to grow and produce new pods all summer, providing the plants are kept harvested. Two plantings about 4 weeks apart in spring should supply you with beans until the fall temperatures drop below 50 degrees. Also,

---

AT A GLANCE

Garden Season: Spring, summer, fall
Days until Harvest: 50-90
Amount to Plant Per Person: Bush beans, 15 feet of row or 7-8 feet of 3-foot-wide row for fresh use, an additional 15 feet of row or 7-8 feet of wide row for storage; pole beans, 5 feet of row for fresh use, an additional 10 feet for storage
Serious Insects: Mexican bean beetle, mites
Serious Diseases: Rust, mildews
Comments: Avoid overfertilizing. Keep well watered; drought-stressed plants may drop blossoms and pods.

Planting bush beans in a wide bed as shown here increases the number of plants you can grow over the traditional row method, so yields are higher.

Bean seeds germinate in about a week in warm, moist soil. If your soil tends to crust over when dry, cover the seeds with sand, vermiculite, or sphagnum peat moss to help seedlings emerge more easily.

because they grow up a trellis, pole beans require less garden space than bush beans.

Many gardeners plant bush beans for the first early harvest, even though it is more work to pick the low-growing beans from a kneeling or stooping position. Then they rely on the easier-to-pick pole beans for later harvests.

Planting and Culture

Begin planting snap and most shell beans just after the last frost, but do not plant limas until 2 weeks later; they need warmer soil. To plant pole beans, sow seeds along a sturdy trellis or other support. Allow 4 feet between trellises. Space seeds 4 to 6 inches apart and cover them with ½ to 1 inch of soil.

Plant bush beans 3 to 4 inches apart at the same depth but in rows that are 3 feet apart. Or plant in 3-foot-wide rows or beds, leaving 1½ to 2 feet between the beds.

You can plant bush beans through midsummer for continuous harvests into fall. Because bush snap beans tend to drop blossoms when temperatures are higher than 90 degrees, time spring plantings so that pods will be set by early summer. Or use heat-tolerant selections such as Contender.

Too much nitrogen can delay maturity or cause excessive vine growth and poor fruiting. On rich, organic soils the preplant fertilization should be sufficient. On other soils, side-dress when young plants develop 3 to 4 leaves, applying about ¼ cup of 10-10-10 per 20 feet of row. Repeat for pole beans after the first harvest.

Water beans regularly. Drought-stressed plants may drop blossoms or pods or may produce partly filled pods with shrivelled tips. Avoid overwatering, as it can also cause plants to drop blossoms and pods.

Harvest

Harvest bush snap beans when pods are 3 to 6 inches long and pole snap beans when 4 to 6 inches long. Pods should be bright green, smooth, and crisp, and should snap with a pop. The seeds inside should still be small. If you leave the pods on the plants until they are lumpy, they may be tough and stringy. At this stage you can shell them and cook as you would Southern peas.

Pole beans mature later than bush beans, but continue producing over a longer period. One or two plantings will provide harvests throughout the summer.

The pods of immature limas are flat, filling out as the beans become fully formed.

Limas, kidney, and pinto beans are ready to harvest for fresh use as soon as the seeds are fully formed in the pods. For more tender limas, pick while beans are small. Mature limas are more "meaty." Horticultural beans and scarlet runner beans may be used as you would snap beans, if you pick the pods while they are young and tender. Or wait until the seeds show in the pods and use as you would lima beans.

Recommended Selections

Selections of bush snap beans recommended for the South include Burpee's Tenderpod, Tenderette, Contender, Bush Blue Lake, Top Crop, Provider, Astro, Roma, and Harvester. Selections of pole snap beans for the South include Kentucky Wonder 191, Dade, McCaslan, Blue Lake, and Kentucky Wonder.

Lima selections with large, meaty seeds include bush types such as Fordhook 242, and pole types such as King of the Garden and Florida Speckled. Butterbeans, which are also called baby limas, have small seeds. Recommended selections include the bush types Henderson, Jackson Wonder, and Dixie Butter Pea, and the pole type Carolina Sieva.

Selections of horticultural beans include Taylor's Dwarf ("October bean"), French, and Cranberry. Selections of pinto beans include Pinto and Pinto 111. Catalogs usually list kidney beans simply as red and white.

Bush snap beans are table-ready 6 to 8 weeks after planting. Pick them as they reach 3 to 6 inches in length, pinching carefully to avoid damaging the plant.

If you plant bush limas in conventional rows, leave 3 feet between rows so you will have room to work once the plants get bushy.

COLD GREEN BEAN SALAD

½ pound new potatoes, peeled and cubed
1 pound fresh green beans
3 tablespoons olive oil
1 tablespoon white wine vinegar
1 tablespoon lemon juice
1 tablespoon fresh basil or 1 teaspoon whole basil
½ teaspoon salt
⅛ teaspoon garlic powder
⅛ teaspoon coarsely ground black pepper

Cook potatoes in enough boiling water to cover 15 to 20 minutes; drain well, and set aside.

Remove strings from beans; cut beans into 1½-inch pieces. Wash thoroughly. Cover beans with water, and bring to a boil. Reduce heat, cover, and simmer 8 to 10 minutes or until crisp-tender. Drain.

Combine potatoes and beans, tossing gently. Combine remaining ingredients, stirring well; pour over vegetables, tossing gently to coat. Cover and chill at least 4 hours. Yield: 4 to 6 servings.

GREEN BEANS WITH BASIL

1 pound fresh green beans
2 cups water
Salt
½ cup chopped onion
¼ cup chopped celery
2 tablespoons butter or margarine
1 clove garlic, minced
1½ teaspoons minced fresh basil or ½ teaspoon dried whole basil
¼ teaspoon minced fresh rosemary or ½ teaspoon dried whole rosemary

Remove strings from beans; cut beans into 1-inch pieces. Wash thoroughly. Place 2 cups water, salt to taste, and beans in a medium saucepan, and bring to a boil. Reduce heat, cover, and simmer 10 minutes; drain. Stir in remaining ingredients; cover and simmer 20 additional minutes or until tender. Yield: 3 to 4 servings.

SWEET AND SOUR GREEN BEANS

2 pounds fresh green beans
1 quart water
Salt
5 slices bacon
¼ cup chopped green onions
¼ cup water
1 tablespoon vinegar
1 tablespoon cornstarch
1 tablespoon sugar
¼ teaspoon salt
Dash of pepper

Remove strings from beans; cut beans into 1½-inch pieces. Wash thoroughly. Place 1 quart water and salt to taste in a medium saucepan, and bring to a boil. Add beans; reduce heat, cover, and simmer 10 to 12 minutes or until beans are crisp-tender. Drain well and set aside.

Cook bacon in a large skillet until crisp; remove bacon, reserving 1 tablespoon drippings in skillet. Crumble bacon, and set aside. Sauté onions in bacon drippings until tender.

Combine ¼ cup water, vinegar, and cornstarch, stirring until smooth. Pour cornstarch mixture over onions; cook, stirring often, over medium heat until thickened. Stir in sugar, ¼ teaspoon salt, and pepper. Add green beans, stirring to coat. Top with reserved bacon. Yield: 6 to 8 servings.

GREEN BEANS GOLDENROD

2 pounds fresh green beans
1½ quarts water
Salt
2 hard-cooked eggs
2 teaspoons butter or margarine
2 teaspoons all-purpose flour
½ cup milk
¼ teaspoon salt
⅛ teaspoon pepper
½ cup mayonnaise

Cut beans into 2-inch pieces, and wash. Bring 1½ quarts water, salt to taste, and beans to a boil. Reduce heat, cover, and simmer 20 to 30 minutes or until tender. Drain; set aside.

Chop egg whites; set whites and yolks aside.

Melt butter in a heavy saucepan; add flour, stirring until smooth. Cook 1 minute, stirring constantly. Gradually add milk; cook over medium heat, stirring constantly, until thickened and bubbly. Stir in ¼ teaspoon salt, pepper, and chopped egg white. Remove from heat; stir in mayonnaise.

Arrange beans in a serving dish; spoon sauce over top. Sieve egg yolks and sprinkle over sauce. Yield: 6 to 8 servings.

SAUCY GREEN BEAN BAKE

1 pound fresh green beans
½ cup chopped onion
⅓ cup chopped green pepper
1 clove garlic, minced
2 tablespoons butter or margarine, melted
1 (8-ounce) can tomato sauce
2 tablespoons chopped pimiento
1 tablespoon prepared mustard
⅛ teaspoon pepper
¾ cup (3 ounces) shredded process American cheese

Cut beans into 2-inch pieces, and wash thoroughly. Cook beans, covered, in boiling water 20 minutes or until tender; drain well, and set aside.

Sauté onion, green pepper, and garlic in butter until onion is tender. Add beans, tomato sauce, pimiento, mustard, and pepper; stir well. Spoon into a 1¾-quart casserole. Bake at 350° for 20 minutes; top with cheese; bake 5 additional minutes or until cheese melts. Yield: 4 to 6 servings.

Beets

Beets are grown mainly for their roots, but many Southerners also enjoy the bonus of their tender, fresh greens, either cooked or raw in salads. They are a good crop for small gardens because they produce a lot in a limited space and are relatively pest-free.

If your idea of a beet is a round, red root, you will be surprised by the variety available. There are "baby" beets, which are small roots popular for serving whole; cylindrical roots that provide many uniform slices; and a golden-colored beet that does not "bleed" like red beets do. In addition, there are some selections that are especially popular for their tasty, solid-green tops.

Planting and Culture

For the best texture and flavor, beets need the cool weather of early spring and fall. Roots grown in hot weather become tough and woody and may develop alternate white and red or yellow circles.

In spring, begin sowing seeds 2 to 4 weeks before the last frost. Instead of sowing all the seeds at once, make 2 additional sowings spaced 2 to 3 weeks apart for a steady supply of roots and greens in spring. For fall and winter crops, plant seeds in late summer and make 3 successive sowings about 2 weeks apart.

Beet seeds germinate slowly, but soaking them overnight helps speed the process. Before planting, work ½ cup of 10-10-10 per 10 feet of row into the soil. Scatter the seeds over a 15-inch-wide bed, or sow 2 inches apart in single rows that are spaced 1 foot apart. Cover with ½ to 1 inch of soil. Water gently and thoroughly to keep the soil moist for good germination.

Beet seeds are actually clusters of seeds and each cluster produces 4 to 6 seedlings. When the seedlings are about 1 inch tall, thin the clusters to 1 plant every 2 to 4 inches. Early thinning is important because crowding results in small, tough, stringy roots. Instead of pulling up each plant, simply pinch it off near ground level; it will not come back.

To produce the best roots, beets must grow quickly and steadily. Four to six weeks after planting, side-dress plants with ½ cup of 10-10-10 per 10 feet of row.

Harvest

Beet greens can be harvested when they are 6 inches tall. Snap off the outer leaves, but do not disturb the inner ones so that more leaves will be

---

AT A GLANCE

Garden Season: Early spring, fall
Days until Harvest: 55-80
Amount to Plant Per Person: Roots, 5 feet of row or 2-3 feet of 18-inch-wide row for fresh use, an additional 10 feet of row or 4-6 feet of wide row for storage; greens, 3 feet of row or 2 feet of wide row for fresh use, an additional 6 feet or 4 feet of wide row for storage.
Serious Insects or Diseases: None
Comments: Soak seeds overnight to speed germination.

Grow beets for the greens as well as the roots. But be sure to plant extra for this purpose, because continually picking the leaves keeps roots from forming properly.

produced for later harvests. If you plan to harvest greens regularly, be sure to plant additional beets for this purpose alone, as continual harvesting of greens keeps roots from forming properly.

Pull roots when they are 1 to 3 inches in diameter. If they are larger than this, the roots are sweeter but tougher. Beets that mature in the fall may be left in the ground until you are ready to use them. If the soil normally freezes hard in your area, spread a 4- to 6-inch layer of mulch over the row before frost to protect the beets and to make pulling them easier. In the Upper and Middle South, you may prefer to pull the beets before the first hard freeze and store them. (*See page 115.*)

Recommended Selections

Recommended selections include Detroit Dark Red; Little Ball; Green Top Bunching (grown primarily for greens); Lutz Green Leaf; and Burpee Golden Beet.

COLD BORSCHT

  1 pound fresh beets
  4 medium potatoes, peeled and cubed
  1 green onion, chopped
  1 medium carrot, scraped and sliced
  2 quarts water
  1 (8-ounce) carton commercial sour cream
  1 (10½-ounce) can chicken broth, undiluted
  ¾ teaspoon salt
  ¼ teaspoon white pepper
  2 teaspoons lemon juice

Leave root and 1 inch of stem on beets; scrub with a vegetable brush. Place beets in a saucepan; cover with water and bring to a boil. Reduce heat, cover, and simmer 20 minutes. Drain. Pour cold water over beets; drain. Trim beet roots and stems and rub off skins; cut beets into cubes.

Place beets, potatoes, onion, and carrot in a large Dutch oven; add 2 quarts water, and bring to a boil. Reduce heat, cover, and simmer 30 to 35 minutes or until vegetables are tender. Drain, reserving 1 cup liquid.

Puree vegetables in food processor or blender. Combine next 5 ingredients; mix well. Stir in vegetable puree and 1 cup reserved vegetable liquid, blending well. Chill. Yield: 6 cups.

ORANGE GLAZED BEETS

  2 pounds fresh beets
  ¼ cup butter or margarine
  ⅓ cup sugar
1½ teaspoons grated orange rind
  ¼ cup orange liqueur

Leave root and 1 inch of stem on beets; scrub with a vegetable brush. Place beets in a saucepan; cover with water, and bring to a boil. Reduce heat, cover, and simmer 35 to 40 minutes or until tender. Drain. Pour cold water over beets, and drain again. Trim off beet roots and stems, and rub off skins; cut beets into julienne strips, and place in a serving dish.

Melt butter in a small saucepan; add sugar, and stir to dissolve. Add orange rind; pour glaze over hot beets.

Place orange liqueur in a small, long-handled pan; heat just until warm. Ignite with a long match, and pour over beets. Yield: 6 servings.

• To keep fresh beets from losing their color during cooking, do not peel until after cooking. Also leave 1 to 2 inches of stem attached.

Harvest beet roots when they are 1 to 3 inches in diameter, firm, and deeply colored.

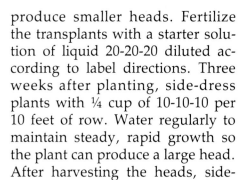

Broccoli

Many Southern gardeners grow two crops of broccoli, one in spring and one in fall. To produce the large heads you see in seed catalogs or in the grocery requires a longer period of mild weather than we have over most of the South. But you can usually expect plants to bear heads at least 4 inches across; and if the season is without extreme temperature fluctuations, heads may reach their maximum size (up to 8 inches for some selections).

Planting and Culture

Always start broccoli from transplants to get a head start on the growing season. Broccoli does not grow well after warm weather arrives in spring, and a hard freeze in fall will kill plants. In spring, plant 4 weeks before the last frost. For a fall crop, plant in late summer or early fall.

Set plants 18 to 24 inches apart in rows 2 to 3 feet apart. Space properly, as crowded plants produce smaller heads. Fertilize the transplants with a starter solution of liquid 20-20-20 diluted according to label directions. Three weeks after planting, side-dress plants with ¼ cup of 10-10-10 per 10 feet of row. Water regularly to maintain steady, rapid growth so the plant can produce a large head. After harvesting the heads, side-dress again to encourage production of side shoots.

Harvest

The time to harvest broccoli is when the hundreds of tiny green flower buds that form the head are still green and tightly closed. Cut the stem 5 to 6 inches below the head. You can harvest anytime after the head forms; but when the florets begin to open, exposing the yellow petals, the broccoli is overmature. Its flavor and texture will be inferior.

In addition to the large, central head, broccoli forms small flower clusters or side shoots about 1 inch in diameter along the stem. These shoots are usually ready to harvest 2 to 3 weeks after

---

AT A GLANCE

Garden Season: Early spring, fall
Days until Harvest: 60-85 after transplanting
Amount to Plant Per Person: 3-5 plants for fresh use, an additional 5-7 for storage
Serious Insects: Cabbage looper, imported cabbageworm
Serious Diseases: Black rot, downy mildew
Comments: Best as a fall crop. To produce large heads, do not crowd plants in the row, and be sure to water and fertilize regularly for uninterrupted growth.

Cut the central head when it is still green and the flower buds (florets) are tightly closed.

Plant three to five broccoli plants per person for fresh use and another five to seven to have some to freeze.

Harvest

Harvest sprouts when they are about 1 inch in diameter. Removing the lower leaves may make it easier to twist the buds off the stem. Some gardeners believe that removing the leaves also hastens maturity and increases production, but there is no agreement on this.

Brussels sprouts can survive occasional hard freezes, and frost sweetens their flavor. Where winters are mild, such as along coastal areas, they will produce all winter and into early spring. Elsewhere in the Lower South, the plants will overwinter without producing new sprouts until the next spring; then they may produce a few before they bolt. Winter temperatures below 26 degrees can kill the plants.

Recommended Selections

Selections of brussels sprouts recommended for the South include Jade Cross Hybrid and Long Island Improved.

Harvest sprouts when they are about 1 inch in diameter.

FRIED BRUSSELS SPROUTS

1½ pounds fresh brussels sprouts
1 (13-ounce) can chicken broth, undiluted
4 eggs
2 tablespoons milk
1½ cups Italian-style breadcrumbs
   Vegetable oil

Wash brussels sprouts thoroughly; drop into boiling chicken broth. Cover and simmer 7 minutes or until crisp-tender. Drain well.

Combine eggs and milk, beating well. Dip brussels sprouts into egg mixture; coat in breadcrumbs. Repeat coating procedure twice for each brussels sprout. Drop a few coated sprouts in hot oil (375°); fry 2 to 3 minutes or until golden brown, turning once. Drain on paper towels. Repeat with remaining sprouts. Yield: 6 servings.

SWEET AND SOUR BRUSSELS SPROUTS

1½ pounds fresh brussels sprouts
8 slices bacon
2 tablespoons vinegar
2 teaspoons sugar
½ teaspoon salt
¼ teaspoon garlic powder
⅛ teaspoon pepper

Wash brussels sprouts thoroughly; slash bottom of each crosswise-fashion. Cover with water and bring to a boil. Reduce heat, cover, and simmer 7 minutes or until crisp-tender. Drain well.

Cook bacon in a large skillet until crisp; remove bacon, reserving ¼ cup drippings in skillet. Crumble bacon and set aside. Add next 5 ingredients to reserved drippings; bring to a boil, stirring occasionally. Add brussels sprouts; stir until thoroughly heated. Sprinkle with bacon. Yield: 6 servings.

COCKTAIL BRUSSELS SPROUTS

2 pounds fresh brussels sprouts
1 cup mayonnaise
2 tablespoons lemon juice
2 teaspoons grated onion
2 teaspoons sugar
½ teaspoon curry powder

Wash brussels sprouts thoroughly; slash bottom of each crosswise-fashion. Cover with water and bring to a boil. Reduce heat, cover, and simmer 7 minutes or until crisp-tender. Drain well.

Combine remaining ingredients; stir well. Arrange brussels sprouts on a platter; serve with wooden picks and sauce for dipping. Yield: 16 appetizer servings.

Note: To serve as a side dish, place brussels sprouts in serving dish and top with sauce. Yield: 8 servings.

Vegetables 137

The types of cabbages that you can grow will amaze you: Cabbage heads can be red, green, or white; flat, round, or pointed; and smooth or crinkly. With so many from which to choose, gardeners often grow cabbage for the opportunity to try something different.

Cabbage

Planting and Culture

Cabbage is one of the first plants you set out in spring, as it is quite hardy and must mature in cool weather to produce firm, sweet heads. Set out transplants 4 to 6 weeks before the last frost. Use only healthy transplants with short, strong stems.

Cabbage is especially practical as a fall crop, since it can remain in the garden for several weeks after it has matured. For a fall crop, set out transplants or sow seeds in mid- to late summer (8 to 14 weeks before the first frost). If you grow cabbage for winter storage, you will probably have to grow your own transplants or start from seeds because selections with the best storage quality may not be available as transplants. If you sow seeds directly in the garden, plant them ½ inch deep. Keep the seedbed moist, watering daily if necessary, to ensure good germination.

You can control the size of the head by choice of selection and by altering the spacing in the row. To grow small heads (2 to 4 pounds, 4½ to 6 inches in diameter), set transplants 12 inches apart. For larger heads, allow 15 to 18 inches between plants. Some late-season selections will produce heads 12 inches in diameter if you space plants 24 inches apart. Space all rows about 30 inches apart.

Fertilize transplants with a starter solution of liquid 20-20-20 diluted according to label directions. Three weeks after setting out plants, side-dress with ¼ cup of 10-10-10 per 10 feet of row. Repeat again 3 weeks later. Do not fertilize after cabbage is in the loose-head stage; too much nitrogen can cause heads to split.

Cabbage heads may also split if the plants receive too much water after the heads are solid. To prevent this, reduce watering as heads near maturity.

Harvest

Harvest heads anytime once they are firm and solid, from 4 inches in diameter until they reach full size at 6 to 12 inches in diameter. Harvest before heads begin to split, cutting below the head with a sharp knife. If you leave the bottom leaves in place, the plant may produce several tiny, loose heads for a later harvest.

AT A GLANCE

Garden Season: Early spring, fall
Days until Harvest: Cabbage, 70-105 days after transplanting; Chinese cabbage, 40-70 days after transplanting or sowing seed
Amount to Plant Per Person: Cabbage, 3-4 plants for fresh use, an additional 5-10 for storage; Chinese cabbage, 2 plants for fresh use
Serious Insects: Cabbage looper, imported cabbageworm, slugs
Serious Diseases: Black rot, downy mildew
Comments: Control insects early because they can ruin a crop quickly. As cabbage heads approach maturity, reduce watering to prevent splitting. Chinese cabbage is best as a fall crop.

The spacing at which you set plants will determine the size of the head that develops. Closer spacing produces smaller heads. Remember that you only need three to four plants per person to have plenty for fresh use.

When the first fall frost is predicted, harvest young heads, but leave those that are mature in place until you are ready to use them. In the Upper and Middle South, protect them with a layer of mulch, and harvest before temperatures drop to 20 degrees.

Recommended Selections

Choosing selections with different maturity dates allows you to spread harvests over a longer period. Early-maturing and midseason selections are good for both spring and fall crops. The late-maturing selections are best for the fall garden, because the weather is becoming cooler as they mature.

Cabbage selections recommended throughout the South include the early-maturing selections Red Acre and Early Round Dutch; midseason selections Savoy Ace, Savoy King, and Chieftain Savoy; and the late-maturing selection Danish Ballhead. Chieftain Savoy stands well in the garden without splitting or bursting. Danish Ballhead is a good selection for winter storage.

Recommended for the Upper and Middle South are the early-maturing selections Golden Acre and Stonehead. For the Lower South, Rio Verde is a good midseason selection.

Chinese Cabbage

Chinese cabbage is a must for gardeners who like to stir-fry. There are 2 types, heading and nonheading. The heading types are long and slender or egg-shaped. The inner leaves blanch to light green or nearly white and are thin like mustard greens. Heads mature in about 60 to 70 days. Nonheading types have loose, thick leaves on long, white stalks. Most selections mature quickly, in 45 to 60 days.

Planting and Culture

Chinese cabbage may be grown in early spring, but most selections do best in the fall, so plant in late summer or early fall. In spring, lengthening days (combined with erratic temperature changes) cause plants to bolt. If you plant a spring crop, be sure to start 4 to 6 weeks before the last frost.

You can start Chinese cabbage from seeds sown directly in the garden in the fall, but it is better to start the spring crop from transplants. (*See page 53 for starting transplants.*) Set plants 12

Chinese cabbage is best as a fall crop and can tolerate light frost.

Cabbage is ready to harvest when the head feels firm and does not yield to pressure.

Vegetables 139

to 15 inches apart in rows 24 to 30 inches apart, or sow seeds ½ inch deep and thin to this spacing. Fertilize transplants or seedlings with a starter solution such as liquid 20-20-20 diluted according to label directions.

Side-dress 3 weeks later with ¼ cup of 10-10-10 per 10 feet of row. Keep the soil evenly moist, but avoid overwatering. Too much water or fertilizer can cause heading types to split.

Harvest

Heading-type Chinese cabbage is ready for harvest when the heads are 10 to 12 inches tall. Cut the plant at the base. Harvest nonheading types when the plants are 10 to 14 inches tall. A fall crop will tolerate light frost.

Recommended Selections

Recommended selections include heading-types Michihli and Tropical Pride. Pak Choi, Green Vegetable, and Spoon Cabbage are nonheading types. Tropical Pride is good for spring planting because it tolerates warm weather better, but may bolt in cooler temperatures.

Nonheading types of Chinese cabbage, such as Pak-Choi, mature quickly, in 6 to 7 weeks.

CABBAGE WEDGES WITH SOUR CREAM SAUCE

1 medium cabbage
2 tablespoons butter or margarine
2 tablespoons minced onion
1 tablespoon all-purpose flour
1 (8-ounce) carton commercial sour cream
2 teaspoons vinegar
½ teaspoon sugar
½ teaspoon salt
 Dash of pepper
 Paprika

Cut cabbage into 8 wedges, removing core; cover in a small amount of boiling water and cook 10 minutes. Drain well; place wedges on a serving platter.

Melt butter in a heavy saucepan over low heat; add onion and sauté until tender. Add flour, stirring until smooth. Cook 1 minute, stirring constantly. Gradually add sour cream and vinegar; cook over medium heat, stirring constantly, just until thickened and bubbly. Stir in sugar, salt, and pepper; pour sauce over cabbage. Sprinkle with paprika. Yield: 8 servings.

CABBAGE SCRAMBLE

3 cups shredded cabbage
1 cup thinly sliced carrots
½ cup chopped onion
½ cup water
2 teaspoons vegetable-flavored bouillon granules
¼ teaspoon dried whole oregano

Combine all ingredients in a large skillet; bring to a boil. Reduce heat, cover, and simmer 15 minutes, stirring occasionally. Drain before serving. Yield: 4 servings.

TEX-MEX CABBAGE

1 medium cabbage
2 tablespoons butter or margarine
1 tablespoon sugar
1 medium onion, thinly sliced
1 green pepper, thinly sliced into rings
1 (28-ounce) can tomatoes, drained and quartered
½ teaspoon salt
¼ teaspoon pepper
¾ cup (3 ounces) shredded Cheddar cheese

Cut cabbage into 6 wedges, removing core; cover in a small amount of boiling water and cook 10 minutes. Drain well; place wedges in a lightly greased 2-quart shallow baking dish.

Melt butter in a medium saucepan. Add sugar, onion, and green pepper; cook over medium heat, stirring constantly, until vegetables are tender. Stir in tomatoes, salt, and pepper; pour vegetable mixture over cabbage.

Sprinkle cheese over vegetables, and bake at 350° for 20 to 30 minutes or until thoroughly heated. Yield: 6 to 8 servings.

Preceding page. *Make the most of your spring and summer vegetable crop with Tomatoes Vinaigrette (page 205), Watermelon Rind Pickles (page 169), Cold Green Bean Salad (page 131), Corn Relish (page 155), and Garden Stuffed Yellow Squash (page 199).*

Capture the flavors and bright colors of fresh vegetables in Herbed Carrots (page 145), Creamy New Potatoes (page 185), Glazed Leeks (page 177), and Italian Celery (page 149).

Following page. *Autumn brings a bountiful garden harvest of Superb Pumpkin Bread (page 189), Rutabaga Delight (page 207), Crunchy Radish Salad (page 191), and Sesame Broccoli (page 135).*

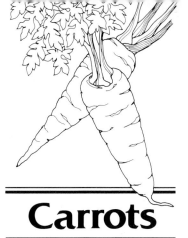

Carrots

The key to growing carrots successfully is loose, deep soil. If your soil is heavy clay or rocky, consider planting in raised beds, and choose selections that grow only 3 to 4 inches long. Long-rooted selections often grow crooked or forked in soil that is less than ideal.

Carrots are a good spring crop and even better for fall. The flavor improves as the weather cools. And you can leave roots in the ground, pulling them as needed until the first hard freeze.

Planting and Culture

For spring harvests, sow seeds about 6 weeks before the last frost. Make 2 or 3 small, consecutive plantings every 10 days to extend the harvest season. For a fall crop, sow in midsummer in the Upper and Middle South and in late summer in the Lower South. Be sure carrots have time to mature by the first hard freeze.

Before planting, work ½ cup of 10-10-10 per 10 feet of row into the soil. Sow the seeds thinly in rows that are 1½ feet apart. Or sow them in blocks or wide beds. Cover with no more than ¼ inch of soil. In soil that crusts over when dry, cover the seeds with sand, peat moss, perlite, or vermiculite instead of soil.

Seeds may take 1 to 3 weeks to germinate and all of them may not come up at the same time. Planting a few radish seeds with the carrots marks the row until the carrots emerge. To help seeds sown in late summer come up more easily, place a board over the row to keep the soil cool. Check frequently, and remove the board as soon as seedlings appear.

Keep the soil evenly moist from the time of planting. Roots will be stunted by competition with other roots, so pull all weeds and thin seedlings to 2 to 4 inches apart when they are 2 inches tall. Thin again 3 weeks later.

Overwatering can cause carrots to crack or split and underwatering can cause them to be tough and hairy, so water only when the top inch of soil is dry. Cover root tops with soil to prevent greening and bitterness.

Harvest

You can harvest carrots from the time the roots first develop until they reach maturity, which depends on the selection. If pulling carrots from the ground is difficult, water the soil. Trim the tops off immediately or the leaves will draw moisture from the roots and leave them limp and rubbery instead of crisp.

Recommended Selections

Recommended selections include Nantes Coreless, Danvers Half Long, Royal Chantenay, Short 'n' Sweet, Little Finger, and Planet.

AT A GLANCE

Garden Season: Early spring, fall
Days until Harvest: 55-75
Amount to Plant Per Person: 5-10 feet of row or 2 feet of 18-inch-wide row for fresh use, an additional 10 feet of row or 2 feet of wide row for storage
Serious Insects: None
Serious Diseases: Leaf blight
Comments: Needs loose, deep soil free of rocks and clumps. Choose short selections for heavy soils.

If you have heavy clay soil, try growing carrots in raised beds to which you have added good topsoil and compost.

HERBED CARROTS

1 pound carrots, scraped and cut into thin strips
½ cup water
¼ cup butter or margarine
2¼ teaspoons minced fresh tarragon or ¾ teaspoon dried whole tarragon
¼ teaspoon salt
Dash of white pepper
Lemon slices (optional)
Fresh tarragon sprigs (optional)

Combine carrots and ½ cup water in a medium saucepan; cover and simmer 10 to 15 minutes or until crisp-tender. Add butter, tarragon, salt, and pepper, stirring well. Cook, uncovered, 2 minutes. Garnish with lemon slices and tarragon sprigs, if desired. Yield: 4 servings.

In the South, cauliflower is the measuring stick of a vegetable gardener's luck and ability. Cauliflower likes mild weather, and fluctuating temperatures present a challenge to gardeners. But in a long, mild spring or fall, plants will form good-sized heads (curds).

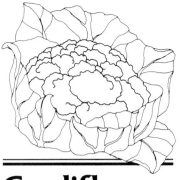

Cauliflower

Special Requirements

To form a large, white curd, cauliflower must grow rapidly under cool conditions. You must provide adequate water and fertilizer to encourage steady growth. A poor harvest will result if anything interrupts the vegetable's development. Ideal temperatures for growing cauliflower are between 75 and 80 degrees during the day and 60 to 65 degrees at night, so it is usually most successful as a fall crop. In spring, warm weather sometimes comes too quickly for curds to develop properly. And you have to be careful not to plant too early in the spring: Young plants that are 8 weeks old or less will form tiny heads (buttons) prematurely if exposed to daytime temperatures below 50 degrees for several weeks or below 40 degrees for a few nights.

Planting and Culture

For a fall crop, set out transplants in late summer, 8 to 10 weeks before the first frost, so that the crop will mature before the first hard freeze. For a spring crop, set out transplants 2 weeks before the last frost.

Space plants 18 to 24 inches apart in rows 2 to 3 feet apart. Fertilize transplants with a starter solution, such as liquid 20-20-20, diluted according to label directions.

Keep the soil evenly moist; if it dries out between waterings, cauliflower curds may split. Three weeks after planting, side-dress the plants with ¼ cup of 10-10-10 per 10 feet of row.

If exposed to the sun, cauliflower curds turn brownish yellow. To keep them white, you will

---

AT A GLANCE

Garden Season: Early spring, fall
Days until Harvest: 50-68 after transplanting
Amount to Plant Per Person: 3-5 plants for fresh use, an additional 8 plants for storage
Serious Insects: Cabbage looper, imported cabbageworm
Serious Diseases: Downy mildew, black rot
Comments: Best as a fall crop, but does not tolerate frost. Keep soil evenly moist to prevent curds from splitting.

Space plants 18 to 24 inches apart so they will have enough room to develop properly.

One way to protect curds from the sun (blanch them) is to secure the leaves over the head with a clothespin.

need to blanch them. When the curd is 2 inches in diameter, gather the outer leaves to the top of the plant so that they shade the curd; fasten them together with a clothespin or tie them loosely with soft twine. You should be able to check the head without untying the leaves. Be careful not to tie too tightly or moisture may become trapped, causing the curd to rot.

Harvest

If the weather is cool, the curd should be ready for harvest about 2 weeks after you begin blanching it. In warmer weather, it will be ready in a few days. Harvest when the curd is snowy white and firm, before the buds loosen. Cut the stem at the base of the leaves with a sharp knife. Do not judge maturity by the size of the head. Because growing conditions in the South are not ideal, curds are usually smaller than those found in supermarkets. If the curd looks yellowish or soft, it is becoming overmature.

Recommended Selections

For best results, plant fast-maturing hybrids such as Snow King, a heat-tolerant selection, and Snow Crown. Snowball selections and Self Blanche are also recommended but may mature 2½ weeks later than the hybrids.

To harvest cauliflower, cut when the curd is snowy white and firm. Size of the head is no indication of maturity.

TANGY CAULIFLOWER

1 medium head cauliflower
¼ cup mayonnaise
1 tablespoon plus 1 teaspoon prepared mustard
1 cup (4 ounces) shredded Cheddar cheese

Wash cauliflower and remove green leaves; cover with water and bring to a boil; cover and cook 10 minutes or until tender. Drain. Place cauliflower in a lightly greased 1-quart casserole.

Combine mayonnaise and mustard; mix well. Spread over cauliflower. Sprinkle cheese on top; bake at 350° for 10 to 15 minutes or until thoroughly heated. Yield: 4 servings.

CREAMY CAULIFLOWER SOUP

1 medium head cauliflower
3 cups water
2 chicken-flavored bouillon cubes
⅔ cup chopped onion
2 tablespoons butter or margarine, melted
2 tablespoons all-purpose flour
2 cups half-and-half
½ teaspoon Worcestershire sauce
¾ teaspoon salt
1 cup (4 ounces) shredded Cheddar cheese
Chopped fresh parsley

Wash cauliflower and break into flowerets. Add 3 cups water and bring to a boil. Reduce heat, cover, and simmer 10 minutes. Remove from heat and add bouillon cubes; set aside.

Sauté onion in butter 3 to 5 minutes or until tender; add flour, stirring until smooth. Cook 1 minute, stirring constantly. Gradually add cauliflower-bouillon mixture; cook over medium heat, stirring constantly, until mixture comes to a boil. Stir in half-and-half, Worcestershire, and salt; cook over low heat until thoroughly heated. Add cheese, stirring until melted. Garnish with parsley. Yield: 5 cups.

FANTASTIC CAULIFLOWER SALAD

1 medium head cauliflower
½ cup mayonnaise
½ cup commercial sour cream
¼ cup (1 ounce) shredded Cheddar cheese
¼ cup chopped green onions
¼ cup thinly sliced radishes
½ teaspoon Worcestershire sauce
Dash of salt
Dash of pepper

Wash cauliflower and break into flowerets. Cover with water and bring to a boil. Reduce heat, cover, and simmer 4 minutes or until crisp-tender. Drain and cool.

Combine remaining ingredients; stir well. Stir in cauliflower. Cover and chill at least 1 hour. Yield: 4 servings.

Celery

If you enjoy a challenge, celery may be the crop for you. Grown commercially in Florida in muck soils, it is one of the more difficult crops to grow at home because it needs more moisture and fertilizer than other vegetables. Also, home-grown stalks of celery are likely to be smaller and in looser bunches than those you find in the grocery. The keys to growing it are a constant, plentiful water supply and a very rich organic soil.

Grow this vegetable in the cool weather of early spring and fall. Celery grown in spring does tolerate warm weather once plants are established. The fall crop withstands light frost but will be killed by a hard freeze.

Planting and Culture

Transplants may be hard to find except in Florida, so be prepared to grow your own. (*See* *page 53 for instructions.*) For spring planting, set out plants 4 weeks before the last frost. Plants should be about 5 inches tall with at least 3 leaves. For a fall crop, set out transplants about 13 to 14 weeks before the first frost.

To prepare the soil for planting, dig to a depth of 18 inches and work in as much rotted manure, compost, and peat moss as possible. (It is possible to grow celery in a mixture of these 3 materials only.) Also, work into the soil 1 cup of 10-10-10 per 10 feet of row.

Set seedlings so that the crown is level with the soil. Space plants 7 inches apart in rows 24 inches apart.

To keep the soil well watered, a drip or trickle irrigation system is best. It supplies moisture to the roots slowly and steadily. If the plants do not receive enough moisture, the stalks will be small and stringy, and they will spread outward instead of forming a tight bunch. You may need to

---

AT A GLANCE

Garden Season: Early spring, fall
Days until Harvest: 100 to 115 after transplanting
Amount to Plant Per Person: 3 plants for fresh use
Serious Insects: None
Serious Diseases: Early blight, late blight
Comments: Needs very rich organic soil and frequent watering.

You can pinch off a few celery leaves during the season to add to salads.

To grow more celery in less space, plant in staggered rows, allowing 7 to 12 inches between plants each way.

water every day in sandy soils and every 2 days in heavier soils. However, be careful to avoid waterlogging the soil.

Celery needs plenty of fertilizer. Side-dress every 4 weeks with ⅓ cup of 10-10-10 per 10 feet of row.

Blanching used to be a common practice. Although it may make the flavor of the stalks a little milder, blanching also lowers nutritional value. If you choose to blanch celery, pile hay, straw, or leaves around the stalks when they are 12 to 15 inches tall; these materials block the light while permitting air circulation. Avoid mounding soil around the plants because the soil may contain diseases that will cause the stalks to rot. Blanching takes about 14 days.

Harvest

You can begin cutting the outer stalks when they are large enough to use. Plants will produce more stalks from the center. Or cut the entire plant at the base of the stalk.

Homegrown celery is likely to be smaller and in looser bunches than that which is commercially grown. You can harvest the outer stalks as they become large enough to use, or pull up the whole plant when it is mature.

Recommended Selections

Recommended selections include Summer Pascal; Florida strains; Utah 52-70; and Golden Self-Blanching, which produces light golden stalks without being blanched.

ITALIAN CELERY

    4 cups diagonally sliced celery
    ½ cup water
    1 medium onion, chopped
    3 tablespoons olive oil
    ¼ cup grated Parmesan cheese
    2 tablespoons chopped fresh parsley
    2 tablespoons diced pimiento
    ¼ teaspoon garlic salt
    ¼ teaspoon pepper

Combine celery and ½ cup water in a medium saucepan; bring to a boil. Reduce heat, cover, and simmer 5 minutes or until crisp-tender. Drain well and set aside.

Sauté onion in oil in a large skillet until onion is tender. Stir in celery and cook until thoroughly heated. Remove from heat and stir in remaining ingredients. Yield: 6 servings.

STIR-FRY CELERY AMANDINE

    2 tablespoons butter or margarine
    ⅓ cup slivered almonds
    6 cups diagonally sliced celery
    2 tablespoons dry white wine
    1 tablespoon instant minced onion
    1 teaspoon chicken-flavored bouillon granules
    ½ teaspoon sugar
    ⅛ teaspoon garlic powder
    ⅛ teaspoon ground ginger

Melt butter in a large skillet or wok. Add almonds; cook over medium-high heat, stirring constantly, until golden brown. Remove almonds and set aside. Add next 7 ingredients and cook, stirring constantly, 3 minutes or until celery is crisp-tender. Stir in almonds; serve immediately. Yield: 8 servings.

CREAMY STUFFED CELERY

    6 stalks celery
    2 (3-ounce) packages cream cheese, softened
    2 tablespoons finely chopped pimiento-stuffed olives
    2 tablespoons finely chopped onion
    2 tablespoons finely chopped sweet pickles
    2 tablespoons finely chopped pecans
    1 tablespoon mayonnaise

Wash celery, and cut into 3-inch pieces. Combine remaining ingredients, mixing well. Stuff the celery pieces with cream cheese mixture. Yield: 18 celery pieces.

Vegetables 149

Swiss chard, which is closely related to beets, is grown for its beautiful, thick, mild-flavored leaves. Unlike beets, it does not produce an edible root. Because chard does not ship well, you are not likely to see it in the grocery. But it is an especially good summer crop for Southern gardens, providing tender greens long after collards turn bitter and mustard goes to seed. It produces prolifically and tolerates both frost and summer heat.

Swiss chard is also striking enough to be used as an ornamental. In addition to the plants grown for harvest, you can use it for texture and color in the vegetable garden. The selection Rhubarb is especially good for this purpose.

Swiss Chard

Planting and Culture

A single planting in spring will give you harvests until early winter. But if you prefer, you can plant in spring, 2 to 4 weeks before the last frost, and again in summer for a fall crop. Although you may start chard from transplants, direct seeding is easier. Soak seeds overnight to speed germination. Sow in wide beds or in single rows spaced 18 to 24 inches apart.

Chard seeds, like beet seeds, are actually clusters of seeds, so several plants will come up where you sow a single seed. When plants are about 1 inch tall, thin each cluster to one plant every 3 to 4 inches. Instead of pulling the plants, which will disturb the roots of the ones remaining, you can pinch off the extra seedlings near

---

AT A GLANCE

Garden Season: Spring, summer, fall
Days until Harvest: 50-60
Amount to Plant Per Person: 3 feet of row or 1-2 feet of 18-inch-wide row for fresh use, an additional 3-5 feet or 1-2 feet of wide row for storage
Serious Insects: Leaf miner
Serious Diseases: None
Comments: Soak seeds overnight to speed germination.

Water plants regularly; if subjected to drought, they may bolt.

Foliage remains tender and tasty in spite of summer heat.

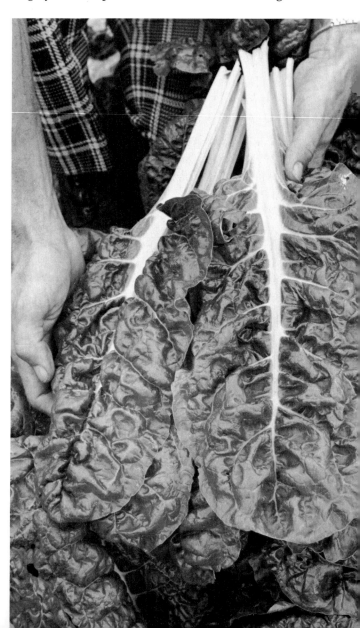

ground level. They will not grow back. When plants are large enough to touch each other, thin to 1 plant every 9 to 12 inches. Set out transplants 9 to 12 inches apart at the same time that you would sow seeds.

Water regularly, as dry weather can cause the plants to bolt. If you harvest continuously, sidedress every 4 to 6 weeks with ¼ cup of 10-10-10 per 10 feet of row.

Harvest

Harvest the outer leaves when they are 4 to 10 inches long by breaking off the stalks at the base of the plant. More foliage will be produced from the center of the plant. Or cut all of the foliage 2 to 3 inches above the ground, and plants will send up new leaves. Foliage is most tender when young, but you can also use the large, older leaves.

Harvest Swiss chard by breaking off the stalks at the base.

Recommended Selections

Recommended selections include Fordhook Giant, Geneva, and Lucullus, which have white stalks; and Rhubarb, which has red veins and stalks.

INDIVIDUAL SWISS CHARD CUSTARDS
½ pound Swiss chard leaves
2 tablespoons butter or margarine
2 eggs
½ cup whipping cream
½ cup milk
½ teaspoon salt
⅛ teaspoon freshly ground black pepper
    Dash of ground nutmeg

Wash chard thoroughly; drain. Remove and discard ribs from larger leaves. Cut leaves diagonally into 2- x ¼-inch strips.

Melt butter in a large skillet. Add chard; toss gently. Cover and simmer 3 to 4 minutes or until chard is wilted. Uncover and cook over medium heat, stirring constantly, until chard liquid is evaporated. Remove from heat; cool.

Lightly grease four 6-ounce custard cups; divide chard evenly among cups. Combine remaining ingredients; beat with a wire whisk. Pour egg mixture evenly over chard in cups; stir each cup gently. Place cups in an 8-inch square pan; pour 1 to 1½ inches boiling water in pan around cups. Bake at 350° for 25 minutes or until set. Remove cups from pan; let stand 5 minutes. Invert onto serving dishes. Yield: 4 servings.

SWISS CHARD WITH TOMATOES
2 pounds Swiss chard leaves
¼ cup chopped onion
2 cloves garlic, minced
¼ cup olive oil
1½ cups chopped, peeled fresh tomatoes
¼ teaspoon salt
    Dash of freshly ground black pepper

Wash chard thoroughly; drain. Remove and discard ribs from larger leaves. Coarsely chop chard.

Sauté onion and garlic in oil in a large skillet until tender. Add chard and tomatoes; cover and cook over medium heat 12 to 15 minutes, stirring occasionally. Sprinkle vegetables with salt and pepper; stir well. Yield: 4 servings.

• Chard ribs tend to darken when they are cooked.

• Young, tender Swiss chard leaves can be substituted for spinach in salads.

Collards and Kale

Collards and kale are dependable, nutritious greens that stay in the garden long after cold weather kills many other leafy vegetables. In fact, they taste better when harvested after frost touches the leaves. The plants tolerate temperatures of 15 to 20 degrees and can survive temperatures as low as 0 degrees if the drop is gradual and the plants are protected by mulch or snow. Collards and kale do not actually grow in such cold, but plants that are full-sized by winter can remain in the garden to be harvested as you need them. In spring, plants that were in the garden all winter will bolt.

AT A GLANCE

Garden Season: Early spring, fall
Days until Harvest: Collards, 80 from seed or 50 after transplanting; kale, 55-75 from seed
Amount to Plant Per Person: Collards and kale, 5 feet of row or 2 feet of 18-inch-wide row for fresh use, an additional 5 feet or 2 feet of wide row for storage
Serious Insects: Cabbage looper, imported cabbageworm
Serious Diseases: Downy mildew, black rot
Comments: Control insects early. Plants overwinter over most of the South. Flavor is sweeter after frost.

Collards

Collards also tolerate summer temperatures in the 90s, so it is possible to keep harvesting an early-spring planting through summer. But because collards develop a strong, slightly bitter flavor in hot weather, it is better to harvest the spring crop before the weather gets hot. Plant again in late summer and early fall for fall and winter harvests.

Planting and Culture

Start collards from seeds or transplants. Space transplants 14 to 18 inches apart in rows 2½ feet apart; thin seedlings to the same spacing. Fertilize transplants and seedlings with a starter solution of liquid 20-20-20 diluted according to label directions. Three weeks after planting, side-dress the rows with ¼ cup of 10-10-10 per 10 feet of row. Repeat every 4 to 6 weeks during the growing season.

Harvest

Begin harvesting leaves when they are 6 to 10 inches long; harvest the lower leaves first, and work your way up the plant. Old leaves are tough and woody. Do not remove the terminal tip, which will continue producing new leaves. In cold weather, even frozen leaves may be

Although collards tolerate summer heat well, they are most flavorful in fall and winter.

Kale is quite hardy and will overwinter if mulched. Severe cold will make leaves harvested in winter taste even sweeter.

harvested. They quickly thaw indoors for cooking. A frozen plant is brittle; to avoid damaging it, cut the leaves instead of snapping them off.

Recommended Selections

Vates, which grows to 1½ to 2 feet tall, withstands cold well and is the best selection for fall and winter harvests. Georgia, which grows to 3 feet tall, tolerates heat and is best for spring and summer gardens.

Kale

Grow kale as you would collards, except that you will probably have to start from seeds, as transplants may be hard to find. Sow seeds in the garden ½ inch deep and 3 inches apart in rows that are 2½ feet apart. When seedlings are 3 inches tall, thin to 8 inches apart and fertilize with a starter solution of liquid 20-20-20 diluted according to label directions.

You can harvest kale by cutting only the lower leaves while they are young and tender (4 to 8 inches long), letting the terminal tip continue to grow. Or you can cut the whole plant at its base and strip the leaves from the stem.

Over most of the South, kale will overwinter if mulched, although a period of severe cold may kill the leaves back to the crown. Side-dress in late February in the Lower South and in mid-March in the Upper and Middle South, applying 10-10-10 at the rate recommended above. New

growth will produce harvests until May, when the plants flower.

Recommended Selections

Recommended selections include Dwarf Blue Curled Vates (low-growing plants with frilly leaves) and Dwarf Siberian (low-growing and especially hardy, with broad, thick leaves).

LIGHT SOUTHERN COLLARDS

About ¾ pound lean ham hock
1 quart water
5 pounds collard greens
½ to 1 teaspoon salt
¾ teaspoon minced fresh basil or ¼ teaspoon dried whole basil

Rinse salt from meat; place meat in a large Dutch oven. Add 1 quart water and bring to a boil; reduce heat, and simmer, uncovered, 30 to 45 minutes or until meat is tender. Remove and discard ham hock (reserve any meat for use in other recipes). Strain broth and chill until fat rises to surface and hardens. Remove and discard fat.

Wash collards thoroughly; drain well and chop. Place collards, broth, salt, and basil in Dutch oven; bring to a boil. Reduce heat, cover, and simmer 30 to 45 minutes or until collards are tender. Yield: 8 to 10 servings.

COLCANNON

¾ pound fresh kale
3 cups mashed potatoes
1 tablespoon minced fresh parsley
½ teaspoon ground mace
⅛ teaspoon pepper
4 slices bacon
1 large onion, chopped
¼ cup soft breadcrumbs
2 tablespoons butter or margarine, melted

Remove stems from kale. Wash leaves thoroughly; tear into bite-size pieces. Place in Dutch oven (do not add water); cover and cook over high heat 5 minutes. Drain. Combine potatoes and kale; stir in parsley, mace, and pepper.

Cook bacon until crisp; remove bacon, reserving drippings. Crumble bacon and set aside. Sauté onion in reserved drippings until tender. Add kale mixture and heat thoroughly; spoon into a lightly greased 1-quart casserole. Sprinkle with breadcrumbs; pour melted butter over top. Bake at 450° for 15 minutes or until top is golden brown. Sprinkle bacon over top. Yield: 4 servings.

Harvest kale by breaking off the lowest leaves.

Vegetables 153

Corn

What Southerner does not love tender, juicy sweet corn, steaming hot and dripping with melted butter? And the best you will ever eat is that which you grow in your own garden.

If you time your planting properly, you can enjoy fresh corn nearly every day of the summer. For the first harvest, plant early-maturing selections after the last frost. Two to four weeks later, follow this planting with a midseason selection; and in late spring or early summer, plant a late-maturing selection to harvest in late summer.

A second way to enjoy a long season of harvests is to make several plantings of a single selection. Begin after the last frost and make each succeeding planting when the previous one has 3 to 4 leaves.

Note that extrasweet selections do not germinate well in cool soil and should not be planted until 2 weeks after the last frost. Supersweet types designated as EH (Everlasting Heritage), however, germinate well in cooler soils.

Pollination

Corn depends primarily on the wind to carry the pollen released by the tassels to the silks. Each silk leads to a potential kernel inside the husk. For each silk that's not pollinated, the ear will have a missing kernel. To help ensure complete pollination, plant corn in blocks of 4 or more rows to create a high concentration of pollen. When corn is planted in a single row, pollen is too easily blown away from the plants.

When different selections release pollen at the same time, they cross-pollinate readily. Extra-sweet hybrids should not be allowed to cross-pollinate with other selections, or the ears of both types will be starchy. It is essential to isolate the extrasweet selections, such as Early Xtra Sweet, by planting them at least 200 feet away from other types. Or stagger planting times by 4 weeks so the different selections do not tassel at the same time. (Extrasweet selections do not have to be separated from each other.)

Cross-pollination between other sweet selections, including the supersweet Everlasting Heritage hybrids, will not affect the flavor, although it may affect the appearance. A white selection pollinated by a yellow one will have some yellow kernels.

Planting and Culture

Before planting, work 1 cup of 10-10-10 per 10 feet of row into the soil. Plant seeds in furrows 4 to 6 inches deep, spacing seeds about 6 inches apart. Cover seeds with only 1 to 1½ inches of soil. As the plants grow, fill in the furrow and hill the soil around the stems to help support the plants. Space rows of early-maturing types 2½ feet apart and of mid- and late-season selections 3 to 3½ feet apart.

Seedlings are grasslike when they first emerge. When plants are 6 inches tall, thin to about 1 foot apart. Crowded corn bears fewer, smaller ears.

Fertilization is important, because once plants are stunted, they never fully recover. Side-dress

---

AT A GLANCE

Garden Season: Summer
Days until Harvest: 70-92 days
Amount to Plant Per Person: 10-15 feet of row for fresh use, an additional 20-30 feet for storage
Serious Insects: Corn earworm, wireworm
Serious Diseases: Northern and Southern corn leaf blights
Comments: Plant in blocks of 4 or more rows to ensure good pollination. Water is especially important during tasseling, because drought causes plants to produce smaller ears with missing kernels.

Unfilled kernels at the tip of the ear could be the result of incomplete pollination or of drought.

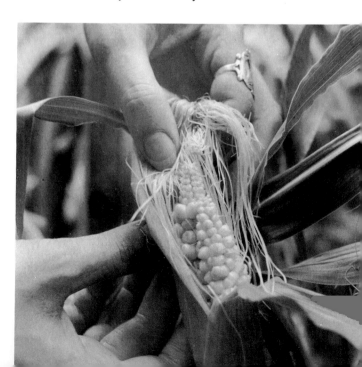

twice, when the plants are about 8 inches tall and again when they are 18 inches tall. Apply ⅓ cup of 10-10-10 per 10 feet of row each time.

Water regularly, especially when the corn is tasseling. Drought-stressed plants produce smaller ears with missing kernels and poorly developed tips.

Harvest

Use the number of days to maturity indicated on the seed packet as a guide but remember that in hot weather (up to 100 degrees), corn matures quickly; in cooler weather, it grows more slowly.

Corn is usually ready for harvest when the silks turn brown and dry. Remove the ear by breaking it off with a sharp twist. Be careful not to damage the stalk. Test the ear for maturity by puncturing a kernel with your thumbnail. If it squirts an opaque, milky liquid like skim milk, the corn is mature. Clear, watery juice indicates that the corn is immature, and you should delay harvesting ears of a similar size for at least a day. If the liquid is white and thick like cream, the ear is overmature and will taste starchy. Usually, the top ear matures a day or two before any below it.

The sugars of most types begin turning to starch as soon as the ear is harvested. If you do not plan to eat the ears right away, refrigerate them (unshucked) immediately. It is best to use them within 24 hours, but extrasweet selections may keep in the refrigerator for several days without losing their sweetness. Ears of Everlasting Heritage hybrids can stay on the plants for 10 to 14 days without losing their quality.

Recommended Selections

Among the many selections recommended for the South are Sundance and Early Extra-Sweet, early yellow selections; Seneca Chief, Merit, Bonanza, and Jubilee, midseason yellow selections; Silver Queen, a favorite late-season white corn; Bi-queen, a late-season bicolor; Florida Staysweet, a late extrasweet selection; and Kandy Korn E.H., an Everlasting Heritage selection.

CORN RELISH

About 18 ears fresh corn
7 quarts water
1 small head cabbage, chopped
1 cup chopped onion
1 cup chopped green pepper
1 cup chopped sweet red pepper
1 to 2 cups sugar
2 tablespoons dry mustard
1 tablespoon celery seeds
1 tablespoon mustard seeds
1 tablespoon salt
1 tablespoon ground turmeric
1 quart vinegar (5% acidity)
1 cup water

Remove husks and silks from corn. Bring 7 quarts water to a boil; add corn. Bring water to a second boil; boil 5 minutes. Cut corn from cob, measuring about 2 quarts of kernels.

Combine corn kernels and remaining ingredients in a large saucepan; simmer over low heat 20 minutes. Bring mixture to a boil. Pack into hot sterilized jars, leaving ¼-inch headspace.

Cover at once with metal lids, and screw bands tight. Process in boiling-water bath 15 minutes. Yield: about 6 pints.

ZESTY CORN ON THE COB

6 ears fresh corn
   Grated rind of 1 lemon
   Juice of 1 lemon
¼ cup sugar
   Butter or margarine

Remove husks and silks from corn. Place corn in a large saucepan or Dutch oven. Cover with water and stir in next 3 ingredients; bring to a boil. Boil 3 minutes; remove from heat, cover, and let stand 10 minutes. Remove corn from water; serve hot with butter. Yield: 6 servings.

Most types of corn are sweetest when taken straight from the garden to the kitchen and dropped into a pot of boiling water. (New Everlasting Heritage hybrids, however, can stay on the plants up to 2 weeks with little loss of quality.)

For crispy texture and cool flavor, a homegrown, freshly harvested cucumber easily surpasses the wax-coated ones found in the grocery. And it does not take many plants to keep you supplied for most of the summer.

Planting and Culture

Cucumbers are sensitive to cold, so plant 2 weeks after the last frost, when the soil and weather are warm. Plant again in midsummer to extend the harvest through early fall.

To save space and make harvesting easier, grow cucumbers on a trellis. You can train the

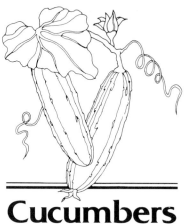

Cucumbers

vines to climb almost any structure that provides support for the tendrils. (*See page 88.*) Sow seeds along the base of the trellis, planting them ½ to 1 inch deep and 4 to 6 inches apart. Thin to 8 to 12 inches apart. As the vines begin to run, guide them up the supports.

To grow cucumbers without trellising, sow seeds in hills spaced 4 feet apart. Sow 4 to 6 seeds per hill and thin to the strongest 2 or 3 seedlings.

Although most cucumbers produce long vines, there are new bush types that produce shorter vines. Sow their seeds 6 inches apart in rows or hills spaced 3 feet apart. Thin seedlings to 12 inches apart in rows and to 2 to 3 seedlings in hills.

Before planting, work ½ cup of 10-10-10 per 10 feet of row into the soil. One week after blossoming begins, side-dress plants with ½ cup of 10-10-10 per 10 feet of row. Repeat 3 weeks later.

To help prevent fruit from developing a bitter taste, keep the soil consistently moist. Bitterness is a genetic trait found in most cucumbers, but it usually does not appear unless plants are subjected to stress from too much or too little water. Mulch the plants well and water every 3 to 5 rainless days.

AT A GLANCE

Garden Season: Summer
Days until Harvest: 50-60
Amount to Plant Per Person: 1-2 hills or 2-3 feet trellised for fresh use, an additional 3-5 hills or 5-7 feet trellised for pickling
Serious Insects: Mites, cucumber beetle
Serious Diseases: Anthracnose, mildews
Comments: Keep well watered to prevent bitterness, and harvest regularly to prolong production.

Cucumbers grown on an upright support are easier to care for and to harvest than those that are allowed to vine on the ground.

You may need to gently twine the cucumber vine onto the support in order to get it started climbing.

Harvest

Begin harvesting cucumbers for slicing when they are longer than 3 inches, firm, and a good green color. Depending on the selection, slicing cucumbers may grow 12 to 16 inches long. It is better to harvest them when they are smaller, however, because as cucumbers approach maturity, the seeds become larger and harder. For making sweet pickles, harvest cucumbers when they are 2 to 4 inches long. For dills, pick fruit when it is 6 inches long. Do not leave any fruit on the vine to ripen and turn dull, puffy, and yellow or orange; they will be overmature and the plant will stop producing.

Recommended Selections

Cucumber selections developed especially for pickling are usually smaller than those developed for slicing. But slicing types can also be used for pickling if you harvest them while they are small.

Hybrid selections for slicing include Gemini 7, Comanche, Cherokee 7, Victory, Sweet Slice, and Sweet Success. Hybrid selections for pickling include Carolina, Liberty, County Fair, and Saladin. Victory and Saladin are gynoecious types; that is, they produce all female blooms, thus bearing more fruit than monoecious plants.

Once the flower is pollinated, the fruit will need only a few days to reach harvesting size. Note how the flower has begun to wither.

Since several seeds of a pollinator (male) are included in the seed packet of a gynoecious selection, be sure to plant all the seeds.

Nonhybrid selections recommended for the South include Ashley and Poinsett 76. Bush types to try include Patio Pik, Bush Champion, and Spacemaster.

CUCUMBERS IN SOUR CREAM

2 medium cucumbers
1 large onion, thinly sliced and separated into rings
¾ cup water
¾ cup vinegar
1½ teaspoons salt
1 teaspoon sugar
½ cup commercial sour cream
1 teaspoon dillseeds
1 or 2 drops hot sauce
 Dash of coarsely ground black pepper

Peel one cucumber; thinly slice both cucumbers. Combine cucumber and next 5 ingredients; mix well. Let stand at room temperature for 1 hour. Drain well.

Combine remaining ingredients; stir well. Add to cucumber; toss gently. Cover and chill at least 1 hour. Yield: 4 to 6 servings.

PICNIC SALAD ROLLS

¾ cup chopped, seeded cucumber
½ cup chopped, seeded tomato
½ cup chopped celery
¼ cup chopped green pepper
2 tablespoons chopped onion
2 tablespoons chopped parsley
2 tablespoons chopped dill pickle
⅓ cup garlic-flavored sour cream dip
¼ cup mayonnaise or salad dressing
¼ teaspoon salt
6 hard rolls

Combine first 7 ingredients, tossing well. Combine dip, mayonnaise, and salt; mix well, and fold into vegetable mixture. Set aside.

Split tops of rolls lengthwise; scoop out center, leaving a ½-inch shell. Spoon vegetable mixture into rolls; wrap each tightly with plastic wrap, and chill until serving time. Yield: 6 servings.

MINTED CUCUMBERS AND YOGURT

2 medium cucumbers, peeled and diced
1 tablespoon chopped fresh mint or 1 teaspoon dried whole mint
2 (8-ounce) cartons plain yogurt
 Lemon-pepper seasoning to taste
 Coarsely ground black pepper to taste
 Lettuce leaves

Combine all ingredients, except lettuce; chill. Serve over lettuce leaves. Yield: 4 servings.

Vegetables 157

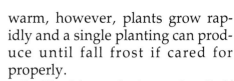

Eggplant

There is more to eggplant than big purple fruit. In fact, the plant was named for a small white type that looks like a swan's egg. There are also selections with oblong or roughly pyramidal shapes, black-fruited types, slender Oriental selections, and even large white-fruited ones.

Oriental eggplant has thin, tender skin; fruit are slow to develop seeds, so they stay sweet tasting even when 10 to 12 inches long. White eggplant also has a mild flavor. In spite of the differences in their appearances, all the types are grown the same way.

Planting and Culture

Eggplant is sensitive to cold weather so do not plant it until daytime temperatures are in the 70s, about 2 to 6 weeks after the last frost. Even a light frost can kill them. Once the air and soil are warm, however, plants grow rapidly and a single planting can produce until fall frost if cared for properly.

In Florida and along the Gulf Coast, you can start from seeds; but over most of the South, it is best to start from transplants. Normally, garden centers have transplants of one or two standard selections. If you want to grow the white or Oriental types, you will have to start your own plants. (*See page 53 for starting transplants.*)

Space transplants 2 to 3 feet apart in rows that are 2 to 2½ feet apart. Oriental and small-fruited white selections are smaller plants and can be spaced 1½ to 2 feet apart. At planting time, apply a starter solution of liquid 20-20-20 diluted according to label directions. It is a good idea to stake plants to help keep fruit off the ground and reduce the possibility of stem breakage. Put 3- to 4-foot stakes in place at planting time.

When the first blossom on each plant appears, some gardeners pinch it off. This lets the plant become stronger before it bears fruit, so that it will be more productive.

For succulent, full-sized fruit, plants must grow without interruption. If growth slows,

---

AT A GLANCE

Garden Season: Summer
Days until Harvest: 55-85 after transplanting
Amount to Plant Per Person: 2 plants for fresh use
Serious Insects: Flea beetle, mites
Serious Diseases: Verticillium wilt
Comments: Water and fertilize regularly for steady growth; otherwise, fruit may be small and bitter.

Harvest eggplant while the skin is still glossy. The fruit should yield slightly to gentle pressure from your thumb.

Eggplant blooms and produces fruit until night temperatures fall below 60 to 65 degrees.

fruit will be small and inferior. To maintain steady growth, keep the soil evenly moist and side-dress every 4 to 6 weeks during the season with ¼ cup of 10-10-10 per 10 feet of row.

Harvest

Harvest eggplants when fruit are 3 to 5 inches long, or let them grow to their maximum size, which depends on the selection. (The smallest white selections are egg sized; Oriental types may grow 4 to 12 inches long.) Be sure to harvest while the skin is still glossy and well colored; purple selections should be dark and white selections should be a clean white. If the fruit has a dull sheen, it is overripe; it will contain many tiny, hard seeds and may have a bitter flavor. Overmature small, white types turn yellow and become rock hard.

To harvest, cut the woody stem that connects the fruit to the plant, leaving an inch or so of the stem on the fruit. You will need to use a knife or a pair of garden clippers. Handle the fruit carefully to avoid bruising them, and keep plants harvested to encourage continued production.

In the fall, growth slows or stops as soon as the weather turns cool. When frost is predicted, harvest all the fruit or pull up the entire plant and hang it in a cool dry place until you are ready to remove the fruit.

Recommended Selections

Recommended selections for the South include Black Beauty, Florida Market, Classic Hybrid, Dusky Hybrid, Ichiban Hybrid (an Oriental type), Easter Egg (a small white selection), and White Beauty (a large white selection). For container gardening, try Morden Midget.

EGGPLANT FRIES

1 medium eggplant
2 eggs, beaten
¼ cup water
1 cup fine cracker crumbs
½ cup grated Parmesan cheese
¾ teaspoon salt
¾ teaspoon celery salt
¾ cup all-purpose flour
  Vegetable oil

Peel eggplant and cut into 2- x ½- x ½-inch strips. Combine eggs and ¼ cup water; beat well. Combine next 4 ingredients; mix well. Dredge eggplant strips in flour; dip in egg mixture and roll in cracker crumb mixture. Fry in hot oil (325°) until golden brown, turning once. Drain on paper towels. Yield: 4 servings.

EGGPLANT ROLL-UPS

2 large eggplants
2¼ cups soft breadcrumbs
⅓ cup grated Parmesan cheese
⅓ cup milk
2 eggs, beaten
1 teaspoon salt
⅛ teaspoon garlic powder
¼ teaspoon pepper
2½ pounds lean ground beef, divided
1 (32-ounce) jar commercial spaghetti sauce

Peel eggplants; slice each lengthwise into twelve ¼-inch-thick slices. Cook 8 slices at a time in boiling water for 4 to 5 minutes or until limp; drain slices on paper towels.

Combine next 7 ingredients and 2 pounds ground beef; mix well. Shape into 24 portions; place one portion of meat mixture on each eggplant slice. Roll eggplant slices up around meat mixture; place seam side down in a 18- x 12- x 1-inch jellyroll pan. Set aside.

Cook remaining ½ pound ground beef until browned, stirring to crumble; drain. Stir in spaghetti sauce. Pour sauce mixture over eggplant rolls; cover and bake 30 minutes. Remove cover and bake 30 additional minutes. Yield: 12 servings.

The stems are woody, so use a knife or garden clippers to cut the fruit from the plant.

Vegetables 159

If you are the kind of gardener who takes pride in making an outstanding salad, you will want to try these "secret ingredients." Little-known greens such as cress, endive, celtuce, and corn salad are easy to grow and add zip to your salads. Nasturtiums add bright color to both garden and salad bowl, as both the leaves and the red, yellow, pink, or orange blossoms are edible.

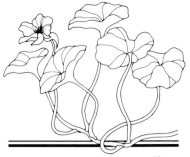

Unusual Greens

Celtuce

Celtuce stalks are eaten like celery and its young leaves look like lettuce, thus the name celtuce. When the plant is young, it produces a rosette of beautiful spring-green leaves, which may be added to salads. Older leaves contain a bitter milky sap.

As the plant grows, it forms a thick central stem. Cut the stem when it is 1 inch in diameter at the base (usually when the plant is 8 to 12 inches tall) and peel the outer skin, which also contains a bitter sap.

AT A GLANCE

Garden Season: Spring, fall (except corn salad—winter, early spring)

Days until Harvest: Celtuce, 14-21 for greens, 90 for stalks; corn salad, 45-50; cress, 10; endive and escarole, 80-90; nasturtiums: 30-40

Amount to Plant Per Person: Experiment with small amounts until you determine your favorites

Serious Insects: Endive and escarole, same as lettuce; others have no serious pests

Serious Diseases: Endive and escarole, same as lettuce; others, none

Comments: Sow small amounts of cress weekly for continuous harvests. Soak nasturtium seeds before planting.

During the first few weeks of growth, you can harvest celtuce leaves and add them to salads. When plants are as large as those in the photo, however, the leaves contain a bitter milky sap.

Grow celtuce as you would lettuce in spring and fall. Thin seedlings to 18 inches.

Corn Salad

Corn salad, also called lamb's lettuce, fetticus, or maches, provides fresh greens through winter into early spring. The spoon-shaped leaves have a mild flavor and delicate texture.

In early fall, sow seeds in 18-inch-wide rows or in single rows that are 12 inches apart, covering seeds with ½ inch of soil. When seedlings are 2 to 3 inches tall, thin to 4 inches apart and apply a starter solution of liquid 20-20-20 diluted according to label directions. During dry weather, water regularly. Begin picking leaves as soon as they reach a usable size.

Garden Cress

Garden cress adds a hot, tangy flavor to sandwiches, soups, salads, and omelets. Also called peppergrass or curlicress, garden cress is easier to grow than watercress and winter cress.

Plant garden cress outdoors in early spring or fall. Sow seeds thinly, barely patting them into the soil. They need light to germinate. Neither thinning or fertilizing is necessary. Since plants are ready for harvest in only 10 days, make several successive sowings. To harvest, simply pull up the tiny plants. About a month after planting, cress will bloom; you can still use it, but the stems will not be tender.

Corn salad, also called lamb's lettuce, gives you fresh salad greens through winter and into early spring. The leaves have a mild flavor and delicate texture.

Endive and Escarole

Endive is a frilly salad green that has a stronger flavor than lettuce. Escarole is a type of endive, with broader less crinkled leaves.

Sow seeds for a spring crop 2 to 4 weeks before the last frost. For a fall crop, set out transplants in late summer. Space plants 18 inches apart in rows 24 inches apart. Water and fertilize as for lettuce.

To harvest, remove the outer leaves; the inner ones keep growing. Or cut the entire plant at the base when the heads are full and leafy. As warm weather approaches, the leaves may develop a slightly bitter taste. For a milder flavor, blanch the head before harvest, tying the large outer leaves over the head. After about a week, the head should be ready for harvest. In fall, harvest before a hard frost occurs.

Selections recommended for the South include Florida Deep Heart, Full Heart Batavian, Ruffec, Green Curled Ruffec, and Salad King.

Nasturtiums

Nasturtium leaves have a peppery flavor similar to cress. The flowers are hot and peppery like radishes. Use them in salads, sandwich spreads, or in making vinegar. (*See page 216.*)

Plant nasturtiums in a sunny spot after danger of frost is past. (In Florida and the Gulf South, plant in fall.) They flower best in poor, dry soil; in rich soil, plants will produce more leaves than flowers.

Sow seeds ½ to 1 inch deep and 1½ to 3 inches apart. Thin seedlings to 4 to 10 inches apart. To use the foliage, pick the young growth at the stem tips. Harvest flowers at any stage.

CELTUCE TOSS

2 tablespoons vegetable oil
4 to 6 stalks celtuce, sliced diagonally into 2-inch pieces
1 cup chicken broth
¼ teaspoon salt
2 tablespoons chopped fresh parsley
1 tablespoon chopped pimiento

Heat oil in a large skillet; add celtuce and sauté 2 minutes. Add broth and salt; bring to a boil. Reduce heat, cover, and simmer 12 to 14 minutes or until crisp-tender; drain. Sprinkle celtuce with parsley and pimiento; toss gently. Yield: 6 to 8 servings.

ENDIVE CONTINENTAL

6 stalks endive
1 tablespoon lemon juice
3 large onions, chopped
2 cloves garlic, minced
¼ cup olive oil
3 small tomatoes, peeled and chopped
1 teaspoon salt
1 teaspoon minced fresh basil or ¼ teaspoon dried whole basil

Trim base from endive stalks; wash leaves thoroughly. Place endive in a large saucepan and cover with water; add lemon juice. Bring to a boil; reduce heat, cover, and simmer 10 minutes. Drain well.

Sauté onion and garlic in olive oil until onion is tender; add tomatoes, salt, and basil. Cover and simmer 10 minutes. Add endive; cover and simmer 15 minutes. Yield: 8 servings.

CRESS AND CHEESE SALAD

½ pound curly cress, torn into bite-size pieces
1 medium head lettuce, torn into bite-size pieces
8 ounces Swiss cheese, cut into julienne strips
⅓ cup thinly sliced carrot
⅓ cup thinly sliced radishes
¼ cup mayonnaise
2 tablespoons olive oil
1 tablespoon red wine vinegar
1 tablespoon Dijon mustard
½ teaspoon paprika

Combine greens, cheese, carrot, and radishes; toss gently. Combine remaining ingredients, stirring well; pour over salad. Toss until coated. Yield: 8 servings.

The leaves and flowers of nasturtiums add a peppery flavor to salads and sandwich spreads, and can be used in making vinegars.

Vegetables   161

Jerusalem Artichokes

Jerusalem artichoke (also called sunchoke) is a relative of the sunflower. It is grown for its tubers, which are knobby and thin-skinned with a crispy white flesh similar to a water chestnut. The name is misleading because the vegetable is nothing like the true artichoke, the globe artichoke. The tubers are often used as a non-starchy, low-calorie potato substitute.

Jerusalem artichokes are easy to grow. In fact, they can become a nuisance, especially in the Middle and Lower South. They are a native perennial wildflower; and once planted, they come back every year, multiplying each time. To keep them from becoming weedy and taking over, place them in a confined area or to one side of the garden. Digging the tubers every year and replanting only the recommended amount may also help control their spread.

Planting and Culture

Jerusalem artichokes grow in any kind of soil, but plants produce the largest tubers in loose, light soil. Plant in spring as soon as you can work the soil or in fall before the first frost. (Planting in fall is simply for convenience. Tubers set out then do not grow over the winter, so they do not produce harvests any earlier than those planted in the spring.)

Before planting, work 1 cup of 10-10-10 per 10 feet of row into the soil. Plant tubers whole, or cut them into pieces with at least one eye on each piece. Set them 3 to 4 inches deep and 6 to 8 inches apart. Space rows 3 to 4 feet apart. As the plants grow, pull the soil to the stems to form hills. This provides extra support for the stalks, which may grow to 8 feet or taller.

Jerusalem artichokes thrive with no special care. However, to grow large tubers, water during dry weather and keep weeds removed. Also, side-dress about 6 weeks after planting with ¼ cup of 10-10-10 per 10 feet of row.

AT A GLANCE

Garden Season: Perennial, growth begins in spring
Days until Harvest: Dig in fall, after frost
Amount to Plant Per Person: 1 tuber for fresh use, an additional 1-2 for storage
Serious Insects or Diseases: None
Comments: Plant in a confined area because plants may become weedy, especially in the Middle and Lower South. Crowding results in smaller tubers; for large ones every year, dig and replant every fall.

Plant Jerusalem artichokes in a confined area such as a bed defined with crossties or other border. These plants have grown to half their mature size.

The flowers tell you that Jerusalem artichoke is a member of the aster family. It is hardy throughout the South.

Harvest

After plants die in fall, you can begin to harvest the artichokes. The tubers will be along either side of the plants rather than directly beneath them. Lift the plants and roots with a fork or simply use a trowel to dig the tubers.

Tubers stay crisp and plump in the ground all winter, and you can dig as you need them. When frost kills the tops, leave the stalks in place so you will know where to dig for tubers. If moles, mice, termites, or other underground pests are a problem in your garden, you may want to dig all the tubers at once, as these pests may eat your crop.

Freezing does not hurt the tubers, but winter digging may be difficult where the ground freezes hard. In the Upper South, you may need to dig and store the tubers for winter use.

In spring, any tubers left in the ground will send up new plants and the next season's crop is on its way. To limit the spread of your planting, you can pull up or cut back unwanted plants after growth begins. You may need to cut them back more than once. This also helps prevent crowding so that tubers will be larger.

After the plants die back in fall, you can begin harvesting the tubers. Dig them through the winter as you need them, using a trowel or turning fork.

ARTICHOKE SOUP

2 pounds Jerusalem artichokes
¼ cup butter or margarine
2 medium onions, sliced
3 cups hot water
½ teaspoon salt
¼ teaspoon coarsely ground black pepper
2 cups milk
1 cup half-and-half
⅛ teaspoon ground cardamom
⅓ cup slivered almonds, toasted
2 tablespoons chopped fresh parsley

Peel and slice artichokes. Melt butter in a heavy saucepan (do not use cast-iron pan); add artichokes and onion. Sauté 8 to 10 minutes; add 3 cups hot water, salt, and pepper. Simmer 5 minutes; pour into container of electric blender. Process until smooth. Return to saucepan; stir in milk, half-and-half, and cardamon. Cook over low heat, stirring constantly until thoroughly heated. Top with almonds and parsley. Yield: about 6 cups.

ARTICHOKE MEDLEY

1 pound Jerusalem artichokes
Dash of salt
3 tablespoons butter or margarine
1 cup chopped celery
1 small onion, chopped
2 cloves garlic, minced
¼ cup grated Parmesan cheese
3 tablespoons chopped fresh parsley

Peel and slice artichokes. Cover with water and add salt; cover and cook over medium heat 5 to 7 minutes. Drain well.

Melt butter in a heavy skillet; add celery, onion, and garlic and sauté until tender. Add artichokes, stirring well. Sprinkle with cheese and parsley. Toss gently. Yield: 4 servings.

JERUSALEM ARTICHOKES IN CREAM

1 pound Jerusalem artichokes
2 tablespoons butter or margarine
2 tablespoons all-purpose flour
1½ cups milk
¾ teaspoon salt
¼ teaspoon pepper
2 tablespoons minced fresh parsley
2 teaspoons grated lemon rind

Peel and slice artichokes. Cover with water and cook, covered, 5 to 7 minutes. Drain. Place in serving dish.

Melt butter in a heavy saucepan over low heat; add flour, stirring until smooth. Cook 1 minute, stirring constantly. Gradually add milk; cook over medium heat, stirring constantly, until thickened and bubbly. Stir in salt and pepper. Pour over artichokes; sprinkle with parsley and lemon rind. Yield: 4 servings.

Vegetables 163

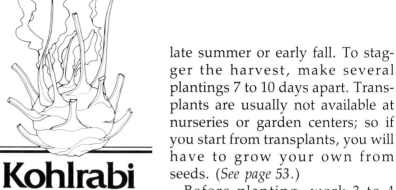

Kohlrabi

Despite its odd looks, kohlrabi is easy to grow. And if you like the flavor of turnip roots or cabbage, you will also like this unusual vegetable. It is a member of the cabbage family; its flavor is similar to both of those vegetables but milder. The edible part is the firm bulblike stem that develops at ground level.

The keys to growing crisp, succulent kohlrabi are fertile, well-drained soil, full sun, and plenty of moisture. Poor soil or drought results in slow growth and woody-textured bulbs.

Planting and Culture

For a spring crop, set out transplants or sow seeds directly in the garden 2 to 4 weeks before the last frost. For fall harvests, plant or sow in late summer or early fall. To stagger the harvest, make several plantings 7 to 10 days apart. Transplants are usually not available at nurseries or garden centers; so if you start from transplants, you will have to grow your own from seeds. (*See page 53.*)

Before planting, work 3 to 4 inches of compost or manure into the soil; or work in ½ cup of 10-10-10 per 10 feet of row. Set transplants 3 to 6 inches apart in rows 18 inches apart, or sow seeds ¼ to ½ inch deep and thin to this spacing. Thinning is important, because crowding limits growth and results in undersized, woody bulbs.

At the time of transplanting or thinning, apply a starter solution of liquid 20-20-20 diluted according to label directions. Do not let the soil dry out. When plants are 3 to 4 inches tall, side-dress with ¼ cup of 10-10-10 per 10 feet of row.

AT A GLANCE

Garden Season: Early spring, fall
Days until Harvest: 45-60
Amount to Plant Per Person: 3-5 feet of row or 1 foot of 18-inch-wide row for fresh use, an additional 3-5 feet of row or 2 feet of wide row for storage
Serious Insects: Aphids, slugs, imported cabbageworm
Serious Diseases: Downy mildew, black rot
Comments: Water and fertilize regularly so that bulbs will be crisp and succulent; poor growth results in woody bulbs.

The flavor of kohlrabi may remind you of cabbage and turnips.

Harvest kohlrabi by cutting the stems at the soil line, or by pulling the whole plant as you would a turnip. Do not let them become oversized (3 to 6 inches in diameter), because they will be fibrous and woody.

Harvest

To harvest, cut the stems at the soil line or pull the bulbs when they are golf ball-sized to 3 inches in diameter. Unharvested bulbs will swell to 6 inches or more, but they will be fibrous and woody. Kohlrabi is as cold tolerant as cabbage and tastes sweeter when exposed to the cool days and frosty nights of late fall. As bulbs reach the proper size, harvest right away, trim the leaves, and store them in the refrigerator.

Recommended Selections

Recommended selections include Grand Duke Hybrid and Prima Hybrid, which are slightly more tolerant of hot weather and dry conditions than some of the older selections such as Early White Vienna. Also, try one of the purple-skinned selections, such as Azur Star or Early Purple Vienna. Their flavor is the same, and the flesh is creamy white like the other selections.

Kohlrabi is best when bulbs reach golf ball-size. Trim the leaves and store the bulbs in plastic bags in the refrigerator.

MARINATED KOHLRABI

1½ pounds kohlrabi
½ cup olive oil
3 tablespoons lemon juice
½ teaspoon salt
⅛ teaspoon coarsely ground black pepper
¼ teaspoon dry mustard
Lettuce leaves

Trim off kohlrabi roots and tops; peel, and cut into ¼-inch slices. Cover with water and bring to a boil. Reduce heat, cover, and simmer 20 minutes or until tender. Drain well. Combine next 5 ingredients and pour over warm kohlrabi. Chill several hours. Serve on lettuce leaves. Yield: 6 servings.

CANDIED KOHLRABI

2 pounds kohlrabi
½ cup firmly packed brown sugar
½ cup light corn syrup
⅓ cup butter or margarine, melted

Trim off kohlrabi roots and tops; peel, and cut into quarters. Cook, covered, in a small amount of boiling water 20 minutes or until tender; drain well. Combine remaining ingredients; spoon over kohlrabi. Cook over low heat, stirring gently, 10 minutes or until glazed. Yield: 6 to 8 servings.

SIMPLE KOHLRABI

1 pound kohlrabi
2 tablespoons vegetable oil
1 tablespoon butter or margarine, melted
1 tablespoon sugar
1 teaspoon all-purpose flour
½ cup chicken broth
¼ teaspoon salt
⅛ teaspoon pepper
¼ teaspoon minced fresh parsley

Trim off kohlrabi roots and tops; peel, and cut into ¼-inch slices. Combine oil and butter in a heavy skillet; stir in sugar. Cook over medium heat, stirring constantly, until sugar is golden brown. Add kohlrabi and stir until coated. Reduce heat, cover, and simmer 15 to 20 minutes or until tender. Add flour, stirring until smooth. Gradually add broth; cook over medium heat, stirring constantly, until thickened and bubbly. Stir in salt, pepper, and parsley. Yield: 4 servings.

• Use raw kohlrabi in stir-fry dishes.

• Kohlrabi is an excellent side dish for meats and is delicious in mixed salads.

Lettuce is very productive and easy to grow, and there is none fresher than that which you grow yourself. In addition, its green or red leaves are quite ornamental and provide a nice border for the spring and fall garden. It is also well suited to clay pots or other containers.

Lettuce

Types of Lettuce

Of the three basic types of lettuce (leaf, semiheading, and heading), leaf and semiheading are best for the South. They mature in half the time of head lettuce and are not as sensitive to heat. Leaf lettuce, which produces thick bunches of leaves, tolerates more shade and slightly warmer temperatures than other types. Semiheading lettuce, also called Bibb, loosehead, or butterhead lettuce, forms a loose head of thick leaves with a chewy spinachlike texture. Cos or romaine lettuce also forms a loose head, but its leaves have a coarse, crispy texture.

AT A GLANCE

Garden Season: Spring, fall
Days Until Harvest: 45-90 (from seed)
Amount to Plant Per Person: 8 feet of row or 2 feet of 18-inch-wide row
Serious Insects: Aphids, slugs
Serious Diseases: Downy mildew
Comments: Do not sow seeds too deeply; pat into ground. Tolerates light frost in fall.

Leaf lettuce grown in wide rows forms a thick cover of foliage, which acts as a natural mulch.

Paris Island Cos forms a loose head of crispy, coarse-textured leaves.

Heading lettuce performs erratically in the South. It needs about 3 months of cool weather to head fully. However, you can use the small, loose heads as leaf lettuce.

Planting and Culture

Begin planting lettuce 4 to 6 weeks before the last spring frost. Always start head lettuce from transplants; start leaf and semiheading lettuce from either seeds or transplants. Since leaf and semiheading types mature faster, you can make 3 or 4 successive plantings of these 2 weeks apart to extend the harvest.

Begin planting the fall lettuce crop in late summer and make successive plantings every 2 weeks into early fall. Use transplants at first since lettuce seeds germinate poorly when the soil is too warm (80 degrees or higher). If you do not have transplants, germinate the seeds before sowing: Wrap them in a moist paper towel and put the towel in a plastic bag in the refrigerator for about five days.

If you plant lettuce in blocks or wide rows, broadcast seeds thinly over the seedbed. Space single rows 1½ feet apart. Pat seeds gently into the soil, as some selections need light to germinate. Water regularly to keep the soil moist.

Set transplants or thin 1- to 2-inch-tall seedlings to the following spacing: leaf lettuce, 4 to 8 inches; semiheading types, 6 to 8 inches; and heading types, 12 to 18 inches. Fertilize transplants with a starter solution of liquid 20-20-20 diluted according to label directions.

Three to four weeks later, side-dress with ¼ cup of 10-10-10 per 10 feet of row. Keep the soil evenly moist. Drought-stressed plants may taste bitter.

Harvest

Lettuce is ready for harvest when it is large enough to use. To harvest leaf lettuce and cos, break off the outer leaves near the base. New ones will form from the plant's center. Or let plants grow until they are leafy and full, and pull the whole plant. For semiheading lettuce, harvest the entire rosette, cutting the plant at ground level. Head lettuce may be harvested in the same way when the heads are softball sized or larger; be sure to harvest before the weather gets hot. In fall, lettuce survives until the first hard freeze.

Be sure to harvest mature lettuce before plants bolt (flower); bolting lettuce grows over 1 foot tall and becomes bitter. Bolting is most likely to occur in spring, hastened by lengthening, warm days; but it may also occur in fall.

Recommended Selections

Recommended selections of leaf lettuce for the South include Salad Bowl, Black Seeded Simpson, Grand Rapids, Ruby, Prizehead, and Green Ice. Also try Slobolt, Hot Weather, and Oakleaf, which are slower to bolt in spring than most other selections. The most popular butterhead selections are Buttercrunch and Bibb. Of the heading types, choose Great Lakes or Minetto. For cos, try Paris Island.

CREAMY ICEBERG SOUP

2½ cups coarsely chopped iceberg lettuce
2 (½-inch-thick) slices onion
1 (3-inch) slice celery
1 tablespoon sugar
1 tablespoon cornstarch
3 cups chicken broth, divided
1 (13-ounce) can evaporated milk
1 tablespoon butter or margarine
1 teaspoon salt

Combine lettuce, onion, celery, sugar, cornstarch, and 2 cups broth in container of electric blender; process until smooth. Pour lettuce mixture into a saucepan; add remaining 1 cup broth, and stir well. Bring to a boil. Reduce heat, and simmer 10 minutes, stirring constantly. Stir in evaporated milk, butter, and salt; simmer 3 to 5 minutes, stirring occasionally. Yield: about 5 cups.

WILTED BIBB SALAD

3 medium heads Bibb lettuce
5 slices bacon
¾ cup sliced green onions
⅓ cup vinegar
¾ teaspoon sugar
⅛ teaspoon coarsely ground black pepper
1 beef-flavored bouillon cube
½ cup water

Line a salad bowl with 5 or 6 large outer leaves of lettuce. Tear remaining lettuce into small pieces; place in salad bowl. Set aside.

Cook bacon in a large skillet until crisp; remove bacon, reserving drippings in skillet. Crumble bacon and set aside. Stir next 6 ingredients into bacon drippings; bring to a boil. Pour over lettuce; add bacon and toss gently. Serve immediately. Yield: 6 servings.

This butterhead or semiheading lettuce was planted in staggered rows across the width of the planting bed to make the best use of space.

Melons

Nothing says "summer" better than melons. Cantaloupe and honeydew are a cool treat on hot summer days. And sweet, juicy watermelon is as indispensable to the Fourth of July as fireworks. The South has the long, warm growing season melons need to develop their sweetest flavor.

Melons used to be limited to large gardens as the rambling vines require a lot of space. But new bush-type selections, which are actually short vines, make it possible to grow melons in a medium-sized garden.

Planting and Culture

Plant melons only after the soil is warm; seeds will rot in cold soil. Experienced melon growers like to wait until daytime temperatures are into the 80s before they plant.

Before planting, work ½ cup of 10-10-10 per 10 feet of row into the soil. Melons are usually planted in hills. Make them 5 to 6 feet apart for vining watermelons, 3 to 4 feet apart for cantaloupes and honeydews. Space bush types 3 feet apart. Sow seeds ½ to 1 inch deep, 4 to 6 per hill; thin seedlings to the healthiest 1 or 2 per hill.

To avoid being inundated with melons, make 2 or 3 plantings 2 weeks apart, or plant selections with different maturity dates.

To grow the most flavorful melons, keep the leaves free of insects and diseases. The plants need abundant, healthy foliage to produce fruit with a high sugar content, so planting disease-resistant selections is especially important.

When the vines begin to run, side-dress with ¼ cup of 10-10-10 per 10 feet of row. Also, keep the soil evenly moist through the season. Dry weather followed by heavy rains just before harvest can dilute the sugars in watermelons so that the flavor is less sweet. But if dry days follow the rain, you can leave fruit on the vine a few days to help concentrate the sugars.

For cantaloupes, reduce watering as harvest approaches. Too much water at this stage can dilute the sugars, and they will not reconcentrate as they will in watermelons.

Growing Tips

Poor fruit set or misshapen fruit may be caused by poor pollination. Remove deformed melons from the vine to allow normal fruit to form. Some melons may shrivel after the plants set fruit. This is a normal process by which the vine sheds extra fruit it cannot support.

Some gardeners lift ripening melons off the ground onto upside-down plates or aluminum pans. This exposes them to the sun so they can ripen. But melons will ripen just as well without this process.

Harvest

Determining when melons are ready for harvest takes some practice. To test cantaloupes, sniff the stem end for the characteristic aroma. Look for a pronounced netting and a change in

---

AT A GLANCE

Garden Season: Summer
Days until Harvest: 68-110
Amount to Plant Per Person: Cantaloupes and honeydews, 10-15 feet of row or 5-7 hills; watermelons, 8 feet of row or 4 hills
Serious Insects: Mites
Serious Diseases: Mildews, leaf spots, fusarium wilt (watermelons)
Comments: To produce the sweetest fruit, plants need plenty of healthy foliage; fertilize as directed and control diseases. Avoid overfertilizing, however, because too much nitrogen can cause poor flavor.

If you have a medium-sized garden, try bush-type or icebox selections of watermelons. However, bush types are susceptible to fusarium wilt, so they may not do well in parts of the Southeast where the disease is a problem.

skin color from green to yellow or tan. Also, check for a crack between the stem and fruit. It indicates that you can separate the stem from the fruit with slight pressure. This is called the "full slip" stage and is the best time to harvest. Fruit picked early will not mature off the vine.

Harvest most honeydew selections when the blossom end is slightly soft or springy and the skin has turned from green to ivory or greenish white, depending on the selection.

The best signs of ripeness for watermelons are when the shiny surface dulls and the underside of the melon (where it rests on the ground) turns from whitish to creamy yellow. The thump test, when a thump produces a muffled sound, tells you that the melon may be ripe—or overripe. Some growers harvest watermelons when the tendril at the stem end dries up and curls. But in some selections, this occurs 7 to 10 days before the melons are ripe, so it is not a completely reliable indicator. Handle melons carefully at harvest to avoid bruising them.

Recommended Selections

Growing the sweetest melons depends partly on cultural practices and partly on the selection. Selections with an asterisk were noted for their extrasweet flavor in studies at the Agricultural Research Center in Leesburg, Florida.

Healthy cantaloupe vines bear up to five juicy melons. Some gardeners lift melons onto aluminum pans or empty plastic margarine tubs to help them ripen.

Cantaloupes	
Ambrosia Hybrid*	Edisto 47*
Burpee Hybrid	Hale's Best Jumbo
Busheloupe (bush type)	Planter's Jumbo
Earlidew*	Saticoy Hybrid*

Watermelons	
Large, oblong types:	Dixie Queen
Calhoun Gray*	Garrisonian
Charleston Gray	Jubilee
Congo	Smokylee*
Crimson Sweet*	Sugarlee*
Dixielee*	Sweet Favorite
Seedless types:	
Triple Sweet*	Tri-X 313
For smaller gardens:	
Small icebox types:	
Sugar Baby	Sweet Baby
Sugar Doll	Yellow Baby*
Bush types:	
Baby Fun	Kengarden

Honeydew	
Honey Dew	Honey Dew Green Flesh
Oliver's Pearl Cluster (bush type)	

WATERMELON RIND PICKLES

1 large watermelon, quartered
  Pickling salt
2 tablespoons plus 2 teaspoons whole cloves
16 (1½-inch) sticks cinnamon
½ teaspoon mustard seeds
8 cups sugar
1 quart vinegar (5% acidity)

Remove flesh from melon (reserve for other uses); peel watermelon. Cut rind into 1-inch cubes.

Place rind in a large crock or plastic container. Add water by the quart until it covers the rind; add ¼ cup pickling salt for each quart water, stirring until salt dissolves. Cover and let stand in a cool place overnight. Drain well.

Place rind in a 10-quart Dutch oven; cover with cold water. Bring to a boil, and boil until rind is almost tender. Drain and set aside.

Tie cloves, cinnamon, and mustard seeds in a cheesecloth bag. Combine spice bag, sugar, and vinegar in a Dutch oven. Bring to a boil; remove from heat, and let stand 15 minutes. Add rind to syrup. Bring to a boil; reduce heat to low, and cook until rind is transparent. Remove spice bag.

Pack rind into hot sterilized jars, leaving ½-inch headspace. Cover at once with metal lids, and screw bands tight. Process in boiling-water bath 5 minutes. Yield: about 6 pints.

Vegetables 169

One of the first leafy vegetables ready for harvest in early spring is mustard. The nutritious greens reach full size in only 4 to 6 weeks, but can be harvested even earlier. In fact, the first pot of mustard greens is usually made up of the "thinnings."

Mustard

Planting and Culture

For spring harvests, plant 2 to 4 weeks before the last frost. A single spring planting produces until the plants bolt when warm weather arrives. To extend the harvest of tender young greens, make a second planting 2 to 3 weeks after the first. Once the plants flower, the leaves will have a strong, peppery flavor and be tough and stringy. For fall harvests, sow again in late summer or early fall. A light frost sweetens the flavor of the leaves.

You may start from transplants, but direct seeding is best. Before planting, work ¼ cup of 10-10-10 per 10 feet of row into the soil. Sow seeds thinly ½ inch deep in rows spaced 2 feet apart, or broadcast the seeds over a wide bed. Thin seedlings to 4 to 8 inches apart. Three to four weeks after planting, side-dress with ¼ cup of 10-10-10 per 10 feet of row. Be sure to keep the soil evenly moist. If it dries out, the leaves may taste peppery.

Harvest

To harvest, break off the outer leaves when they are 4 to 5 inches long and let the inner ones

---

AT A GLANCE

Garden Season: Early spring, fall
Days until Harvest: 28-40
Amount to Plant Per Person: 5-10 feet of row or 1½ feet of 18-inch-wide row for fresh use, an additional 5-10 feet or 1½ feet of wide row for storage
Serious Insects: Cabbage looper, imported cabbageworm
Serious Diseases: Downy mildew
Comments: If soil dries out between waterings, leaves may taste hot. Light frost in fall sweetens the flavor but hard frost kills plants.

For lush, vigorous growth, side-dress plants 3 to 4 weeks after planting. Keep the soil moist so leaves will not taste peppery.

You can choose either curly-leaved or smooth-leaved mustard. Curly-leaved types are a little more difficult to clean because soil and grit lodge in the curls.

keep growing. Young leaves are mild enough to eat raw in salads. Larger leaves (up to 10 inches) tend to have a strong flavor when cooked. If you grow mustard in wide rows, one way to harvest is to thin the row by pulling up whole plants when they are large enough to use. In fall, be sure to finish picking leaves before a severe freeze, which will kill the plants.

Recommended Selections

Recommended selections include Florida Broadleaf (very large leaves), Green Wave (slow bolting), Southern Giant Curled (a little more difficult to clean because soil lodges in the curly leaves), and Tendergreen (matures in 35 days, 10 days earlier than other selections).

• To conserve nutrients in mustard greens, do not overcook, and use only a small amount of water. Often the water clinging to the leaves after the greens are washed is enough.

One way to harvest is to snap off the outer leaves when they are 5 to 10 inches long. Let the inner ones keep growing. A patch of mustard 9 feet square (3 feet x 3 feet) can produce enough greens for two people to enjoy all season.

SWEET AND SOUR MUSTARD GREENS

1½ pounds mustard greens
¼ pound fresh mushrooms, thinly sliced
2 hard-cooked eggs, sliced
2 small tomatoes, cut into wedges
¼ cup thinly sliced green onions
¼ cup vegetable oil
2 tablespoons vinegar
2 tablespoons catsup
2 tablespoons brown sugar

Remove stems from mustard greens; wash leaves thoroughly and tear into bite-size pieces.

Combine greens, mushrooms, egg, and tomato; toss gently. Combine remaining ingredients in a jar; cover tightly and shake vigorously. Pour over salad and toss. Yield: 6 to 8 servings.

MUSTARD GREENS WITH RUTABAGA

3½ pounds mustard greens
1 medium rutabaga, peeled and diced
Salt to taste

Remove stems from mustard greens. Wash leaves thoroughly; tear into bite-size pieces. Place greens in a large Dutch oven (do not add water); cover and cook over medium heat 10 minutes. Add rutabaga and salt; cover and cook 30 minutes or until rutabaga is tender. Yield: 8 servings.

It is no wonder that okra is almost exclusively a Southern vegetable—it thrives in our long hot summers. Okra is at its best in July and August, but it continues to bear until frost. Unlike other vegetables, okra does well in heavy clay soil. It also tolerates a wide pH range and grows easily in Texas and other areas with alkaline soils.

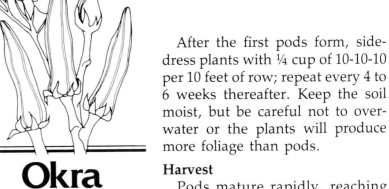

Okra

Planting and Culture

Do not plant okra until the soil is warm, at least 75 degrees. It is easy to grow but the seeds are hard to germinate; so before you plant, soak them in warm water for 6 to 24 hours. Also, before planting, work ½ cup of 10-10-10 per 10 feet of row into the soil. Sow seeds ½ to 1 inch deep and about 2 inches apart in rows 3 to 4 feet apart. When seedlings are 2 inches tall, thin to 6 to 12 inches apart.

After the first pods form, side-dress plants with ¼ cup of 10-10-10 per 10 feet of row; repeat every 4 to 6 weeks thereafter. Keep the soil moist, but be careful not to over-water or the plants will produce more foliage than pods.

Harvest

Pods mature rapidly, reaching harvesting size as quickly as 4 days after the flowers open. Cut pods from the plants when they are about 3 inches long. If over 5 inches long, they usually become tough and stringy. Use a sharp knife to cut the pods; pulling them off may damage the plants.

Harvest every day so the plants will continue to produce; if you leave pods to mature, the plants will stop producing. If plants are well fertilized and watered, they may grow to 15 feet

---

AT A GLANCE

Garden Season: Summer
Days until Harvest: 53-60
Amount to Plant Per Person: 4-6 feet of row for fresh use, an additional 6-10 feet of row for storage
Serious Insects or Diseases: None
Comments: Soak seeds overnight before planting. Harvest daily for continuous production.

If you water and fertilize okra properly, plants may grow 6 to 15 feet tall. So be sure to plant where they will not shade other vegetables.

Each flower forms a pod that is ready to harvest as quickly as 4 days after the bloom opens.

tall; even dwarf selections can reach 6 feet. Since okra bears new pods toward the top, plants this tall are difficult to harvest. Some gardeners cut back okra to about 4 to 5 feet when it gets too tall. This encourages branching from the bottom of the plant and may increase production. However, the bushy plants may also be more difficult to harvest.

Recommended Selections

If size could be a problem in your garden, choose a dwarf selection such as Lee, which has smooth, spineless pods, or Dwarf Green Long Pod. Other selections for the South include Clemson Spineless, Clemson Spineless 80, Jefferson, Emerald, and Louisiana Green Velvet, all of which are spineless. Park's Candelabra is a new branching type with an open growth habit that makes harvesting easy.

FRESH OKRA AND TOMATO

    2 tablespoons butter or margarine
    ½ cup finely chopped onion
    ½ cup finely chopped green pepper
    1 clove garlic, minced
    2 cups sliced fresh okra
    1 cup chopped, peeled tomato
    ⅛ teaspoon dried whole oregano
      Salt and pepper to taste

Melt butter in a large skillet; sauté onion, green pepper, and garlic until vegetables are tender. Add okra; cook 5 minutes, stirring often. Stir in tomato and oregano; cover, and simmer 10 mintues. Stir in salt and pepper. Yield: 4 servings.

OKRA PUFFS

    2 cups sliced fresh okra
    1 egg, beaten
    ½ cup evaporated milk
    ½ cup cornmeal
    ¾ teaspoon minced fresh marjoram or ¼ teaspoon
        dried whole marjoram
    ¾ teaspoon minced fresh thyme or ¼ teaspoon
        dried whole thyme
    ¼ teaspoon salt
    1 large onion, chopped
      Vegetable oil

Combine okra and next 7 ingredients, stirring well. Carefully drop okra mixture by rounded teaspoonfuls into hot oil (375°). Fry 3 to 5 minutes, or until puffs are golden, turning once. Drain on paper towels. Yield: about 2½ dozen.

SCRAMBLED OKRA

    2 cups sliced fresh okra
    1 teaspoon salt
    ½ cup cornmeal
    4 slices bacon
    ½ cup sliced fresh mushrooms
    3 eggs, beaten

Sprinkle okra with salt; add cornmeal, stirring until okra is coated. Set aside.

Cook bacon in a 9-inch skillet until crisp; remove bacon, reserving drippings. Crumble bacon and set aside. Add okra to bacon drippings. Cover and cook over medium heat 10 minutes or until okra is tender. Stir in mushrooms; cook, stirring often, 5 minutes. Add eggs; cook over low heat until eggs are set but still moist. Sprinkle with bacon before serving. Yield: 4 servings.

• The acidity of tomatoes cuts the sticky texture of okra, and the flavors are complimentary.

Pods are tenderest when 3 to 5 inches long.

For the sweetest onion to slice or add to a salad, you need to grow your own. Generally, the selections with the mildest flavor are available only to the gardener. Except for the Vidalia, most onions you can buy are strong-flavored, because they are the types that store and ship best.

Onions

Planting and Culture

Onions can be started from sets, transplants, or seeds. Transplants produce the fastest results; those started from seeds take the longest to mature. The number of seed selections available, however, is greater than the selection of sets or commercially available transplants.

Sets

Sets, which are young onions, are easier to plant than seeds or transplants—you simply put them into the ground. The key to growing good onions from sets is to choose sets that are firm, well shaped, and ½ to ¾ inch in diameter. The larger ones are likely to bolt instead of bulbing.

For late-spring harvests, plant sets 4 weeks before the last frost. In the Lower South, an early fall planting will produce green onions for late fall; plants not harvested then may overwinter and form bulbs in late spring.

Push sets into the ground, pointed ends up, so that the tips are just covered with soil. Space sets 2 to 4 inches apart. Each set will send up young leaves. For longer white portions to use as scallions, plant as you would leeks.

Transplants

Choose transplants that are at least pencil-sized, with a firm stem and healthy leaves. Do not buy those that are slimy, slick, or odorous; they are rotting.

Set out transplants 4 weeks before the last spring frost. In the Lower South, you can also plant in fall for harvests the following spring. Set the base of the transplant 2 inches deep; firm soil around the plant so that it stands upright. Space plants 3 inches apart in beds or in single rows spaced 1 to 2 feet apart.

Seeds

Onions started from seeds take longer to form bulbs than those started from sets or transplants. For spring-sowed onions, you will have to wait at least 4 months to harvest. A fall sowing will not produce mature onions until the following spring, because plants do not grow over winter. To shorten the time plants take up garden space, buy seeds and grow your own transplants to set out in spring. (*See page 53.*)

In the Lower South, sow seeds in the fall. In the Upper and Middle South, sow in spring 6 to 8 weeks before the last frost.

AT A GLANCE

Garden Season: Early spring, fall
Days until Harvest: Onions, 110-180 from seed, 85 from sets, 65 from plants; leeks, 110-150 from seed
Amount to Plant Per Person: Onions, 3-5 feet of row or 1½ feet of 18-inch-wide row for fresh use, an additional 10-15 feet of row or 1½ feet of wide row for storage; leeks, 5-10 plants for fresh use, an additional 5-10 for storage
Serious Insects: Onion thrips
Serious Diseases: Purple blotch
Comments: As bulbs develop, brush soil away from top to let them expand. Mulch to prevent sunburn, which turns bulbs green. For large leeks, thin to recommended spacing and mound soil up to where leaf blades branch.

Plant firm, well-shaped sets that are ½ to ¾ inch in diameter. Space them 2 to 4 inches apart and cover the tip with soil.

Sow seeds ½ inch deep in wide rows or in single rows that are 1½ feet apart. Spring-sowed seeds may take 2 weeks or longer to germinate in the cool soil. At first, seedlings are hard to see; they have narrow leaves that often form a loop as they emerge from the ground. When the seedlings are about 6 inches tall, thin to 2 to 4 inches apart.

When onion sets, transplants, or seeds are planted too early in the fall, they may bloom the following spring. Such flowering either prevents bulbing or causes the bulb to be small with a hollow heart. To avoid this, be sure to plant at the recommended time so that the plants are no larger than ¼ inch in diameter when cool weather arrives. If flowering does occur, use the onions as scallions.

To produce full-sized bulbs, plants need enough fertilizer to support plenty of foliage growth. In addition to a preplant application of ¼ cup of 10-10-10 per 10 feet of row, side-dress plants 4 to 6 weeks after planting and again when bulbs begin to form. Apply ¼ cup of 10-10-10 per 10 feet of row each time.

Keep the soil evenly moist. As the bulbs develop, carefully brush away the soil to expose the top two-thirds. (Be careful not to damage the roots.) This gives the bulbs more room to expand. Mulch the exposed part to protect it from sunburn, which turns onions green.

Harvest

When the tops of about half the crop turn yellow and fall over, the onions are mature. If you want to harvest all the onions at once, bend the remaining tops down and stop watering to allow tops and bulbs to dry. (However, this can cause rot. An alternative is to dig under the onions with a fork and lift them slightly to break some of the roots.) After the leaves wither and die, pull the onions and spread them out in a shaded, warm (80 to 85 degrees), well-ventilated place to cure. This helps prevent rot and mold during storage. After 2 to 3 weeks, the skins should be papery and the roots dry and wiry. Immature onions have thick necks and are susceptible to rot in spite of curing, so be sure to use them first. Mature onions have dry, narrow necks and may be stored in a cool dry place (45 to 55 degrees, 65 percent relative humidity). Sprouting indicates that temperatures are too warm.

Bunching onions produce a cluster of stems. Harvest them like any type of green onion.

To give onion bulbs room to expand to full size, gently brush away the soil as they develop to expose the top ⅔ of the bulb.

Recommended Selections

To grow onions successfully, you must choose selections adapted to your region. Onions are sensitive to day length and will not bulb properly if exposed to too much or too little light.

Onion selections recommended for the Gulf South include short-day selections such as Yellow Bermuda, White Bermuda, Texas Grano, Granex 33 (the Vidalia onion from Georgia), Excel, Crystal White Wax Bermuda, and Creole C-5. Excel and Creole C-5 keep well in storage. Selections recommended for the Upper South are long-day selections such as Ebenezer, Sweet Spanish, and Brown Beauty. In the Middle and Lower South, you can grow both long- and short-day selections, so choose any of those recommended for the other two regions. All of the recommended selections can be grown for mature dry bulbs or harvested early for green onions.

There is also a type of onion especially suited to use as green onions. Called a bunching onion, it produces a long, white, thick stem but does not form a bulb. Some selections such as Evergreen Long White Bunching, grow in clusters with several stalks per plant. You can treat these as perennials. Harvest stems as you need them in spring and summer; in fall, divide and replant the clumps for more plants the next spring.

Other types of bunching onions, such as Stokes Early Mild Bunching, form single stems. For both types, sow seeds in spring or summer for fall harvests; summer-planted ones will overwinter and give early spring harvests.

Shallots

Prized for their unique, delicate flavor, shallots are expensive to buy but easy to grow. The small bulbs, which resemble garlic cloves, grow in clusters; but each bulb has its own papery covering.

Some catalogs offer shallots, but you can also buy the sets at the grocery. Plant in early spring for midsummer harvests. Before planting, work ¼ cup of 10-10-10 per 10 feet of row into the soil. Plant the sets 1 inch deep and 4 to 6 inches apart in rows 12 inches apart. Side-dress with ¼ cup of 10-10-10 per 10 feet of row 4 weeks after planting and again as bulbs form.

Each set produces a cluster of bulbs, which pushes up through the soil until the shallots are almost entirely aboveground. When the tops die back, harvest the clusters and cure and store them as you would bulb onions. Do not divide the clusters before storing. In spring, divide them and replant the individual sets.

Leeks

Although the leek is related to the onion, it does not develop a bulb; it is grown for its long, straight neck which becomes up to 2 inches thick and 6 to 8 inches long. Its flavor is somewhat milder and sweeter than that of an onion.

To harvest leeks, dig them with a spade or shovel. Although you can harvest once plants bloom, it is best to dig leeks while they are still in the bud stage.

Before planting, work ¼ cup of 10-10-10 per 10 feet of row into the soil. Sow seeds in late winter or set out transplants in early spring. Leek shanks will be more tender if you mound soil around them to blanch them white. To make blanching easier, plant in a trench. Dig trenches 3 to 4 inches deep and 2 feet apart. In the bottom of the trench, set transplants, firming soil around them to hold them upright; or sow the seeds, barely covering them with soil. Thin seedlings to 3 to 5 inches apart. Set transplants at this spacing also.

As leeks grow, fill in the trench, mounding the soil around the shanks to an ultimate height of 4 to 5 inches. However, be careful not to cover the point where the leaf blades branch. Fertilize 6 weeks after planting with ¼ cup of 10-10-10 per 10 feet of row.

Leeks are quite hardy, so you can leave them in the ground over the winter and dig them as needed. The necks should be 1 to 2½ inches in

diameter. Wash them thoroughly before using, because sandy grit works its way into the edible portions. Broad London (Large American Flag) is a good selection for overwintering. Titan is known for its especially long shanks and slightly bulbous base.

GLAZED LEEKS

6 medium leeks
2 tablespoons butter or margarine
2 tablespoons brown sugar

Remove roots, tough outer leaves, and tops from leeks; wash leeks thoroughly. Place leeks in a large heavy skillet; cover and cook over medium heat in a small amount of boiling water 8 to 10 minutes or until tender. Drain; remove leeks from skillet, and set aside.

Combine butter and sugar in skillet; cook over low heat, stirring constantly, until sugar dissolves. Return leeks to skillet; cook over low heat, turning frequently, just until glazed. Yield: 3 servings.

GOURMET ONIONS

⅓ cup butter or margarine
5 medium onions, sliced and separated into rings
½ cup dry sherry
½ teaspoon sugar
½ teaspoon salt
¼ teaspoon pepper
2 tablespoons grated Parmesan cheese

Melt butter in a large skillet; add onion and sauté 5 to 8 minutes, stirring often. Add sherry, sugar, salt, and pepper; reduce heat, and simmer 2 to 3 minutes, stirring constantly. Sprinkle with cheese. Yield: 6 to 8 servings.

HONEY GLAZED ONIONS

24 small white onions, peeled
¼ cup hot water
3 tablespoons butter or margarine, melted
2 tablespoons catsup
2 tablespoons honey
Dash of salt
Dash of red pepper

Place onions in a lightly greased 2-quart casserole. Stir together remaining ingredients and pour over onions. Cover and bake at 350° for 1 hour. Yield: 6 to 8 servings.

Although leeks look like oversized green onions, they are milder and sweeter in flavor than onions.

Peas

The sweet flavor of English peas and the crunchy texture of edible podded peas are best found in those that are fresh from the garden. After growing your own, you may never want to eat canned or frozen peas again.

English Peas

The key to growing English peas is to plant early, as soon as you can work the soil. Late-planted English peas that are beginning to bloom when warm weather arrives will not set fruit, and pods that have already formed will develop slowly. Spring frosts will not damage young plants, but a late frost when plants are blooming may kill them.

AT A GLANCE

Garden Season: Early spring, fall
Days until Harvest: 62-70
Amount to Plant Per Person: 15-20 feet for fresh use, an additional 25-40 feet for storage
Serious Insects: Mites
Serious Diseases: Powdery mildew
Comments: Plant as early as the ground can be worked. Once warm weather arrives, plants stop setting fruit.

Planting and Culture

Smooth-seeded, extraearly selections are hardier than wrinkled-seeded selections, so plant them first, about 6 to 8 weeks before the last frost (around Christmastime in the Gulf South). To extend harvests, plant a wrinkled-seeded selection 2 weeks later. Sow no deeper than 1 inch.

Growing a fall crop may be difficult, especially in the Upper South. You must plant in late summer while the soil is still warm in order to harvest before the first frost causes blossoms to drop. To improve your chances of success, start about 12 weeks before the first frost, and use an early-maturing selection. Sow thickly and 1½ to 2 inches deep and mulch rows lightly to cool the soil. Keep plants watered.

Tall selections that grow to 6 feet require a trellis for support. (*See page 88 for types of trellises.*) You can sow seeds 2 to 3 inches apart along both sides of a trellis, or sow them about 1 inch apart in a double row on one side of the trellis. Dwarf selections that grow 1½ to 3 feet tall do not need to be trellised. Broadcast the seeds in a 4- to 6-inch-wide band, leaving 2 to 3 feet between bands. The plants will support each other, but it is a good idea to push 3-foot-tall sticks into the ground among the plants to

Tall-growing selections of English peas must be supported. Sow seeds along both sides of the trellis as shown here, or in a double row on one side of the trellis.

Harvest English peas when the pods are bright green and rounded. Pinch carefully to avoid tearing the vine.

help hold them erect. Keep the soil evenly moist. Side-dress with ¼ cup of 10-10-10 per 10 feet of row when plants are 4 to 6 inches tall.

Harvest

Pick when pods are bright green and almost rounded. Flat, dark-green pods are immature, while yellow, hard ones are overmature. Remove all mature pods so that plants will continue producing.

Recommended Selections

A recommended smooth-seeded selection is Alaska. Wrinkled-seeded selections include Little Marvel, Wando, Laxton's Progress, Thomas Laxton, Dark Skin Perfection, Alderman, and Freezonian.

Edible Podded Peas

Edible podded peas or snow peas grow in spring and fall like English peas. As a fall crop, they may be slightly more successful than English peas because the plants tolerate late summer heat better. Harvest the wide, flat pods when they are 1½ to 2½ inches long and before the peas begin to fill out.

Sugar Snap peas are a hybrid between a mutant English pea and edible podded peas. You can use them as edible podded peas, or shell and use them like English peas. Pick pods at the stage you desire, but do not let the peas become overmature or they will be starchy.

Recommended Selections

Selections of edible podded peas include Dwarf Gray Sugar; Mammoth Melting Sugar; Sugar Snap; and Sugar Bon, an earlier-maturing, dwarf Sugar Snap type.

BAKED PEAS IN LETTUCE

3 to 4 pounds fresh English peas
3 to 4 large lettuce leaves
¼ cup butter or margarine
½ pound fresh mushrooms, sliced
8 green onions, chopped
1 (10½-ounce) can consommé, undiluted
1½ teaspoons salt
1 teaspoon sugar
¾ teaspoon minced fresh marjoram or ¼ teaspoon ground marjoram
½ teaspoon ground nutmeg
¼ teaspoon pepper
1 tablespoon chopped fresh parsley

Shell and wash peas; set aside. Line a 1½-quart casserole with lettuce leaves; set aside.

Melt butter in a medium skillet; sauté mushrooms and onions until tender. Remove from heat and stir in peas. Pour into lettuce-lined casserole; set aside.

Bring consommé to a boil. Remove from heat and stir in next 5 ingredients; pour over peas. Sprinkle with parsley. Cover and bake at 375° for 55 to 60 minutes or until peas are tender. Remove lettuce, if desired. Stir before serving. Yield: 6 to 8 servings.

SIMPLE SAUTEED SNOW PEAS

1 pound fresh snow peas
1 tablespoon minced shallots or green onions
1 tablespoon vegetable oil
1 tablespoon minced fresh basil or 1 teaspoon dried whole basil
1½ tablespoons beef broth

Wash pea pods; trim ends, and remove any tough strings.

Sauté pea pods and shallots in oil in a large skillet 3 to 5 minutes or until pods are crisp-tender. Stir in basil and beef broth; cook, stirring constantly, 1 minute. Yield: 4 to 6 servings.

Harvest edible podded peas when they are 1½ to 2½ inches long and still flat.

When you say "Pass the peas, please" in the South, what you are likely to get is some kind of Southern pea: Black-eyed, crowder, and cream peas are the most common. The same request in other parts of the country would probably land you a bowl of English peas.

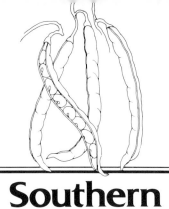

Southern Peas

Planting and Culture

Also called cowpeas, Southern peas are actually more closely related to beans than peas, and their culture is similar. They thrive in our long, hot summers and are one of the most drought-tolerant vegetables you can grow. They even do well in poor soil, provided it is well drained.

Southern peas are sensitive to frost, so plant 1 or 2 weeks after the last frost. Planting early can also encourage excessive vine growth. Make successive plantings every 3 weeks until midsummer for continuous harvests.

Sow seeds in rows spaced 2 feet apart or in 18-inch-wide beds. Plant them 1 inch deep in clay soils, 2 inches deep in sandy soils. Thin seedlings so they stand 6 to 12 inches apart. Southern peas are bush or semibush types and do not need to be trellised.

Southern peas need little or no fertilizer. In poor soils, you may wish to incorporate ½ pound of 5-10-10 per 25 feet of row into the soil before planting. Too much nitrogen encourages vine growth and delays pod set. Although drought tolerant, peas prefer evenly moist soil. But avoid overwatering, especially at blooming time, as this can delay pod set. Plants may also stop setting pods if daytime temperatures remain over 95 degrees for about a week; but they will begin again when temperatures drop.

AT A GLANCE

Garden Season: Summer
Days until Harvest: 56-90
Amount to Plant Per Person: 10-15 feet for fresh use, an additional 20 feet for storage
Serious Insects: Cowpea curculio, mites, nematodes
Serious Diseases: Mosaic viruses
Comments: Need little or no fertilizer. Tolerate dry weather better than most vegetables.

Seeds are large enough to handle easily; sow them 3 to 6 inches apart and 1 inch deep in clay soil, 2 inches deep in sandy soil.

Southern peas survive drought better than most vegetables, but for best production, keep the soil evenly moist. Depending on the selection, you may get four harvests from a single planting if you keep the pods picked.

Harvest

Peas are ready for harvest in 56 to 90 days, depending on the selection. The key to the best harvesttime is the color of the pod. Purple-hulled selections are ready when the ends and almost half of the pod have turned from green to purple. If the pod is completely purple, the seeds will be too dry.

Harvest other types when the pods begin to change from green to yellow, tan, or purple. The peas should be green inside the pod.

If left unharvested, peas will become "rattle dry" in a few days. Be sure to harvest before they reach this stage so that plants will continue producing. Depending on the selection, you may get four harvests from a single planting.

Recommended Selections

Selections recommended for the South include the crowder types Mississippi Silver, Mississippi Purple, and Dixielee; black-eyed types Queen Anne and Magnolia Blackeye; cream types White Acre and Texas Cream 40; and Pink Eye Purple Hull.

Harvest Southern peas when the pods begin to change color. But if pods turn completely purple or tan, the peas will be too dry.

There is also a variation of the Southern pea called asparagus bean. Its long vines bear pods up to 30 inches long. If harvested when immature (15 to 18 inches long), the pods may be used as snap beans.

SOUTHERN COUNTRY PEAS

2 cups shelled black-eyed or purple hull peas, washed
½ teaspoon salt
1 cup cubed, cooked ham
2 tablespoons vegetable oil
¼ cup minced onion
1 tablespoon minced green pepper
2 medium tomatoes, cut into wedges

Combine peas and salt in a 2-quart saucepan. Cover peas with water, and cook over low heat 1 hour or until tender.

Cook ham in a small skillet just until browned. Add oil, onion, and green pepper; cook over medium heat 2 minutes. Add ham mixture to peas and cook, uncovered, 5 to 10 minutes over low heat or until liquid is reduced. Garnish with tomato. Yield: 4 to 6 servings.

CORN AND PEAS WITH SAVORY

3 cups shelled field peas, washed
3 tablespoons butter or margarine
½ cup chopped celery
¼ cup chopped onion
1 (17-ounce) can whole kernel corn, drained
2 tablespoons chopped fresh parsley
¼ to ½ teaspoon dried whole savory
½ teaspoon salt
⅛ teaspoon pepper
½ cup commercial sour cream

Place peas in a 2½-quart saucepan. Cover peas with water and cook over low heat 1 hour or until peas are tender. Drain well.

Melt butter in a skillet; add celery and onion and sauté until tender. Stir in peas and remaining ingredients, except sour cream, stirring constantly; cook until bubbly. Stir in sour cream; cook, stirring often, just until heated. Yield: 6 servings.

FRESH CROWDER PEAS

3 slices bacon, diced
2 quarts shelled crowder peas, washed
1 medium onion, chopped
1 teaspoon coarsely ground black pepper
½ teaspoon salt
2 beef-flavored bouillon cubes

Cook bacon in a 3½-quart saucepan until crisp; stir in next 5 ingredients. Add enough water to cover peas. Bring to a boil. Reduce heat, cover, and cook over low heat, stirring occasionally, 1 hour or until peas are tender. Yield: 12 to 14 servings.

Vegetables 181

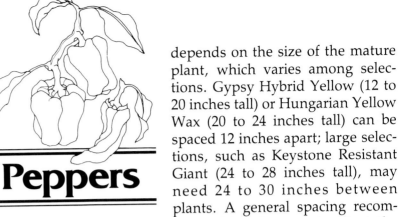

Peppers

Peppers are ideally suited to the South's long growing season. As long as you keep harvesting them, the plants will produce from early summer until fall.

Types of Peppers

Although peppers come in many shapes, sizes, and colors, they fall into one of two groups: sweet or hot. Both types are grown the same way.

Planting and Culture

Select only small, healthy transplants with dark-green foliage and no blooms. Transplants that are blooming when you buy them will not be as productive.

Peppers are sensitive to cold, so do not set out transplants until weather and soil are warm. The distance at which you set pepper transplants depends on the size of the mature plant, which varies among selections. Gypsy Hybrid Yellow (12 to 20 inches tall) or Hungarian Yellow Wax (20 to 24 inches tall) can be spaced 12 inches apart; large selections, such as Keystone Resistant Giant (24 to 28 inches tall), may need 24 to 30 inches between plants. A general spacing recommendation is 18 to 24 inches apart; adjust the spacing in subsequent years according to your own experience.

It is a good idea to stake plants to keep them from breaking or falling over under the weight of the fruit. (*See page 90 for staking.*) Fertilize transplants at planting time with liquid 20-20-20 diluted according to label directions.

After the first few fruit enlarge to about ⅓ their mature size, side-dress with ¼ cup of 10-10-10 per 10 feet of row. Overfertilizing, however, can cause blossom drop.

Keep the soil evenly moist, especially when plants are blooming and setting fruit. Drought causes blossom drop and blossom end rot. Without adequate water, fruit will also be smaller.

AT A GLANCE

Garden Season: Summer
Days until Harvest: 55-75
Amount to Plant Per Person: 3-5 plants for fresh use, an additional 3-5 for storage
Serious Insects: None
Serious Diseases: Leaf spots
Comments: Keep soil evenly moist to prevent blossom drop and blossom end rot. Overfertilizing also causes blossom drop.

Bell peppers require frequent watering during dry weather to produce large, well-shaped fruit. Do not overfertilize peppers; this encourages foliage growth instead of fruit production.

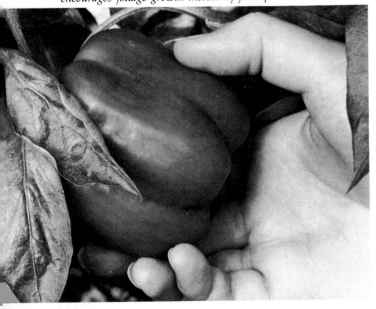

Hot peppers come in all shapes and sizes. Generally they produce better in hot weather (temperatures over 90 degrees in the daytime) than sweet peppers do.

Plants may also drop blossoms when night temperatures are lower than 55 degrees or higher than 75 to 80 degrees, or when day temperatures exceed 90 degrees. (In general, hot peppers are more tolerant of high temperatures than sweet peppers.) They will resume setting fruit when temperatures return to normal.

Harvest

You can harvest peppers as soon as they reach a usable size, or let them grow to the mature size typical of that selection. Cut the woody stems with shears or a sharp knife rather than pulling or twisting the peppers off the plant. Leave about ½ inch of stem on the fruit. For a stronger and sweeter flavor, you can also let bell-type peppers ripen until they turn red or yellow (depending on the selection) but this will decrease future production. When frost is predicted, pick all the peppers and store them in the refrigerator. Use the smaller ones first; healthy ones that are nearly full sized will stay fresh for several weeks. Hot peppers intended for drying should turn completely red before you harvest them.

There are both sweet and hot selections of yellow banana peppers. Pick them while they are still green or yellow to encourage continued production.

Recommended Selections

Recommended selections of sweet peppers include Bell Boy, Keystone Resistant Giant, Yolo Wonder, Sweet Banana, and Pimiento. Gypsy Hybrid Yellow, an All-America Selection, is especially good for container gardening and small gardens because it produces a lot of peppers on small plants. Dutch Treat, another All-America winner, is both ornamental and edible.

Hot pepper selections recommended for the South include Dr. Greenleaf Red Hot Tabasco, Long Slim Cayenne, Long Red Cayenne, Hungarian Yellow Wax, Jalapeño, Anaheim Chili, and Red Chili.

BAKED GREEN PEPPER AND ONION

2 large green peppers, seeded and sliced into ¼-inch rings
2 large onions, sliced
2 tablespoons butter or margarine
¼ teaspoon salt
⅛ teaspoon pepper

Place green pepper and onion in a 1½-quart casserole. Dot with butter and sprinkle with salt and pepper. Cover and bake at 350° for 35 to 40 minutes or until desired doneness. Yield: 4 to 6 servings.

FRIED PEPPER RINGS

6 medium-size green peppers, seeded and sliced into ¼-inch rings
1 egg, beaten
¾ cup fine, dry breadcrumbs
Vegetable oil
Salt

Dip green pepper rings into egg and then in breadcrumbs. Fry rings in hot oil (375°) until golden brown. Drain on paper towels. Sprinkle with salt. Yield: 8 servings.

VEGETABLE-STUFFED PEPPERS

6 medium-size green peppers
1½ cups fresh corn cut from cob, drained
1 cup chopped, peeled tomato
½ cup soft breadcrumbs
¼ cup chopped celery
2 eggs, slightly beaten
2 tablespoons margarine, melted
1 tablespoon minced onion
¾ teaspoon salt
⅛ teaspoon pepper

Cut off tops of green peppers; remove seeds. Combine remaining ingredients; mix well. Fill peppers with vegetable mixture; place peppers in a 10- x 6- x 2-inch baking dish. Pour ½-inch boiling water in dish around peppers. Cover and bake at 350° for 1 hour. Yield: 6 servings.

Vegetables 183

Potatoes

Irish potatoes have an undeserved reputation for being fattening and requiring lots of garden space. Neither accusation is true. They are nutritious, have only 80 calories per medium-sized potato, and will fit into nearly any size garden. You can even grow them in containers.

Seed Potatoes

Except for some new selections (one of which is Explorer) that are started from true seeds, Irish potatoes are started from seed potatoes (potatoes that you cut into pieces for planting). To help prevent disease, plant only certified seed potatoes, which have been grown in carefully controlled, disease-free conditions. It is best not to use grocery store potatoes, as they may carry diseases and are often chemically treated to prevent sprouting. Potatoes may be grown in fall as well as spring. Purchase enough seed potatoes in early spring for both crops. Store them in the refrigerator. A week before planting, remove from the refrigerator and keep them at room temperature for 4 to 5 days before cutting them.

Cut large seed potatoes into 1½- to 2-ounce pieces (about the size of an egg). Each piece should have one or two eyes (recessed growth buds), and should not be too small, as they provide energy for the sprouts until these reach the sunlight. Plant seed potatoes whole if they are egg sized or smaller.

Before planting, some gardeners let the cut seed pieces sit at room temperature for 2 or 3 days. This allows a corky layer or callous to form to prevent rotting.

Planting and Culture

Hot weather keeps tubers from developing, so for a late-spring harvest, plant 2 weeks before the last frost. A late frost may nip young plants back, but they usually recover. For a fall crop, plant again in mid- to late summer, to harvest before the first hard freeze, which kills the plants.

Before planting, work ¼ cup of 10-10-10 per 10 feet of row into the soil. Plant seed pieces about 12 inches apart in furrows spaced 3 feet apart. Set them 3½ inches deep in clay soil and 6 inches deep in sandy soil, making sure the eyes face upward. Be careful not to crowd plants in the row, or they will produce lower yields and smaller potatoes.

As the plants grow, mound the soil around the stems to a height of about 8 inches. Since potatoes form at the level where the seed piece is planted or slightly higher, mounding encourages plants to produce more tubers. And it protects the potatoes from exposure to light, which turns them green. The green areas should be peeled or cut away before the potato is cooked.

An alternative method is to grow potatoes in mulch. Set the seed pieces only 1 inch deep. Then cover them with 6 to 12 inches of aged sawdust, leaves, hay, or pine straw. The potatoes developing in this organic layer are smoother, cleaner, and easier to harvest than soil-grown potatoes. This is particularly good for gardens with heavy soil or poor drainage.

Potatoes need evenly moist soil, especially when tubers begin to form. This usually occurs 6

AT A GLANCE

Garden Season: Early spring, fall
Days until Harvest: 100-115 after planting seed pieces
Amount to Plant Per Person: 10 feet of row for fresh use, an additional 15 feet for storage
Serious Insects: Colorado potato beetle
Serious Diseases: Early blight, late blight
Comments: Plant only certified seed potatoes. Hill soil to plants to protect tubers from sunlight. Try Explorer, which grows from true seed, for the fall crop.

Potatoes form at the level of the seed piece or slightly higher. Mounding the soil provides extra room for more tubers to form, and protects them from sunlight.

to 10 weeks after planting. Alternate wet and dry periods can cause potatoes to develop growth cracks, knobs, and hollow hearts (a cavity in the center of the potato).

Too much nitrogen produces lush foliage and poor tubers; too little causes plants to form small tubers prematurely, thus reducing yield. When sprouts break through the soil surface, apply ⅓ cup of 10-10-10 per 10 feet of row.

Harvest

New potatoes are the small, immature tubers prized for their sweetness and tenderness. They are ready for harvest about 8 weeks after planting. To harvest, dig carefully with your fingers several inches below the ground in an area 12 to 18 inches around the plant. Be careful not to uproot the plants. They will continue to mature the remaining potatoes. Remember, though, that the early harvest reduces the number of large tubers that you will harvest later.

Potatoes are mature when the foliage begins to die back, but leave them in the ground 2 to 3 weeks longer. The tougher skin that develops during this period helps protect the potato from damage during harvest and lengthens storage life. To further toughen the skin, cut the dying foliage to the ground.

Dig the tubers carefully, using your hands or a turning fork. Rough handling can bruise them or break the skin, resulting in rot during storage. Some will inevitably be damaged, so set those aside to eat first.

Clean the potatoes by wiping the soil off with a soft brush. Or spread them out and spray with a gentle stream of water. Never wash them in a tub of water, as any decay organisms present can be spread by the water to all the tubers. After washing, place the potatoes in a shaded location until completely dry.

Recommended Selections

It is best to purchase seed potatoes from a local farm supply store or a mail-order source that lists specific selections. Those listed in seed catalogs simply as red or white may not be adapted to the South. Recommended selections include Red Pontiac, Red LaSoda, and La Rouge; and white-skinned potatoes, such as Kennebec, Irish Cobbler, Atlantic, Sebago, and Superior. Kennebec, Irish Cobbler, and Atlantic have a short storage life. Atlantic is usually grown for new potatoes.

Selections grown from true seed, such as Explorer, should be started indoors as you would tomatoes or peppers (*see page 53*) and set out after the last spring frost or 17 weeks before fall frost. The plants produce small- to medium-sized potatoes. While yields are not as high as those of other selections, these types are convenient for late-summer planting if you did not buy enough seed potatoes in the spring.

CREAMY NEW POTATOES

12 new potatoes
¼ cup butter or margarine
2 tablespoons all-purpose flour
½ teaspoon salt
Dash of pepper
1 cup milk
½ cup half-and-half
1 teaspoon chopped fresh chives

Wash potatoes; pare a 1-inch strip around center of each potato. Place potatoes in a large saucepan; cover with water, and bring to a boil. Reduce heat, cover, and simmer 15 to 20 minutes or until tender; drain well.

Melt butter in a heavy saucepan over low heat; add flour, salt, and pepper, stirring until smooth. Cook 1 minute, stirring constantly. Gradually stir in milk and half-and-half; cook over medium heat, stirring constantly, until thickened and bubbly. Pour over potatoes; sprinkle with chives. Yield: 4 servings.

To harvest, push the fork straight into the ground 12 to 18 inches from the plants, then lift carefully to avoid stabbing tubers. If you harvest before the foliage dies back, potatoes may be immature and will have a shorter storage life.

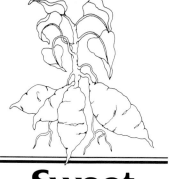

Sweet Potatoes

Sweet potatoes are best for a large garden. They require a lot of space; but if you have it, sweet potatoes are easy to grow. They are one of the few vegetables that truly thrive during the hottest part of the summer.

Sweet potatoes are often called yams to distinguish them from the selections grown in the North, which have a much drier flesh. But the true yam is an entirely different plant that is seldom grown in the United States.

Planting and Culture

You can plant sweet potatoes anytime from 3 weeks after the last frost until early summer, but be sure they have enough time to mature before frost. Start from young plants or slips (also called draws, poles, or transplants). Buy certified, disease-free plants from a seed store or mail-order source. Unpack mail-order plants immediately; if they appear wilted, immerse the roots in water for a few hours prior to planting. If you must delay planting 2 or 3 days, place the roots in moist sphagnum moss.

Be sure the soil is loose and well drained. If grown in heavy clay soils, potatoes may be rough and irregular. It is best to have a soil test made prior to planting, because a potassium deficiency causes the roots to be long and slender rather than short and chunky. Too much nitrogen reduces yield and quality; but in poor, infertile soils, work in ¼ cup of 10-10-10 per 10 feet of row before planting.

Sweet potatoes are grown in mounded rows built 10 inches high and 12 inches wide. Leave 3 to 4 feet between rows. Set plants 4 to 5 inches deep and 12 to 15 inches apart.

Ordinarily, a sweet potato vine produces a few huge roots and several small ones. To grow potatoes of a more uniform size and weight, plant them in staggered double rows 10 inches apart on raised beds that are 10 inches high and 30 inches wide. Set the plants 10 inches from the edges of the bed. Leave 2 feet between the beds.

AT A GLANCE

Garden Season: Summer
Days until Harvest: 100-120 after transplanting slips
Amount to Plant Per Person: 5-10 for fresh use, an additional 10-20 for storage
Serious Insects: Sweet potato weevil, wireworm
Serious Diseases: Scurf, black rot
Comments: Use only certified, disease-free plants. For high yields of short, chunky roots, provide the correct balance of nitrogen and potassium as indicated by a soil test.

Sweet potatoes are easy to grow, but require a lot of space because of their vining growth habit.

To know when to harvest sweet potatoes, dig a few tubers about 100 to 120 days after planting. If most have reached a good baking size, harvest the crop. Dig deeply below the plants to avoid injuring the tubers.

Be sure to record the planting date so you will know when to begin harvesting.

Keep the soil moist until the slips are established. Once they are growing, sweet potatoes can withstand more dry weather than many other vegetables. But a constant moisture supply will prevent cracking, which occurs when the roots take in a lot of water after a long, dry period.

Harvest

Sweet potatoes should reach maturity between 100 and 120 days after planting, but they will keep growing larger until you harvest them or until frost kills the plants. Near the expected maturity date, check to see if the soil has begun cracking and dig a few potatoes to see if they have reached a good baking size. If so, harvest the crop, digging carefully to avoid injuring them. If potatoes are cut or bruised, they will be more likely to rot in storage. Very small potatoes may not store well either, so plan to use them first. Be sure to harvest before a frost. In fact, if plants are exposed to temperatures below 50 degrees, the potatoes will be of poor quality.

Let sweet potatoes dry a few hours on the ground; then cure them to help prevent rot during storage and to improve flavor. Uncured sweet potatoes taste musty and earthy. To cure, spread the potatoes in a dark, well-ventilated place where temperatures are above 70 degrees. Near a furnace, water heater, or clothes dryer is a good place. After 5 to 10 days, they should be ready for storage. (*See page 115, Harvesting, Storage, and Preservation.*)

Recommended Selections

Selections recommended for the South include Centennial, Porto Rico, Bush Porto Rico, and Jewel.

SWEET POTATO BALLS

2½ cups mashed, cooked sweet potatoes (about 2 pounds)
2 tablespoons butter or margarine, melted
½ teaspoon salt
Dash of pepper
⅓ cup honey
1 tablespoon butter or margarine
1½ cups chopped pecans

Combine first 4 ingredients. Cover and chill 1 to 2 hours; shape mixture into 8 balls. Set aside.

Combine honey and remaining tablespoon of butter in a small skillet; cook over medium heat, stirring constantly, until bubbly. Remove from heat. Roll each potato ball in honey mixture; coat with pecans. Place in a lightly greased 8-inch square pan; bake at 350° for 20 to 25 minutes. Yield: 8 servings.

SHERRIED SWEET POTATOES

3 medium-size sweet potatoes
Vegetable oil
1 cup firmly packed brown sugar
2 tablespoons cornstarch
¼ teaspoon salt
½ teaspoon grated orange rind
1 cup orange juice
½ cup golden raisins
¼ cup plus 2 tablespoons butter or margarine
⅓ cup dry sherry
¼ cup chopped pecans

Wash sweet potatoes and rub with vegetable oil. Bake at 400° for 1 hour or until done. Peel and cut potatoes into 1-inch cubes. Place in a lightly greased 2-quart casserole; set aside.

Stir together sugar, cornstarch, and salt; stir in orange rind, juice, and raisins. Cook over medium heat, stirring constantly, until smooth and thickened. Boil 1 minute, stirring constantly. Add butter, sherry, and pecans; stir until butter melts. Pour over potatoes; bake at 350° for 30 minutes, stirring twice. Yield: 6 servings.

Normally, a vine produces a few huge potatoes and several small ones.

Vegetables 187

Pumpkins are often grown just for the fun of it. If you have a large garden, you can aspire to brag-sized fruit that weigh up to 100 pounds. Even if your space is limited, you can still grow jack-o'-lanterns of a respectable size or ones good enough for pumpkin pie with the new semibush types (actually compact vines).

Pumpkins

Planting and Culture

Plant pumpkins after the soil is thoroughly warm, 2 weeks after the last frost. This planting will be ready for harvest in midsummer in the Lower South and in mid- to late summer in the Upper and Middle South. To harvest later in the fall (by Halloween over most of the South, by Thanksgiving in Florida and South Texas), delay planting until early to midsummer.

Pumpkins are usually grown in hills. Before planting, work about ⅛ to ¼ cup of 10-10-10 into each hill. Allow 6 to 10 feet between hills for vining types, 4 to 6 feet for bush types. Sow 5 or 6 seeds 2 to 3 inches apart and ½ to 1 inch deep in each hill. When seedlings are 2 inches tall, thin to 1 or 2 plants per hill. If you want to grow the largest pumpkin in the neighborhood, leave 1 plant per hill; and after the fruit begin growing, remove all but 1 or 2 from the vine.

You may also grow pumpkins in rows. Sow seeds of vining types 2 to 3 feet apart in rows 8 to 12 feet apart. For bush types, sow seeds 2 to 3 feet apart in rows 4 to 6 feet apart. In a small garden, small-fruited pumpkins can be trained on a trellis if the fruit is supported in a sling.

Pumpkins require a lot of water, so be sure to keep the soil evenly moist. One week after blooms appear, side-dress the vines with ¼ cup of 10-10-10 per hill or ½ cup per 10 feet of row.

AT A GLANCE

Garden Season: Summer, fall
Days until Harvest: 90-120
Amount to Plant Per Person: 1-2 hills
Serious Insects: Squash bug
Serious Diseases: Anthracnose, mildews
Comments: Pumpkins require a lot of water, so keep the soil evenly moist.

Growing large pumpkins like these requires a lot of garden space, about 16 square feet per plant.

Like squash, pumpkins depend on bees to pollinate the blossoms. If bees are not active in your garden, pollinate the flowers by transferring pollen from male to female flowers with an artist's brush. Otherwise, fruit will not form.

Harvest

Pumpkins are ready for harvest when the vines die and the fruit turns a rich orange or the color typical of the selection. If you cannot pierce the skin with your thumbnail, the fruit is mature. Cut the pumpkins from the vines, leaving 3 inches of stem attached. Handle them carefully to avoid bruising or scarring them. Fruit with broken stems or punctured shells will rot in storage, as will pumpkins that are not harvested before a frost.

Pumpkins must be cured before they can be stored. To cure, put them in a well-ventilated, warm (75 to 85 degrees) place for 1 or 2 weeks. (*See page 115 for storage information.*)

Although yields vary according to selection, weather, and cultural conditions, you can usually expect to harvest three to four fruit per plant. Large-fruited selections may yield only one or two fruit per plant.

Recommended Selections

Below are some selections that grow well in the South.

Selection	Size	Purpose
Big Max	up to 100 lbs. and 70" in circumference	carving, contests, pies
Connecticut Field	15 to 25 lbs.	baking, carving, pies
Howden Field	15 to 25 lbs.	baking, carving, pies, storage
Cushaw Green Striped	12 to 25 lbs.	baking, canning, storage
Jack-O'-Lantern	10 to 15 lbs.	carving, pies
Small Sugar	7 lbs.	baking, pies, storage
Lady Godiva	——	seeds only
Triple Treat	6 to 8 lbs.	pies, seeds
Spirit Hybrid*	10 to 15 lbs.	carving, pies
Trick or Treat*	10 to 12 lbs.	pies, seeds

*Semibush selections.

Pumpkins harvested in late summer can be cured by spreading them out in a shady spot for 1 or 2 weeks.

SUPERB PUMPKIN BREAD

1½ cups all-purpose flour
¼ teaspoon baking powder
½ teaspoon baking soda
¼ teaspoon salt
½ teaspoon ground cloves
½ teaspoon ground cinnamon
½ teaspoon ground nutmeg
1 cup sugar
½ cup vegetable oil
2 eggs
1 cup mashed, cooked pumpkin

Combine first 7 ingredients; stir well and set aside. Combine sugar and oil in a large mixing bowl; mix well. Add eggs, one at a time, beating well after each addition. Add pumpkin; mix well. Add dry ingredients and mix until smooth. Pour into a greased and floured 9- x 5- x 3-inch loafpan; bake at 350° for 50 to 55 minutes or until a wooden pick inserted in center comes out clean. Cool in pan 10 minutes; remove from pan, and cool completely. Yield: one 9-inch loaf.

Vegetables 189

Radishes

Ready for harvesting in just 3 to 4 weeks, spring radishes are a quick, easy crop to grow in the cool weather of spring and fall. If you are especially fond of radishes, try the summer and winter types also, which take longer to mature.

Spring Radishes

Spring radishes include the typical red, round, or oblong radish as well as white, round, or icicle-shaped types. Their crisp texture and mildly hot flavor depend partly on cool weather, so begin planting 2 to 6 weeks before the last frost and continue until 4 weeks after it. The quality declines with warm weather in late spring. For a fall crop, plant in early fall, 6 weeks before the first frost, and continue up to 4 weeks before.

Because spring radishes mature in only 20 to 30 days, sow a few seeds every 10 days to enjoy continuous harvests. These radishes are also ideal for interplanting with other crops, particularly those that are slow to germinate, such as carrots and salsify. The radishes help mark the rows and are ready for harvest by the time the main crop begins growing.

Summer Radishes

Summer radishes are sometimes called all-season radishes because they tolerate some warm weather. However, since they take about 45 days to mature, they are best grown for fall harvests in the South. They are long and firm like carrots, with a mild flavor. Plant in late summer, about 8 weeks before the first frost.

Winter Radishes

Winter radishes, which require 55 to 60 days to mature, are larger and firmer than spring radishes. They grow about 3 inches in diameter and have a crisp, mildly pungent flesh that keeps well in storage without becoming pithy. Because they require cool weather at the end of their growing season, plant them only as a fall crop. Sow seeds at least 4 weeks before the first fall frost. (If you sow them in spring, they may flower before forming roots.)

Planting and Culture

Radishes need loose soil so they can swell rapidly; if they grow slowly, roots will be tough and stunted. If your soil is heavy clay, work in sand and compost.

AT A GLANCE

Garden Season: Spring, fall
Days until Harvest: Spring radishes, 20-30 days; summer radishes, 45 days; winter radishes, 55-60 days.
Amount to Plant Per Person: 3-5 feet of row or 1-2 feet of 18-inch-wide row
Serious Insects or Diseases: None
Comments: Must have loose soil for good growth. Thin seedlings when first true leaves appear, as crowding prevents good roots from forming.

White Icicle radishes literally push themselves out of the ground when they are ready to be harvested.

Spring radishes are best if harvested when the roots are ¾ to 1½ inches in diameter. White Icicle, however, can grow up to 5 inches long and still be edible.

Sow spring radishes in rows 6 to 12 inches apart and cover seeds with ½ inch of soil. Space rows for summer radishes 10 to 15 inches apart and sow seeds ¾ inch deep. Sow winter radishes at the same depth, but space rows 18 to 20 inches apart.

If you sow seeds over a wide row, thin to the same spacing as for those growing in a row. Thin plants soon after they emerge, as crowding prevents good roots from forming. Thin spring radishes to 2 inches, summer radishes to 3 to 5 inches, and winter radishes to 6 inches.

When the first true leaves develop, side-dress plants with ¼ cup of 10-10-10 per 10 feet of row. Keep the soil evenly moist. Excessive or uneven moisture may cause radishes to split or to be hot and pithy.

Harvest

Spring radishes are ready to harvest when they are ¾ to 1½ inches in diameter. White Icicle pushes up out of the ground when it is ready to be pulled. Do not leave spring radishes in the ground too long after they reach harvesting size, or they will become oversized, hot, and woody.

Pull summer selections when the roots are 6 to 12 inches long. Harvest winter types when the roots are about 3 inches in diameter. Both types usually push out of the ground about an inch when they are ready for harvest. Unlike spring radishes, summer and winter types can be left in the ground for several weeks after they mature without becoming woody. Winter types also withstand light frost.

Recommended Selections

Recommended selections of spring radishes include Cherry Belle, Scarlet Globe, White Icicle, Champion, and Sparkler. Summer radishes include All Seasons White and Summer Cross Hybrid. Winter radishes include White Chinese (Winter Celestial), Chinese Rose, and Round Black Spanish.

CRUNCHY RADISH SALAD
4 cups shredded cabbage
3 tomatoes, peeled and chopped
1 green pepper, chopped
1¾ cups chopped celery
1¼ cups sliced radishes
¾ cup sugar
¼ cup vinegar
¼ cup vegetable oil

Combine vegetables in a large bowl, tossing gently; set aside. Combine remaining ingredients in a medium saucepan; bring to a boil over low heat, stirring occasionally. Set aside to cool. Pour dressing over vegetables, tossing gently. Yield: 8 to 10 servings.

CREAMY CUCUMBER-RADISH SALAD
1 cucumber, peeled and thinly sliced
2 cups sliced radishes
2 small onions, thinly sliced
½ cup commercial sour cream
1 tablespoon vinegar
1 teaspoon salt

Combine vegetables in a medium bowl, tossing gently; set aside. Combine sour cream, vinegar, and salt, mixing well. Toss vegetables with sour cream mixture just before serving. Yield: 6 to 8 servings.

RADISH-GREEN ONION CHEESE SPREAD
1 (8-ounce) package cream cheese, softened
¼ cup butter or margarine, softened
½ teaspoon celery salt
½ teaspoon Worcestershire sauce
1 cup finely chopped radishes
¼ cup finely chopped green onions

Combine cheese and butter, mixing until smooth; add salt and Worcestershire sauce. Stir in radishes and onions; chill several hours or overnight. Yield: about 1½ cups.

Winter radishes require 55 to 60 days to mature, but can be left in the garden until the first hard frost without becoming woody.

Rhubarb is a vegetable you can serve for dessert. Its long, pink leaf stems (petioles) are used to make pies, preserves, and sauces with a special tart, sweet flavor.

This hardy perennial is best suited to the Upper and Middle South (especially the mountainous areas), where the ground freezes hard during winter. In the Lower South, you will need to take precautions to protect it from summer heat. In the Coastal South and Florida, rhubarb will be killed by disease during the hot, humid summers, but you can grow it as an annual. Plants grown in warmer regions will not be as large or vigorous as those in cooler parts of the South.

Planting and Culture

Rich, well-drained soil is essential to success with rhubarb; if planted in soggy ground, it will rot. In the Lower South, plants fare better in

Rhubarb

summer if planted where they receive partial shade in the afternoon. Also, be sure to plant at the edge of the garden where the plants will not be disturbed by other garden activities.

Rhubarb is usually started from crowns (underground stems with attached roots); purchase large healthy ones with at least 1 bud on each. Plant in spring 2 weeks before the last frost or in fall, a week before the first frost.

Like asparagus, rhubarb stays in the same place year after year, so initial soil preparation is very important. To prepare the planting bed, dig a trench 18 inches deep and 18 inches wide. At the bottom of the trench, mound compost and rotted manure, making a mound for each crown. Space the mounds 4 feet apart. In heavy clay soil, build the mounds so that the bud will be 1 inch below the soil surface. In sandy soil, the bud should be about 3 inches below the surface. Position a crown on each mound and spread the roots out carefully. Mix the backfill soil with rotted manure and compost and fill in the trench to ground level. Keep the bed well watered. After the plants come up, mulch them to help keep the soil cool.

Once established, rhubarb needs little care except watering. Every year after the last harvest and again after the first fall frost, spread a 1- to 2-inch layer of rotted manure or compost over

---

AT A GLANCE

Garden Season: Perennial, comes up in early spring
Days until Harvest: 2 years after planting, except in Gulf South, where it grows as an annual and is harvested 4-5 months after transplanting
Amount to Plant Per Person: 1-2 roots
Serious Insects: None
Serious Diseases: Crown rot
Comments: Work in plenty of compost and well-rotted manure before planting. If you turn under a cover crop or vegetable debris, wait 6-8 weeks before planting; decaying organic matter promotes disease.

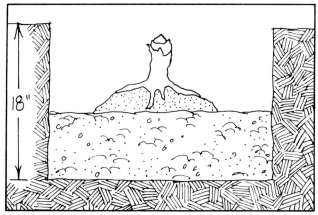

Dig a trench 18 inches deep, mixing the soil with rotted manure and compost. Set each crown on a mound of soil so the bud is 1 to 3 inches below the soil surface; fill the trench to ground level.

A hardy perennial, rhubarb grows best in the Upper and Middle South. Plant it at the edge of the garden, where other activities will not disturb plants.

the bed. Side-dress each plant with ⅛ cup of 10-10-10 after growth begins in the spring.

When flower stalks appear in spring, cut them off at the base. If allowed to develop, they will limit future harvests.

Every 4 or 5 years, rhubarb needs dividing in fall. Crowding reduces yields and causes plants to produce small, thin leaf stalks. Separate the youngest, healthiest plants into clumps with at least 1 bud on each. Replant them 4 feet apart at the same depth they were growing previously.

Tips for the Gulf South

Although you can grow rhubarb as an annual as far south as Central Florida (and possibly South Florida as well), you probably will not be able to obtain crowns early enough for spring planting. In this case, you can start from seeds, using the selection Victoria. Start seeds in pots in September and transplant them to the garden in November. Set the plants at the same depth they were growing previously, spaced 4 feet apart. Keep them well watered and mulched.

Plants started from seed in fall should be ready for harvest from February to April. (*See Harvest.*) Victoria produces green stems rather than red ones; but the stems are as large as those of red selections grown further north, and the eating quality is the same. Victoria grows especially well in Florida's muck soils. Growth is poor in dry, sandy soils, so be sure to prepare the planting bed properly.

Harvest

When rhubarb is grown as a perennial, it needs 2 years to become well established, so it is best not to harvest any stalks the first year. The second spring, harvest lightly for no longer than 2 weeks. The third year and following years, harvest for 6 to 8 weeks or until the plants start producing thin, tough stalks.

Pick older stalks when they are 18 to 24 inches long and allow the younger, smaller ones to keep growing. Pull them from the base of the plant instead of cutting them; cutting may provide entry for diseases. Remove the leaves and discard them; they contain oxalic acid, which is harmful if eaten.

After the last harvest, apply a 1- or 2-inch layer of compost or manure around plants and allow the foliage to continue growing until a fall frost kills it back.

Recommended Selections

Recommended selections include Victoria and Canadian Red. The intensity of color in Canadian Red stalks (and those of other red selections) depends on temperature; in cooler areas, the stalks will be red or pink, while in warmer areas, they will be greenish.

ROSY STRAWBERRY-RHUBARB COBBLER
1 cup sugar
3 tablespoons cornstarch
⅛ teaspoon salt
2 cups sliced rhubarb
1 pint fresh strawberries, sliced
1 tablespoon lemon juice
1 tablespoon butter or margarine
1 (10-ounce) package refrigerated biscuits
1 teaspoon sugar
½ teaspoon ground cinnamon

Combine 1 cup sugar, cornstarch, and salt in a 2-quart saucepan; add rhubarb, strawberries, lemon juice, and butter. Cook over medium heat until bubbly and thickened, stirring constantly.

Pour mixture into a 1¾-quart baking dish. Cut biscuits in half, and arrange around edge and center of dish. Combine remaining teaspoon of sugar and cinnamon; sprinkle over cobbler. Bake at 400° for 15 to 20 minutes or just until biscuits are browned. Yield: about 4 to 5 servings.

Harvest the older, outer stalks when they are 18 to 24 inches long. Pull the stalks from the base of the plant rather than cutting them.

If you like the flavor of oysters, you will want to grow salsify. Also called vegetable oyster or oyster plant, its carrot-shaped white roots take on a delicate oysterlike flavor after exposure to several frosts. Grow it as a fall crop in the same way you would carrots.

Salsify

Planting and Culture

Since salsify takes 16 weeks to develop full-sized roots, plant in mid- to late summer. The roots will be a good size for har-

vesting by the first fall frost. Salsify will grow in spring if you plant 2 to 4 weeks before the last frost, but the texture and flavor are inferior because it matures in warm weather.

Since salsify stays in the ground so long, plant it in an out-of-the-way spot so that it will not interfere with other gardening activities. Dig the soil to a depth of 12 inches. In hard clay or rocky soil, remove all rocks, break up clods, and incorporate sand and organic matter into the soil. Or plant in a raised bed or row of amended soil mounded 12 inches high. Unlike most vegetables, salsify prefers a neutral to slightly alkaline soil. A soil test will indicate whether you need to add lime to raise the pH to around 7.0. Also, work in ½ cup of 10-10-10 per 10 feet of row.

Be sure to use fresh seeds every year, because old seeds germinate poorly. Store seeds in an airtight plastic container in the refrigerator until you are ready to plant them.

AT A GLANCE

Garden Season: Fall
Days until Harvest: 112
Amount to Plant Per Person: 5 feet of row or 2 feet of 18-inch-wide row for fresh use, an additional 5 feet or 1-2 feet of wide row for storage
Serious Insects or Diseases: None
Comments: Always use fresh seed and keep soil moist after planting; seeds are slow to germinate. Texture and flavor of roots are best after frost; leave them in the ground until you are ready to use them.

To have enough salsify for fresh use all winter, plant 10 feet of row per person in your family.

Because salsify stays in the ground at least 4 months, consider planting it in a bed with other vegetables that occupy space for more than one season, such as Jerusalem artichokes.

To speed germination, soak the seeds before planting. Sow them thinly in rows spaced 15 inches apart or broadcast the seeds over a wide bed; cover with ½ to ¾ inch of soil. Because seeds may not germinate well in warm soil, try placing a board over the row to keep the soil cool. Check under the board regularly, and remove it as soon as sprouts appear.

The seedlings resemble young grassy weeds, so weed the bed carefully. When seedlings are 3 inches tall, thin to 3 to 4 inches apart. Salsify has few problems with insects and the only care it needs is water in dry weather.

Harvest

Harvest salsify roots anytime after frost has hit them. But leave the roots in the ground until you are ready to use them, because the flavor fades in storage. Salsify is very hardy and can be left in the ground all winter. In the Upper South, you may need to cover the row with mulch to keep the ground from freezing, which makes harvesting difficult. To harvest, use a trowel to loosen the soil around the roots and dig them.

In spring, salsify will bloom and produce an abundance of cigar-shaped seeds that you can use for the next planting. Be sure to store them properly.

Recommended Selection

The most commonly available selection is Mammoth Sandwich Island.

BATTER-FRIED SALSIFY

1 tablespoon lemon juice
1 quart water
1 pound salsify
1½ cups water
1 egg, beaten
2 tablespoons water
½ teaspoon salt
¼ teaspoon pepper
½ cup all-purpose flour
  Vegetable oil

Combine lemon juice and 1 quart water. Wash salsify; scrape away skins and cut into 2-inch pieces; place in lemon juice mixture. Drain well.

Combine salsify and 1½ cups water in a saucepan. Bring to a boil; cover and simmer 15 to 20 minutes. Drain and cool.

Combine egg, 2 tablespoons water, salt, and pepper; mix well. Dip salsify into egg mixture; dredge in flour. Fry in deep hot oil (375°) until golden brown. Yield: 4 servings.

CANDIED SALSIFY

1 tablespoon lemon juice
1 quart water
1 pound salsify
¼ cup butter or margarine
⅓ cup firmly packed brown sugar
2 tablespoons honey
1½ teaspoons grated orange rind
½ cup orange juice
½ teaspoon salt

Combine lemon juice and 1 quart water. Wash salsify; scrape away skins and cut into thin slices; place in lemon juice mixture. Drain well.

Melt butter in a medium skillet; add sugar and honey. Cook over low heat, stirring constantly, until sugar dissolves. Stir in salsify and remaining ingredients; cover and simmer 20 minutes or until salsify is tender, stirring often. Yield: 4 servings.

Use a trowel to help loosen roots so that you can pull them. The oysterlike flavor fades if you store harvested roots for any length of time.

Spinach is an excellent crop for any size garden. Even a small planting yields an abundance of tender chewy leaves.

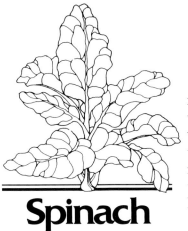

Spinach

Planting and Culture

You can grow spinach in early spring and again in fall. In spring, the key is to start seeds early, 4 to 6 weeks before the last frost. Late-planted spinach bolts (flowers) quickly as days become longer, and warm weather hastens the process. Once plants begin to bolt, the leaves taste strong and bitter. Spinach may also bolt if exposed to streetlights or floodlights. The light triggers the same response as long days. Locate your spinach away from such light sources.

For fall and winter harvests, plant seeds anytime from 4 to 8 weeks before the first frost. Be sure to plant enough to last through winter; although growth stops when cold weather arrives, plants do survive freezing temperatures. Leave them in the garden and harvest as needed through winter. Spinach tastes especially sweet after exposure to frost. To protect plants from severe weather, cover them with a light mulch, such as pine straw. Young plants that overwinter will begin growing again in spring as temperatures rise and will give you extraearly harvests. Because these plants are mature, they will bolt with the first warm spell; so be sure to harvest them early.

Before planting, work in ¼ cup of 10-10-10 per 10 feet of row. Sow seeds thinly in rows spaced 1½ feet apart, or scatter seeds over a wide bed. Cover with ½ inch of soil. Thin seedlings to 4 to 6 inches apart; thinning is important because crowding stunts the plants. When plants have 4 to 5 leaves, side-dress with ¼ cup of 10-10-10 per 10 feet of row.

Harvest

There are 2 ways to harvest spinach. You can pinch off only the large outer leaves when they are 3 to 6 inches long, allowing the plant to produce new leaves from its center. (This method briefly delays bolting in spring by slowing the accumulation of the hormone that causes flowering.) Or you can cut the entire plant at soil level when it reaches 4 to 6 inches in diameter.

Recommended Selections

Spinach selections vary greatly as to how quickly they bolt and how well they tolerate cold. For a spring planting, choose Bloomsdale Long Standing, Avon, or America; they are among the slowest to bolt. In fall, plant Melody Hybrid, Winter Bloomsdale, Bloomsdale Long Standing, Early Hybrid 7, Chesapeake, or Dixie Market; they are among the hardiest selections.

Savoyed (crinkle-leaved) selections have more leaf surface than smooth-leaved types, so they produce more food per planting. But savoyed selections can also be more difficult to clean than smooth-leaved ones, because soil splashes on the leaves and lodges in the curls and crevices. A mulch helps keep these types cleaner.

AT A GLANCE

Garden Season: Spinach, early spring, fall; substitutes, summer, fall

Days until Harvest: Spinach, 40-50 days; substitutes, 70 days

Amount to Plant Per Person: Spinach, 5-10 feet of row or 1½ to 2½ feet of 18-inch-wide row for fresh use, an additional 10-15 feet or 1½ to 2½ feet of wide row for storage; substitutes, 5 feet of row or experiment with small amounts to determine your favorites

Serious Insects: Flea beetle, mites

Serious Diseases: Downy mildew, white rust

Comments: For spring harvests, plant spinach in late winter or very early spring, as longer days and warm weather cause plants to bolt.

Spinach is especially sweet after frost in fall. Mulch plants lightly to protect them from severe freezes, and you can continue harvesting into winter.

Spinach Substitutes

In warm weather, when it is impossible to grow true spinach, you can plant spinach substitutes such as New Zealand spinach, Tampala, and Malabar spinach (also called African climbing spinach or Ceylon spinach). Although they do not taste exactly like true spinach, they are acceptable substitutes that produce in the heat of summer and until the first hard freeze. New Zealand spinach looks and tastes most like true spinach when it is cooked. Tampala and Malabar spinach may be used raw or cooked.

New Zealand spinach grows like a ground cover, spreading to 4 feet. Although the plants grow in warm weather, the seeds need cooler soil to germinate; so plant before late spring. Or start seeds indoors 4 to 6 weeks before the last frost. To help speed germination, soak the seeds overnight before planting. Sow seeds 1 inch deep in rows 3 feet apart. Each seed is actually a cluster of seeds from which several seedlings germinate, so be sure to thin early to a spacing of 12 to 18 inches.

When plants are 6 to 9 inches tall, begin harvesting by pinching about 3 inches of each branch tip. This encourages more branching and new growth. As plants continue to branch, you can increase the amount you harvest at any one time; but do not cut the plant back or pinch out the top, or growth will stop.

Tampala, also known as Chinese spinach or Hinn Choy, will grow to 2 feet tall. It is upright and does not need staking. Sow seeds directly in the garden when the soil and weather are warm. When seedlings are 2 to 3 inches tall, thin to 24 inches apart and keep plants well watered.

About 6 weeks after planting, you can begin harvesting the young leaves. Or if you prefer, broadcast seeds over a wide bed, thinning to 10 to 12 inches: then harvest the entire plant 6 weeks later. If you do this, make successive plantings every week or two for a constant supply of greens.

Malabar spinach is vinelike and needs to grow on a trellis. Seeds can take 2 to 3 weeks to germinate; to help them sprout faster, soak overnight. Sow after the last frost, planting them ½ inch deep. Thin seedlings to 8 to 10 inches apart. When the plants are 6 inches tall, pinch off the bottom leaves. More leaves will develop at those joints. Once plants begin to run on the trellis, pinch the tips of long stems weekly.

• To stem spinach quickly and easily, fold each leaf over lengthwise along its stem so the underside faces you; then pull off the stem with your other hand.

When leaves of spinach become arrow shaped, the plant is getting ready to flower; at this point the leaves will be strong and bitter tasting.

FRESH SPINACH SALAD

2 pounds fresh spinach, torn
1 small head cauliflower, broken into flowerets
1 (4-ounce) jar diced pimiento, drained
1 medium onion, sliced
　Sweet-and-Sour Dressing
6 slices bacon, cooked and crumbled
2 hard-cooked eggs, mashed
½ green pepper, cut into strips

Combine spinach, cauliflower, pimiento, and onion in a large salad bowl; toss lightly. Pour ½ cup Sweet-and-Sour Dressing over vegetables, tossing lightly. Sprinkle bacon, egg, and green pepper over salad. Yield: 8 to 10 servings.

Sweet-and-Sour Dressing:

¾ cup sugar
⅓ cup vinegar
¾ cup vegetable oil
1 teaspoon celery seeds
1 teaspoon paprika
¾ teaspoon salt

Combine sugar and vinegar in a medium saucepan. Bring to a boil; remove from heat. Add remaining ingredients, mixing well. Chill. Yield: about 2 cups.

Squash

Summer squash produces almost faster than you can harvest. And continuously picking the soft-skinned, immature squash keeps them coming for 4 to 8 weeks or longer. In contrast, winter squash produces only one major harvest; but the hard-skinned, mature fruit store for several months, so you can enjoy them in fall and winter.

Summer Squash

The three most popular types of summer squash are yellow (crookneck and straightneck), zucchini, and pattypan. Most selections are bush types, which produce short vines.

AT A GLANCE

Garden Season: Spring, summer, fall
Days until Harvest: Summer types, 40-60; winter types, 75-120
Amount to Plant Per Person: Summer types, 2-3 hills for fresh use, an additional 2-3 hills for storage; winter types, 1-3 hills for fresh use, an additional 1-3 hills for storage
Serious Insects: Squash vine borer, squash bug
Serious Diseases: Anthracnose, mildews
Comments: Control insects and diseases from time of planting. Keep summer squash picked to encourage continuous production. Harvest hybrids Kuta and Jersey Golden Acorn early for use as summer squash and leave some fruit on the plant to mature for use as winter squash.

Planting and Culture

Plant summer squash immediately after the last frost. Plant again 3 weeks later to extend the harvest. A third planting in midsummer will give you late summer and fall harvests, but be prepared to control squash vine borers as soon as seedlings emerge.

Squash is usually planted in hills spaced 3 feet apart on center. Plants depend on bees to pollinate the flowers, so for better pollination and fruiting, plant 2 rows of hills side by side instead of one long row.

Sow 5 to 7 seeds per hill, planting them 1 inch deep. After the seedlings have been up about a week, thin to the strongest 2 plants per hill. Thinning is important because crowded plants produce less fruit and are more likely to develop diseases. Side-dress every 4 weeks after planting with ¼ cup of 10-10-10 per hill.

Harvest

Fruit reach harvesting size quickly, usually 3 to 7 days after the flowers open. Pick yellow squash when they are 4 to 6 inches long, zucchini when 6 to 8 inches long, and pattypan types when 3 to 5 inches in diameter. Leaving fruit on the plants until they are overmature causes less fruit production.

Recommended Selections

Recommended selections of yellow summer squash include Early Prolific Straightneck, Early

Summer squash may produce for 4 to 8 weeks if you pick the fruit continuously and keep the plants healthy.

Squash plants produce both male and female flowers. You can tell them apart by the miniature fruit at the base of the female flower (left). Normally, the first blossoms that appear are male, and will drop off the plants.

Summer Crookneck, Dixie Hybrid, Goldbar Hybrid, and Seneca Butterbar Hybrid. Zucchini selections include Aristocrat, Seneca Gourmet Hybrid, Gold Rush Hybrid, Zucchini Dark Green, and Gourmet Globe. Pattypan selections include Early White Bush Scallop, Scallopini Hybrid, and Peter Pan.

Winter Squash

The different types of winter squash vary greatly in size and appearance, but all are used in much the same way for baking, stuffing, and pies. Spaghetti squash, however, is used as a substitute for pasta. Make a spring planting immediately after the last frost to harvest in midsummer. A second planting in early to midsummer is ready for harvest in late fall.

Planting and Culture

Although many winter squash are vining plants that need more garden space than summer squash, bush and semibush selections of acorn and butternut types are also available. Plant these in hills spaced 3 to 4 feet apart. Plant vining selections of acorn and butternut squash in hills spaced 4 to 5 feet apart. These types produce fruit that weigh 1 to 4 pounds.

Large types, such as banana and hubbard, bear fruit weighing from 12 to 15 pounds or more. They require 5 to 7 feet between hills and 6 to 10 feet between rows.

Planting and culture are the same as for summer squash. Fruit are ready for harvest when you cannot pierce the skin with your thumbnail.

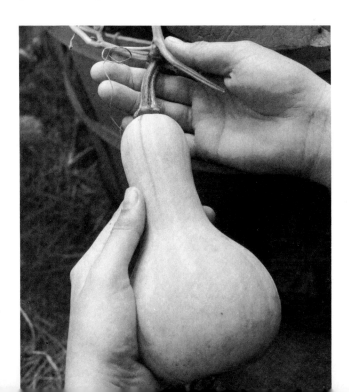

Cut the squash from the vine, leaving 2 to 3 inches of stem attached. Before storing, cure as you would pumpkins.

Recommended Selections

Recommended bush and semibush types include Kuta Hybrid; acorn selections Table King, Jersey Golden, Table Queen, and Table Ace Hybrid, and the butternut selection Burpee's Butterbush.

Vining types of winter squash include Butternut, Waltham Butternut, Early Butternut Hybrid, Royal Acorn, True Hubbard, Improved Green Hubbard, Blue Hubbard, Buttercup, and Pink Banana Jumbo.

GARDEN STUFFED YELLOW SQUASH

6 medium-size yellow squash
1 cup chopped onion
1 cup chopped tomato
½ cup chopped green pepper
½ cup (2 ounces) shredded Cheddar cheese
2 slices bacon, cooked and crumbled
½ teaspoon salt
Dash of pepper
Butter or margarine

Wash squash thoroughly; cover with water and bring to a boil. Reduce heat, cover, and simmer 8 to 10 minutes or until tender but still firm. Drain and cool slightly. Trim off stems. Cut squash in half lengthwise; remove and reserve pulp, leaving a firm shell.

Chop pulp; combine pulp and remaining ingredients, except butter. Place squash shells in a 13- x 9- x 2-inch baking dish. Spoon vegetable mixture into shells; dot with butter. Bake at 400° for 20 minutes. Yield: 6 servings.

NUT-GLAZED ACORN SQUASH

2 medium acorn squash
Salt
¼ cup butter or margarine, divided
2 tablespoons brown sugar, divided
½ cup chopped pecans or walnuts, divided

Rinse squash; cut in half lengthwise and remove seeds. Sprinkle each half lightly with salt; fill each half with 1 tablespoon butter, ½ tablespoon brown sugar, and 2 tablespoons pecans. Place squash in a baking dish; add ½-inch water to dish. Cover and bake at 325° for 1 hour and 15 minutes or until squash is tender. Yield: 4 servings.

Butternut and other winter-type squash grow all summer and are harvested in the fall. Fruit are ready for harvest when the rind cannot be pierced with your thumbnail.

Vegetables 199

The best way to enjoy the full flavor of a juicy, sun-ripened tomato is to grow your own. That unbeatable taste and the plant's prolific production are the reasons for the tomato's popularity in the South. Although tomatoes are easy to grow, you may need to give plants more attention than you do some other vegetables in order to produce the biggest, juiciest fruit. But the results are worth the effort.

Tomatoes

Choosing Adapted Selections

The first step in growing tomatoes successfully is to choose selections recommended for your region. For example, some types are especially tolerant of the warm nights of Florida and the Gulf Coast. Be sure to check with your county Extension agent or local nurseryman for recommendations.

Also look for disease-resistant or -tolerant tomatoes. The initials V, F, N, or T listed after the name indicate resistance or tolerance to the most common tomato problems: verticillium wilt, fusarium wilt, nematodes, and tobacco mosaic.

Your choice is also influenced by your purpose for growing tomatoes. While most types are good for slicing, some have textures better suited for juice, canning, or paste. Some types of tomatoes, such as pink, orange, and yellow ones, are often described as low-acid and therefore unsafe for canning. However, tests show that yellow, orange, and pink tomatoes are as acid as red ones. Among the many selections, differences in acidity are minor; they may be due to climate, soil, cultural practices, and stage of ripeness as much as to selection.

Flavor is affected by a combination of acidity, sweetness, and aroma. Experience will be your best guide in determining your favorites.

Growth Habit

Tomatoes have two basic growth habits, vining and bushlike. Bushy tomatoes, described as determinate in catalogs, usually grow only 3 to 4 feet tall. Generally, they ripen most of their fruit over a short period, which makes them especially convenient to harvest for canning.

Vining tomatoes, which are called indeterminate, can grow from 5 to 12 feet tall, depending on the selection. They grow and bear fruit continuously over several months.

Planting and Culture

Plant tomatoes after the danger of frost has passed. To extend the harvest from early summer until fall frost, plant selections with staggered maturity dates. Or stretch the harvest season by making several successive plantings of your favorite selection every 3 or 4 weeks through midsummer.

Old nylon stockings are good for tying tomato vines to supports. The stockings will not cut into the vines and will stretch to let vines keep growing.

AT A GLANCE

Garden Season: Spring, summer, fall
Days until Harvest: 65-82 after transplanting
Amount to Plant Per Person: 2-3 plants for fresh use, an additional 3-5 for storage
Serious Insects: Tomato fruitworm, mites
Serious Diseases: Blights, wilts, leaf spots, blossom end rot
Comments: Plant deeply. Choose disease- and nematode-resistant selections. Keep the soil evenly moist to prevent blossom end rot.

Start your own transplants from seed (*see page 53*) or buy transplants. Once plants are growing in the garden, you can root suckers for additional plantings. Suckers grow at the junction of the main stem and a leaf branch. (*See Fig. 1.*) Prune 3- to 4-inch-long suckers, remove the leaves from the lower half, and insert each stem in a pot filled with sterile potting soil. Keep them in a bright place but out of direct sunlight and keep the soil evenly moist until new growth appears, indicating that roots have formed.

There are as many methods of planting tomatoes as there are gardeners, but one concept is almost universal: Plant them deeply in well-amended soil. Before planting, work plenty of organic matter into the soil, along with ½ cup of 10-10-10 per 10 feet of row. In calcium-deficient soils, add dolomitic limestone according to soil test recommendations. This will help prevent blossom end rot.

Set stocky plants deep enough so that the lowest leaf is about 2 inches above the ground. For taller plants, strip all but the top 4 leaves from the stem and set the plant so that only the leafy portion is aboveground. (*See Fig. 2.*) Roots will form along the buried stem, producing a stronger root system. Firm the soil and fertilize with a starter solution of liquid 20-20-20 diluted according to label directions.

For leggy transplants over 10 inches tall, you can set the plant horizontally in a trench 2 to 3 inches deep. Strip the leaves from all but the top 2 to 4 inches of the plant and lay the stem in the trench; cover with soil, leaving only the leafy portion aboveground. (*See Figs. 3,4.*) For all planting methods, remember to use cutworm collars at planting time. (*See page 97.*)

Most tomato plants should be supported on some kind of structure. When allowed to sprawl over the ground, they are more likely to become diseased, and they take up more space. Structures for support include stakes, trellises, and wire cages. (*See page 90, Structures.*)

Tomatoes are produced in clusters of fruit called "hands."

The distance at which you set tomato plants depends on how they are supported. Trellised or staked tomatoes may be planted 1 to 2 feet apart in rows 3 feet apart. Tomatoes in cages should be planted 3 feet apart to allow space for the cages and for the plants' prolific growth.

Tomato plants tied to a stake or trellis need to be pruned to 1 or 2 stems. Otherwise, their rampant growth produces so many offshoots that it is nearly impossible to tie them all up.

To prune plants to one stem, pinch off all suckers as they appear. To let 2 stems develop, leave the first sucker below the first flower cluster and remove all others. (*See Figs. 5,6.*) Prune at least weekly. If you remove a lot of foliage all at once, you may expose previously shaded fruit to the sun, which causes sunscald (whitish patches).

After the first fruit are set, side-dress plants with ¼ cup of 10-10-10 per 10 feet of row. Repeat every 4 weeks, but be careful not to overfertilize or you will have a lot of foliage and few tomatoes. Apply a heavy mulch to help keep the soil evenly moist; letting the soil dry out and then soaking it can cause blossom drop or fruit cracking and contributes to blossom end rot.

Harvest

Tomatoes usually reach their peak of flavor 5 to 6 days after the fruit begins to show color. A tomato ready for harvest should be firm, brightly colored, but a little green at the stem end. It will remain in good condition on the vine for about 2 days before beginning to deteriorate. If it is soft, deeply colored, or the skin is crinkly, the tomato is overripe. Use it to make juice or catsup, but not for canning.

Caged tomatoes need less maintenance than staked or trellised ones, because you do not have to prune plants or tie them to their supports.

A healthy sucker will develop a good root system when inserted in sterile potting soil. Rooting suckers is a good way to start plants for the fall garden.

Fig. 1. *Suckers are the shoots that grow at the junction of a leaf branch and the main stem. You can pinch them off and root them to start new plants.*

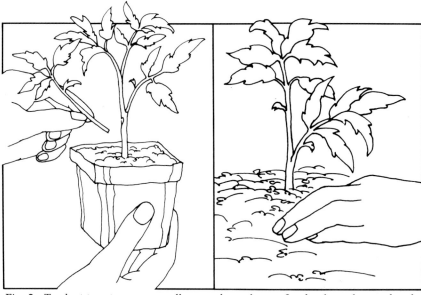

Fig. 2. *To plant tomatoes, remove all except the top leaves. Set the plants deep so that the stem is buried nearly to the lowest leaves, and firm the soil around the plant.*

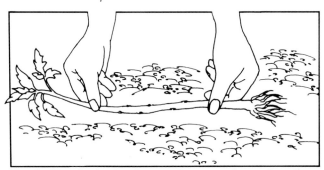

Fig. 3. *Trench planting is a good way to plant tall or leggy transplants. Remove all except the top leaves and lay the stem in a trench 2 to 3 inches deep.*

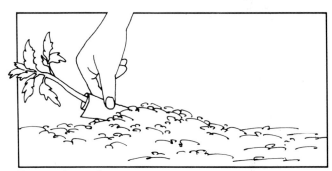

Fig. 4. *Cover the stem with soil, leaving only the leafy part exposed. To protect against cutworms, wrap stiff paper around the stem where it emerges from the soil.*

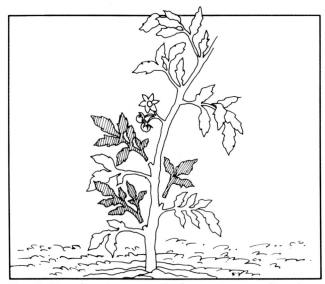

Fig. 5. *To prune plants to a single stem, remove all suckers.*

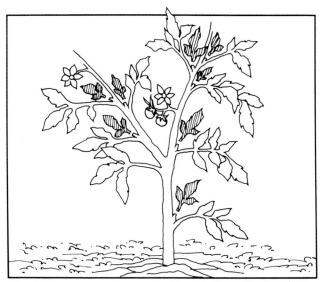

Fig. 6. *To prune plants to a double stem, leave the first sucker below the first flower cluster to develop into the second stem, and remove all others.*

Vegetables   203

If frost is predicted while you still have green tomatoes on the vine, pick them and place them in single layers on shelves in a cool pantry or closet. Or pull up the whole plant and hang it upside down in a dark, cool, dry place. Tomatoes that are whitish green and have formed a corky ring where the stem joins the fruit will ripen slowly indoors.

• A little sugar cooked along with tomatoes counteracts excessive acidity.

• The easiest way to peel fresh tomatoes is to drop them in a pot of boiling water for about 10 to 20 seconds. Then immediately plunge them into cold water and pull the skins off with a small paring knife.

Recommended Selections

Some of the selections recommended for the South include the following.

Selection	Days to Maturity	Growth Habit	Best Use
Small Tomatoes			
Red Cherry	72	indeterminate	canning, salads, slicing
Small Fry VFN Hyb.	65	indeterminate	salads
Sweet 100 Hyb.	65	indeterminate	salads
Medium Tomatoes (4-8 oz.)			
Early Cascade Hyb. VF	60	indeterminate	salads, slicing
Heinz 1350 VF	75	semideterminate	canning
Walter F-1, F-2*	75	determinate	canning, slicing
Roma VF	76	determinate	canning, paste
San Marzano	80	indeterminate	canning, paste
Homestead 24	82	indeterminate	salads
Spring Giant VF Hyb.	68	determinate	salads
Bonus VFN Hyb.	75	determinate	salads
Tropic VF	82	indeterminate	salads, slicing
Large Tomatoes (8-12 oz. or more)			
Beefmaster VFN Hyb.	80	indeterminate	slicing
Beefsteak	80	indeterminate	canning, slicing
Better Boy VFN Hyb.	70	indeterminate	salads, slicing
Floradel	82	indeterminate	salads, slicing
Floramerica VF Hyb.	75	determinate	salads, slicing
Manalucie F	82	indeterminate	canning, salads, slicing
Super Fantastic VFN Hyb.	70	indeterminate	salads, slicing
Park's Whopper VFNT	70	indeterminate	salads, slicing
Terrific VFN Hyb.	70	indeterminate	salads, slicing
Big Set VFN Hyb.	65	determinate	salads, slicing
Fantastic Hyb.	65	indeterminate	salads, slicing
Floradade VF-1, F-2	72	determinate	salads, slicing

* F-1 and F-2 are two races of fusarium wilt.

The selection Sweet 100 produces bite-sized fruit on vining plants that bear all summer.

To grow sandwich-sized tomatoes, be sure to choose large-fruited selections and keep plants well watered and fertilized during the growing season.

TOMATOES VINAIGRETTE

4 large tomatoes
¼ cup plus 2 tablespoons chopped fresh parsley or 2 tablespoons dried parsley flakes
1 clove garlic, crushed
¼ cup plus 2 tablespoons olive oil
2 tablespoons vinegar
1½ teaspoons minced fresh basil or ½ teaspoon dried whole basil
1 teaspoon salt
⅛ teaspoon pepper
Additional chopped fresh parsley (optional)

Slice tomatoes; place in a serving bowl. Sprinkle with ¼ cup plus 2 tablespoons parsley. Combine next 6 ingredients in a jar; cover tightly, and shake vigorously. Pour over tomatoes. Chill 3 hours. Sprinkle with additional parsley, if desired. Yield: 8 servings.

COLD TOMATO RELISH

4 medium tomatoes, peeled and chopped
1½ cups finely chopped onion
2 green peppers, finely chopped
½ cup finely chopped celery
2 tablespoons salt
1 cup sugar
¾ cup vinegar
½ teaspoon mustard seeds

Place vegetables in a large mixing bowl; stir in salt. Let stand 2 hours; drain well. Add remaining ingredients; stir until sugar dissolves. Cover and chill at least 1 hour. Yield: about 2 quarts.

DELICIOUS STUFFED TOMATOES

4 large tomatoes
12 slices bacon
½ cup chopped green pepper
½ cup chopped onion
1½ cups (6 ounces) shredded Cheddar cheese
2 tablespoons shredded lettuce
1 tablespoon plus 1 teaspoon butter or margarine
2 tablespoons crushed Cheddar cheese crackers

Wash tomatoes thoroughly; cut a ¼-inch slice from top of each. Scoop out pulp, leaving shells intact; invert shells on paper towels to drain. Chop tomato pulp; set aside.

Cook bacon in a large skillet until crisp; drain well, reserving 2 tablespoons bacon drippings in skillet. Crumble bacon, and set aside. Sauté green pepper and onion in bacon drippings until tender. Remove skillet from heat; stir in cheese, lettuce, bacon, and tomato pulp. Fill tomato shells with mixture.

Place tomatoes in a lightly greased 8-inch square baking dish; top each with 1 teaspoon butter. Sprinkle with cracker crumbs. Bake at 400° for 15 to 20 minutes. Yield: 4 servings.

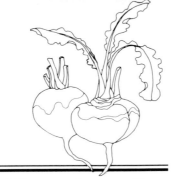

Turnips & Rutabagas

In the South, turnips are grown as much for the greens as for the roots. It is a favorite crop for spring and even more popular for fall, when light frosts make the greens taste sweeter.

Rutabagas are grown primarily for their large roots. The greens may also be eaten, but the stems are bigger and tougher and the leaves are somewhat waxy.

To grow crisp, tender turnip and rutabaga roots, you must provide fertile, loose, well-drained soil and plenty of moisture. In infertile heavy clay or rocky soils, the roots will be tough, woody, and possibly misshapen because their growth will be stunted.

Turnips

Turnips need cool weather. Once daytime temperatures are consistently over 80 degrees, the greens become strong and bitter and roots become pithy.

Planting and Culture

For spring harvests, plant 4 weeks before the last frost. For fall and winter harvests, plant again in August or September.

You can grow turnips in either wide beds or conventional rows spaced 15 to 18 inches apart. Before planting, work ½ cup of 10-10-10 per 10 feet of row into the soil. Sow seeds thinly and cover with ½ inch of soil. Thin seedlings to 1 to 3 inches apart if you are primarily interested in greens; thin to 6 inches apart to allow good-sized roots to develop.

To extend harvests, make 2 or 3 sowings 2 weeks apart. Remember that if you regularly harvest the foliage, good roots will not develop; plant enough to allow for harvesting both tops and roots.

To produce tender roots, turnips need steady growth. Those regularly harvested for greens also need fertilizer to continue producing foliage. Side-dress plants 4 to 6 weeks after planting with ½ cup of 10-10-10 per 10 feet of row.

If turnips develop hollow or gray-brown cores, it may indicate a boron deficiency in the soil. To correct this, apply a borax solution to the soil. Dissolve ⅛ pound of household borax in 5 gallons of water for 1000 square feet of row.

Harvest

To harvest turnip greens, pinch off the outer leaves at the base or cut off all the leaves with a knife. The plant will produce new leaves. Leaves are best when they are 2 to 10 inches long; old ones tend to be tough and strong.

Pull roots when they are about 2 to 4 inches in diameter. If larger, roots may be stronger tasting, pithy, and bitter. Roots tolerate frost, so you can leave them in the ground and dig as needed.

AT A GLANCE

Garden Season: Spring, fall
Days until Harvest: Turnip greens, 27-45; turnip roots, 35-60; rutabagas, 90
Amount to Plant Per Person: Turnip greens, 5-10 feet of row or 1½ to 2½ feet of 18-inch-wide row for fresh use, an additional 5-10 feet or 1-2 feet of wide row for storage; turnip roots, 5-10 feet or 1½ to 2½ feet of wide row for fresh use, an additional 5-10 feet or 1-2 feet of wide row for storage; rutabagas, 10-15 feet of row or 2-3 feet of wide row for fresh use, an additional 10 feet or 2 feet of wide row for storage
Serious Insects: Flea beetle, imported cabbageworm
Serious Diseases: None
Comments: Need loose, well-drained soil for good root development. Fall harvests of rutabagas require planting in midsummer.

In the South, turnips are grown primarily for their greens in both spring and fall. A light fall frost makes the greens especially sweet.

However, alternate freezing and thawing may hurt their quality. In the Upper and Middle South, harvest roots before the first hard freeze.

Recommended Selections

For both roots and greens of good quality, try selections such as Purple Top White Globe, Just Right Hybrid, and Tokyo Cross. Shogoin and Seven Top develop only small roots and are grown primarily for their greens.

Rutabagas

Like turnips, rutabagas are grown in spring and fall.

Planting and Culture

In spring, plant 6 to 8 weeks before the last frost; do not delay, because roots that mature in warm weather are small and pithy. Rutabagas are even better as a fall crop, as frost improves their flavor and texture. Plant in mid- to late summer—they take at least a month longer to mature than turnips.

Sow seeds ½ inch deep in rows that are 18 inches apart, or broadcast seeds over a wide bed. Thin seedlings to 5 to 8 inches apart. Keep the soil evenly moist and side-dress as you would for turnips.

Rutabagas (right) take about a month longer to mature than turnips (left) and are usually larger.

Harvest

Harvest rutabagas when they are large enough to use, about 3 to 5 inches in diameter and 5 to 7 inches in length. You can also cook the greens as you would turnip greens, but they have a stronger flavor and a waxy surface.

Recommended Selection

The best selection for the South is American Purple Top.

RUTABAGA DELIGHT
1 medium rutabaga, peeled and cut into ½-inch cubes (about 4 cups)
3 cups water
1 teaspoon salt
2 tablespoons sugar
1 tablespoon butter or margarine
½ teaspoon ground cinnamon
¼ teaspoon ground nutmeg
⅛ teaspoon pepper
   Chopped fresh parsley

Combine rutabaga, water, and salt in a large saucepan. Bring to a boil; reduce heat, cover, and simmer 30 minutes. Add remaining ingredients, except parsley; cook, uncovered, 10 additional minutes. Pour into serving dish; sprinkle with parsley. Yield: 6 to 8 servings.

MAPLE WALNUT RUTABAGA
2 medium rutabagas, peeled and diced
¼ cup butter or margarine, divided
½ cup walnuts, ground
2 tablespoons maple syrup

Cook rutabaga in a small amount of boiling water 15 minutes or until tender. Drain well; mash with 2 tablespoons butter. Place rutabaga in a shallow 2-quart casserole; set aside.

Sauté ground walnuts in remaining 2 tablespoons butter; stir in syrup. Spread walnut mixture over top of rutabaga. Bake at 400° for 10 minutes. Yield: 6 to 8 servings.

TURNIP PUFF
4 medium turnips, peeled and diced
4 eggs, beaten
½ cup butter or margarine, melted
½ teaspoon salt
½ teaspoon pepper
2 cups (8 ounces) shredded Cheddar cheese, divided

Cook turnips in a small amount of boiling water 20 to 30 minutes or until tender; drain and mash. Stir in next 4 ingredients and 1½ cups cheese; pour into a lightly greased 2-quart shallow baking dish. Bake at 350° for 35 minutes; remove from oven. Sprinkle remaining ½ cup cheese on top; bake 5 additional minutes. Yield: 8 servings.

Herbs

One of the best reasons for growing herbs is that you can rarely buy them fresh. And whether you are a gourmet cook, a gardener on a no-salt diet, or simply an avid gardener, you will find that fresh herbs add interest to your cooking as well as your gardening.

If you have never grown herbs, you may find it a little like cooking eggplant for the first time—you will not know what herbs look like, how to grow them, or how to use them. The best way to learn is by doing. Start with a few familiar ones, such as parsley, mint, dill, chives, and garlic. Soon you will be experimenting with marjoram, burnet, savory, and others, eager for new flavors and aromas.

Designing the Garden

The first step in planning your herb garden is to choose a location that is convenient. You will use herbs more often if they are close to the kitchen. If your mint grows by the back steps, you can freshen each glass of iced tea with a green sprig. But if the ice melts in the glass while you go to the garden, you will seldom bother.

Herbs also combine well with vegetables and flowers in a kitchen garden. This small plot can provide a quick source of salad greens and blooms for a centerpiece as well as fresh herbs.

Many annual herbs such as basil, summer savory, dill, and coriander may be grown in the vegetable garden. However, biennial and perennial herbs must stay in the ground from one year

to the next. (Biennials, such as caraway and parsley, grow leaves the first year; the second year they produce flowers and seeds, then die. Perennials such as sorrel produce foliage, flowers, and seeds year after year.) Since they would interfere with annual gardening chores, plant them in a bed by themselves.

In designing your garden, you must also consider sunlight. In the South, many herbs will grow under partial shade (4 to 5 hours of sun). If shade from trees is too dense, however, growth will be weak, so you will need to thin tree branches to allow more light to reach the plants. Herbs that tolerate partial shade are identified under the individual herbs.

The herb garden must be well drained. If the most convenient location for the garden is also one where runoff is severe or the soil is heavy clay and poorly drained, you can improve drainage by using raised beds. Build the beds of concrete blocks, railroad ties, landscape timbers, or brick. The beds can be any height; if you build them 16 to 20 inches high, the walls will serve as comfortable seating while you work in the beds.

The style of your herb garden may be formal, as are the gardens in many historic restorations; or it may be an informal collage of herbs. Formal gardens are symmetrical, with well-defined borders such as clipped hedges and brick walks. If your herb garden is to be a prominent part of your landscape, consider planting a formal one.

Thyme selections at Melchior residence, Charlotte, North Carolina.

However, if your garden is strictly utilitarian and you have limited time to tend it, you would be better off with an informal garden. Limit its size to just enough space to grow the herbs that you need. That way your plants will fill the bed and shade out the weeds. Then give the garden a permanent edging to keep the bed tidy.

Finally, consider the arrangement of the plants in the bed. Place taller plants toward the back, and low, creeping ones at the front. Plant border herbs such as parsley or chives to soften the edge of the bed. Creeping thyme will overflow the sides of a raised bed and drape down the wall. Interplant annuals with perennials so that when the annuals die, the perennials will have room to spread. For example, you may plant thyme, a perennial, next to summer savory, an annual. By the second season, the thyme will have spread, and you can replant summer savory in another area of the garden.

If you plan to grow mint, remember that it is a rampant spreader and can overrun the herb bed unless you contain it by planting it in clay pots sunk into the soil. Otherwise, plant mint where it can spread freely or where you can contain it with walls, walks, or a deep edging.

If you have limited garden space, plant herbs in containers. In the Middle and Upper South, cold-tender herbs such as bay and rosemary must be grown in containers so they can be moved to a sheltered location in winter.

Blossoms of chives.

Choosing What to Plant

Besides growing the herbs you like to use most, plant those that are most flavorful when fresh; lemon balm, for example, does not keep its flavor well when dried, and you can rarely buy it fresh. Also, grow herbs that you use in quantity: If you make pesto, you will need to grow your own basil; if you bake a lot of breads, include caraway in your herb garden.

Starting Herbs

The easiest way to grow herbs is to purchase plants. The more common herbs are usually available where spring bedding plants are sold. Others can be bought from mail-order sources. (*See pages 264-265.*)

Most herbs also can be grown from seeds sown indoors for transplants, or sown directly in the garden. (*See pages 53-57 for instructions on*

Purple sage.

raising transplants.) But many herbs are best propagated from a growing plant. For example, you do not always get the flavor of mint that you want if you plant seeds.

One way to propagate such plants is by division. This is usually done in the fall, four weeks before the first frost, or in spring. If you live in the Upper South, wait until spring, when the first signs of growth appear. Gulf Coast gardeners can also divide plants during December, January, or early February. Divide clumps of

chives, fennel, sorrel, lemon balm, mint, or winter savory, making sure each has roots and a piece of stem. Gently pull or break the clumps apart and set divisions at the original depth.

You can also root cuttings of many herbs in a soil mix of sphagnum peat moss mixed with an equal part of sand or perlite. Take a 3- to 6-inch cutting, remove the bottom leaves, and dip the cut end in rooting hormone. Make a hole in the soil mix with a pencil, insert the cutting, and water to wash the soil around the cutting. Keep the soil moist and place cuttings in bright indirect light. Rosemary, sage, winter savory, pineapple sage, lemon balm, thyme, and mint should root within a few weeks. However, bay may take three to six months.

Herb garden at Biltmore Country Market, Asheville, North Carolina.

On a small scale, you can root cuttings by arranging them in a drinking glass so that the leaves are above the level of the water. Change the water at least every other day.

Layering is a very simple means of propagating certain herbs because it is done in the garden. Bend down an outside branch of rosemary, thyme, or winter savory until it touches the ground. Dig a small trench and lay the branch in it with the tip exposed. Cover with soil and anchor with a stone, stick, or brick. New roots will form where the stem is covered by the soil. After several weeks, trim the new plant from its mother and transplant to a new location.

A note on spacing herbs in the garden: The spacing given in the "At-A-Glance" for each herb is the distance to allow between plants of the same type when you set out transplants or thin seedlings. But in an herb garden, you may not have more than one plant of a particular herb. To determine how much room it needs to grow, think of the recommended spacing as the mature breadth of the plant rather than as the distance from crown to crown. Lemon balm, for example, has a recommended spacing of 12 inches between plants, so one plant needs a radius of 6 inches; horseradish, with a recommended spacing of 18 inches, needs a radius of 9 inches. If you plant lemon balm next to horseradish, you need to allow 15 inches between the two plants. For a shortcut, add the two recommended spacings, 12 (lemon balm) and 18 (horseradish), and divide by 2.

Preparing, Fertilizing, and Mulching the Soil

Herbs are healthier and more productive when the soil is well prepared. Work amendments such as organic matter and sand into the soil until it is loose, fertile, and well drained. (*See Soils, page 60.*) And, as for the vegetable garden, you need to have a soil test made. Herbs prefer a slightly more alkaline soil than vegetables, with a pH of 6.5 to 7.0. Depending upon where you live in the South, you may have to amend the soil to raise or lower your soil pH. Follow the recommendations given by your soil test results.

Classic herb garden at Agecroft, Richmond, Virginia.

Herbs require a soil that does not stay soggy after a rain. However, they will not survive long periods of dry weather either. Watch for signs of wilting and water as needed to keep the soil evenly moist.

Sage in flower at Old Salem, North Carolina.

Flowers on basil.

If you have acid soil, you may want to build your herb bed of concrete blocks. The lime that leaches out of the concrete helps keep the soil more alkaline, and the herbs thrive. However, you will still need to add lime from time to time.

Herbs require less fertilizer than vegetables. In fact, too much nitrogen causes excessive growth, diluting the flavorful oils in the foliage. Mulching with 1 inch of compost in spring provides enough nutrients for the season. If compost is not available, add 1 to 2 tablespoons of 5-10-10 per square yard of bed in the spring. Herbs that are harvested regularly, such as basil, lemon balm, and summer savory, should be fed with half-strength liquid fertilizer (20-20-20) after each harvest, except the last one in the fall.

Mulch is important to keep the soil from splashing onto the herb foliage. It also insulates the soil from extremes in temperature, shades out weeds, and conserves soil moisture. If you use an acid-forming material, such as pine straw or pine bark, check the soil pH periodically. (*See page 86 for more information on mulches.*)

Tips for Herb Gardening in Florida and South Texas

Growing herbs in Florida and South Texas differs from herb gardening in the rest of the South. One of the major considerations is the diseases that take their toll in July and August. Perennial herbs, such as thyme, garden sage, and tarragon, are grown as annuals in these areas. They are planted in fall and harvested through early summer.

Mild winters also make this region's herb-gardening calendar unique. Herbs that are killed or left bedraggled by winters in colder regions (parsley, chives, and sorrel, for example) are at their best during winter here. Other herbs that should be planted in fall and harvested through the next spring include coriander, burnet, caraway, fennel, garlic, and sweet marjoram. Fall-planted perennials that should remain in the garden several years include mint, oregano, lemon balm, rosemary, winter savory, and chives. These do not seem to be as bothered by disease as others.

Exceptions to fall planting are in areas of North Florida, where repeated freezes occur. Gardeners in this region should follow the planting calendar for the Lower South.

Summer annuals such as basil and dill are grown in summer throughout Florida and in South Texas. However, summer savory grows best in spring or fall; it declines in the summer, yet winter is too cool for good growth.

Some Florida and South Texas gardeners have found that growing herbs under a deciduous tree helps the herbs survive the summer. This provides cooling shade, yet allows sunshine to reach the plants during winter. Mulch is also important to keep the plant roots cool. A 1-inch layer of leaf mold or shredded bark around plants protects the soil from the hot sun.

Controlling Pests

Although you will have fewer problems with insects on herbs than on other plants, you may find that aphids, red spiders, mealybugs, and whiteflies are a problem. The North Carolina Botanical Gardens Herb Volunteers use a spray made by mixing 1 tablespoon of vegetable oil, 1 tablespoon of liquid soap, and 1 quart of water. Check plants every ten days for reinfestation.

Small-scale herb garden. Owners: Mr. and Mrs. Van Chaplin, Birmingham, Alabama.

Formal herb garden. Owner: Dr. Stuart Peery, Charlotte, North Carolina.

Harvesting

Plants can be cut back periodically during the growing season. Flavor is most concentrated near the time of blooming. And by cutting plants before they bloom, you encourage more leafy growth.

Most herbs respond well to pinching and snipping. Each time you cut them, they spring back with tender, new foliage. Whether you are gathering only a few sprigs or cutting a large quantity, the best time to harvest is on a clear sunny morning, after the sun has evaporated the morning dew but before the hottest hours of the day. Do not tear the stems from the plants because you risk injuring or uprooting the plants. Flower shears or kitchen shears are the ideal tool for the job.

If you are harvesting seeds such as dill, fennel, caraway, or coriander, wait until the seeds

Herbs 213

turn light brown and then cut the stalk. By waiting, you risk the ripening seeds dropping into the soil. Hang the stalks upside down in a paper bag to dry until they are crisp. Then shake the seeds into the bottom of the bag.

Capturing the Flavor for Later Use

The flavor of fresh herbs is by far the best, but in winter you will be glad to have the herbs you stored last summer. Drying is the most common method of preservation. To preserve as much flavor and color as possible, dry the foliage slowly and out of the direct sun.

Avoid using a metal screen because it will slightly change the flavor of the herbs; use a nylon screen instead. To air-dry herbs, place them on a screen in a room with low humidity. Prop the screen up to let air circulate above and below the herbs. To dry small quantities of herbs, spread them in a thin layer on paper towels in an air-conditioned room. You can also hang small bunches of herbs on a clothesline in a dry, well-ventilated place such as an attic, screened porch, or air-conditioned room until they are crispy dry. Store leaves as soon as they are dry so that the flavor will not be lost.

Oven drying is much faster, but you must be careful not to use too much heat. If you can smell the herbs, their flavorful oils are being lost. Set the oven at the lowest temperature possible. It is difficult to keep the heat low enough in electric ovens, but the heat generated by the pilot light in a gas oven is fine. Place a screen across the oven rack, and spread a single layer of herbs on it to dry. Leave the door partially open to let moisture escape.

You can also dry small amounts of herbs in a microwave oven. Place four or five leafy stems between paper towels and set the microwave on high power for two to three minutes. Check the herbs and repeat the procedure, if necessary. Some microwaves dry differently, so experiment to perfect your technique.

You can also dry herbs in a dehydrator. It takes about two to three hours to dry them, depending on the thickness of the leaf. Place the herbs on the drying trays with the thermostat set at 100 degrees.

Herbs drying at Mordecai House, Raleigh, North Carolina.

Formal herb garden. Owner: Martha Riddle, Nashville, Tennessee.

A well-kept vegetable and herb garden in front of the house is an attractive landscape feature. A ground cover of strawberries forms the foreground for this one, and annuals add spots of color. Owner: O. G. Touchstone III, Birmingham, Alabama.

Thyme, golden sage, marjoram, and golden oregano.

When your herbs are dry, strip the leaves from the stems and store in an airtight, opaque container or in an airtight jar in a dark place. Check the container in a couple of days. If there is moisture on the sides or lid, return the herbs briefly to a cool oven to finish drying. Most dried herbs will retain their flavor for one year; rosemary and sage will keep for two years.

Freezing Herbs

Some herbs, such as parsley, dill, chives, and basil, keep well frozen. Do not blanch or steam them; just wash and let dry. Then wrap small quantities of the herbs in packets of foil and store in labeled freezer containers.

You can also pack chopped herbs into ice cube trays, with just enough water to freeze into a cube. When the water freezes, put the cubes in labeled plastic bags. Then when you need basil in the spaghetti sauce, just drop in a cube.

Vinegars, Butters, and Bouquet Garni

Another way to capture the flavor of herbs is in an herb vinegar. Simply fill a large jar ¾ full of fresh herbs, either of one kind or a mixture. Pour vinegar over the herbs and let it steep for seven to ten days. Then strain, if desired, bottle, and label. Basil vinegar is a classic with tomatoes, tarragon is good with green salads, and mixtures with chives or marjoram are excellent in stews.

Bouquet garni is a bundle of fresh herb sprigs tied together with a thread and tossed into a simmering soup or stew for the last twenty minutes of cooking. Since you serve hot soup more often in winter, prepare dried bouquet garni by combining the dried leaves of thyme, marjoram, and bay with two or three peppercorns in a cheesecloth bag. Immerse the bag in the pot and remove before serving.

You can make herb butters using either fresh or dried herbs. Beat 1 tablespoon of chopped herbs or combination of herbs into ¼ pound of softened sweet butter, blended with 1 tablespoon of lemon juice. If you use dried herbs, soak them in the lemon juice a few minutes before blending with the butter. Store in small crocks in the refrigerator and use to season vegetables, steak, or breads. Try chive, thyme, savory, or rosemary butter, or combine two or more of your choice.

Tips for Cooking with Herbs

Use herbs to enhance the natural flavor of food, but not to disguise or change it. Too much of an herb can be objectionable; and remember, it is always easier to add more than to subtract.

When experimenting with a new herb, crush some of it and let it warm in your hand; then sniff it and taste it. If it is delicate, you can be bold and adventurous in using it. If it is very strong and pungent, be cautious.

To blend herbs, choose a leading flavor and combine it with one or more less-pronounced flavors. Never emphasize more than one of the strong herbs such as rosemary, sage, or basil.

Keep in mind that the flavor of dried herbs is much more concentrated than the fresh, so use about ⅓ of the dried leaves to replace the fresh. For example, 1 teaspoon of dry leaves is equivalent to 1 tablespoon of fresh. The exception is rosemary; the fresh leaves are more pungent than the dried, so use about half as much.

Most herbs are bitter when cooked too much, but a little heat releases their flavor. So add herbs during the last few minutes of cooking. Bay is an exception; add it at the beginning.

When you serve a meal, remember that parsley is not the only garnish in the garden. The foliage of burnet, dill, fennel, mint, and rosemary can be used, depending on the dish. And do not overlook the flowers of chives, dill, and fennel; all are edible and decorative.

Basil

Basil (*Ocimum sp.*) is so simple to grow that even first-time gardeners can plant it with confidence. And it is indispensable in the kitchen. Its clovelike fragrance and cool taste are a must in summer salads, especially with tomatoes. It is a tender annual, so you will need to replant each spring; but it thrives in hot, humid weather and grows well throughout the South from spring until fall frost.

For best results, plant basil in full sun and a loose, well-drained soil. You can buy transplants of the most common selections at garden centers; but basil grows so easily from seed that you can also grow your own transplants or sow seeds directly in the garden. It will not grow in cold soil, so wait until the ground warms up and all danger of frost is past. Plant seeds in a shallow furrow and cover with ¼ inch of soil. Since basil seeds are covered with a jelly-like coating that makes them float easily, be sure to firm the soil well to keep them from washing away with the first rain. When plants are 2 to 3 inches tall, thin them to 18 to 24 inches apart.

To get an earlier start, sow seeds in flats 6 weeks before the last frost date in your area. Set transplants out when they are 3 to 4 inches tall, spacing them 18 to 24 inches apart.

Plants require little maintenance. For bushier growth, fertilize after a heavy clipping with liquid 18-18-18 or 20-20-20 diluted according to label directions. Also, be sure to keep the soil moist, especially after harvesting. Letting the soil dry out can stunt growth.

For fresh use, you can simply pluck the leaves when you need them. To extend the life of the plants, pinch off the flower buds as they appear. For drying, pesto, or vinegar, harvest just before the flower buds are ready to bloom; clip the plant back to one-third its original size. You should be able to make several harvests in one season before frost kills the plants.

AT A GLANCE

Light: Full sun
Propagation: Seeds, transplants, cuttings
Spacing: 18-24 inches between plants; bush basil, 6 inches
Part Used: Leaves
Type of Plant: Annual
Comments: Dark Opal selection may need partial shade. Basil needs plenty of water, especially after harvest.

A single plant can become quite large and provides more than enough foliage for a family of four.

Selections

Sweet basil (*O. basilicum*) is the most common selection of basil and is good for both drying and fresh use. The plants grow 24 to 30 inches tall with leaves that are about 2 inches long and 1 inch wide. It has the characteristic peppery-clove taste and aroma.

Lettuce Leaf basil (*O. basilicum* Crispum), another common selection, has larger leaves 3 to 4 inches long with smooth edges and crinkled centers. This basil has a good flavor and yields a large amount of foliage for drying. Because the leaves are so large, it is best to pinch them off the stem before drying.

Bush basil (*O. basilicum* Minimum) is a compact form of sweet basil. It grows less than 12 inches tall, with leaves that are ½ inch long or smaller. Its leaves are best used fresh. Space plants 6 inches apart in the garden. Bush basil also grows well in containers.

Lemon basil (*O. basilicum* Citriodorum) grows 18 inches tall and produces light-green leaves with a citrus-clove flavor. The leaves can be used fresh or dry. Lemon basil does not transplant well, so it is best to sow seeds directly in the garden.

To extend the life of your plants, pinch out the flower stalks. The leaves' flavor is strongest just before the flowers open.

Dark Opal basil (*O. basilicum* Purpurescens) is a selection of sweet basil with purplish red leaves and pinkish blossoms. It has a tealike scent and flavor that are not as sweet as those of other basils. It is mostly used fresh, as the color is not good for drying. When the leaves are added to white vinegar, the liquid turns a bright-rose shade. Plant this selection in full sun to partial shade.

BASIL-SQUASH STIR-FRY

2 tablespoons vegetable oil
1 clove garlic, minced
1 large onion, sliced and separated into rings
3 medium zucchini, thinly sliced
3 medium-size yellow squash, thinly sliced
3 medium tomatoes, peeled and cut into wedges
1½ teaspoons minced fresh basil or ½ teaspoon dried whole basil
¾ teaspoon salt
½ teaspoon pepper
2 tablespoons grated Parmesan cheese

Pour oil around top of preheated wok (325°), coating sides and bottom with oil. Add garlic; stir-fry briefly. Add onion; stir-fry 1 minute. Stir in zucchini and yellow squash; cook 2 to 3 minutes or until crisp-tender. Add tomatoes, basil, salt, and pepper; cook 1 minute, stirring gently. Sprinkle cheese over vegetables. Yield: 8 to 10 servings.

BASIL SOUP

1½ tablespoons butter or margarine
1 medium onion, chopped
1½ cloves garlic, minced
3 cups chicken broth
¼ cup uncooked brown rice
½ cup tomato juice
1½ cups diced, peeled tomato
½ pound fresh basil, chopped (about 3 cups)

Melt butter in a Dutch oven. Add onion and garlic and sauté until tender. Add broth; bring to a boil. Stir in rice; return to a boil. Reduce heat, cover, and simmer 35 minutes. Add tomato juice, tomato, and basil; return to a boil. Reduce heat and simmer, uncovered, 10 minutes. Yield: 6 cups.

• Use the leaves, fresh or dry, in tomato dishes, soups, salads, and sauces, and with cucumbers, eggs, and shrimp.

• Add a generous pinch of basil to canned soups or stews before heating.

• For full flavor, add basil during the last 10 minutes of cooking.

Herbs   219

The tree of Greek and Roman legend, bay (*Laurus nobilis*) was used to make laurels with which poets and athletes were honored. For Southerners, it is an important ingredient in soups and stews.

This shrublike tree is an evergreen with glossy, leathery leaves that are 2 to 4 inches long. You can grow it outdoors in Florida and the Gulf South. In the rest of the South, grow it in a container so that you can bring it indoors in the winter. Container-grown bays add a few inches

Bay

each year and can eventually reach 4 to 10 feet in height.

Plant bay in rich, well-drained soil. Although the tree will grow best in full sun, it needs some protection from hot afternoon sun.

Bay is started from cuttings, but since these take at least six months to root, it is best to buy a small plant from a nursery. Because rooting is difficult, the plants are relatively expensive when compared to other herbs. If you want to try starting new plants from an established tree, take cuttings in early summer or late fall. Dip them in a rooting hormone and insert them in a mixture of sand and sphagnum peat moss. Place the cuttings under plastic to prevent the loss of moisture, and set them in a bright location out of direct sunlight.

AT A GLANCE

Light: Full or filtered sun
Propagation: Best to buy a young plant
Spacing: Does not apply; one plant is sufficient
Part Used: Leaves
Type of Plant: Tender perennial
Serious Insects: Scales

In the Upper and Middle South, you can sink a container-grown bay into the ground and leave it in the garden until just before fall frost. If the container is clay, sinking it means you will have to water less often.

Bay must be grown in a container over most of the South. Be sure the container allows for good drainage.

Be careful not to overwater bay. Let the soil dry out between waterings. You can move a container-grown bay outdoors in the summer, but bring it indoors before the first hard freeze. Place it in a cool, sunny room, or in a cold frame or greenhouse for the winter.

You may harvest bay leaves year-round. Just pluck the mature leaves as you need them. Use them fresh or dried, but remember that the fresh leaves are stronger and more aromatic.

Red bay (*Persea borbonia*) is a native Southern tree and the leaves are often used as a substitute for the more familiar bay. It can be used the same way as bay, and some cooks prefer its milder flavor. The dried leaves of California bay (*Umbellularia californica*) are sometimes available in supermarkets. This type has a very different flavor and should not be confused with the other bays; its flavor is much stronger than that of *Laurus nobilis*.

Leaves are easily air dried. Pick them as you need them.

VEGETABLE-BAY STEW

1 pound ground beef
1 medium onion, chopped
1 (16-ounce) can whole tomatoes, undrained and chopped
4 cups water
¾ cup sliced celery
2 beef-flavored bouillon cubes
2 or 3 bay leaves
1 teaspoon salt
1 teaspoon pepper
1 teaspoon Worcestershire sauce
1 (10-ounce) package frozen mixed vegetables
1 cup medium egg noodles, uncooked

Cook ground beef and onion in a Dutch oven over medium heat until meat is browned. Drain meat mixture on paper towels; discard pan drippings. Combine meat mixture and next 8 ingredients in a Dutch oven; bring to a boil. Cover and simmer 30 minutes. Stir in frozen vegetables and noodles. Bring to a boil; reduce heat, and simmer, uncovered, 20 minutes. Yield: about 8 cups.

BLACK BEAN SOUP

1½ cups dried black beans
1½ quarts water or vegetable stock
1 teaspoon salt
2 tablespoons vegetable oil, divided
1 medium onion, chopped
1 medium potato, peeled and grated
1 carrot, grated
2 stalks celery, chopped
2 bay leaves
1 tablespoon minced fresh oregano or 1 teaspoon dried whole oregano
1½ teaspoons minced fresh thyme or ½ teaspoon dried whole thyme
¾ teaspoon minced fresh savory or ¼ teaspoon ground savory
Juice of 1 lemon
1 clove garlic, minced
½ lemon, thinly sliced
1 green onion, chopped

Sort and wash beans; place in a Dutch oven. Add 1½ quarts water, salt, and 1 tablespoon oil. Cover and bring to a boil; reduce heat, and simmer 1½ hours.

Sauté chopped medium onion in remaining tablespoon oil. Add potato, carrot, and celery; cook over medium heat, stirring often, 3 to 5 minutes.

Tie next 3 herbs in a cheesecloth bag; add vegetable mixture and herbs to beans. Simmer 1 hour or until beans are tender. Remove and discard herb bag. Add lemon juice and garlic just before serving. Garnish with lemon slices and green onion. Yield: 9 cups.

Every morning burnet (*Poterium sanguisorba*) glitters with droplets of moisture on the points of each leaflet, adding a beautiful sparkle to the herb garden. And its lacy, fernlike leaves are as refreshing in flavor as they are pleasing to the eye. Young leaves have a mild cucumber taste that is perfect in salads and cool drinks or as a garnish; the herb is also known as salad burnet.

The plant grows as rosettes that form lush mounds of foliage 12 to 24 inches in height. Plant it in full or filtered sunlight and well-drained, fairly dry soil. If the soil is too rich or moist, the rosettes will rot. In the South, burnet seems to do best when mulched year-round and given some shade in summer.

Burnet

Start from seeds in spring or fall. It is best to sow burnet where it is to grow. Although it can be transplanted when young, the plant develops a deep root as it matures and is difficult to move. Sow seeds in a shallow furrow and cover them lightly with soil, but do not bury them. The seeds should germinate in about 10 days. When the seedlings are 2 to 3 inches tall, thin them to 12 to 15 inches apart.

To harvest burnet, simply pick the leaves as needed, clipping an entire stem at a time. Leaves taste best in fall and early spring, and the young leaves are more tender and flavorful than older ones. Since it is evergreen, you can have fresh leaves year-round. Burnet does not dry well, but may be used in herb vinegar.

AT A GLANCE

Light: Full to partial sun
Propagation: Seeds
Spacing: 12-15 inches between plants
Part Used: Young leaves
Type of Plant: Perennial

Burnet has a mild taste that resembles that of cucumber.

The lush mound of foliage may reach 12 to 24 inches in height. Plants need mulch to help cool the soil, but the rosettes will rot if the soil is too wet.

The flowers appear in spring of the second year. They are insignificant, growing on wiry stems and giving the plant a ragged appearance. To keep plants tidy and to encourage better leaf growth, clip the flower stalks as they appear. Although burnet is a perennial, the leaves become bitter after it flowers; so for the best flavor, replant every second or third year. One way to renew the planting is to let burnet flower and reseed. Then thin the seedlings to the recommended spacing and uproot the old plants.

• Use burnet liberally as a garnish in place of parsley.

• Add burnet leaves to wine or cool summer drinks.

Droplets of moisture on the points of each leaflet are the result of a biological process called guttation.

BURNET-CELERY SOUP

6 stalks celery, finely chopped
6 green onions, finely chopped
3 medium potatoes, peeled and cubed
1 quart milk
2 tablespoons chopped fresh burnet or 2 teaspoons dried whole burnet
½ teaspoon salt
⅛ teaspoon pepper
3 tablespoons whipping cream
1 tablespoon butter or margarine
  Sliced celery (optional)
  Fresh burnet leaves (optional)

Combine first 5 ingredients in a large saucepan; simmer 30 minutes (do not boil). Pour half of mixture into blender and process 30 seconds; strain through a sieve. Repeat with remaining mixture. Return to saucepan. Stir in salt, pepper, whipping cream, and butter. Heat thoroughly (do not boil), stirring occasionally. Chill before serving. Garnish with sliced celery and burnet leaves, if desired. Yield: 5 cups.

BAKED POTATOES WITH BURNET CREAM

⅓ to ½ cup chopped fresh burnet
1 (8-ounce) carton commercial sour cream
4 large baking potatoes
  Vegetable oil
¼ cup chopped green onions
½ teaspoon salt
½ teaspoon pepper
½ teaspoon paprika

Combine burnet and sour cream; cover and chill.

Scrub potatoes and rub skins with vegetable oil; bake at 400° for 1 hour or until done. Slice skin away from top of each potato. Carefully scoop out pulp, leaving shells intact. Mash pulp; stir in sour cream mixture, onions, salt, and pepper. Stuff potato shells with pulp mixture; sprinkle with paprika. Bake at 350° for 15 to 20 minutes. Yield: 4 servings.

BURNET FINGER SANDWICHES

4 slices whole wheat bread
2 tablespoons butter or margarine, softened
2 tablespoons cream cheese, softened
1 teaspoon minced fresh burnet

Remove crusts from bread. Spread one side of each slice of bread with butter. Spread two slices of bread with cream cheese (should be spread over butter). Sprinkle burnet evenly over cream cheese; top with remaining slices of bread. Cut into finger sandwiches. Yield: 6 finger sandwiches.

Caraway

Caraway is best known for its flavorful seeds that are used in rye bread, cakes, and cabbage dishes. But growing it in your garden lets you enjoy its edible foliage and roots too. Caraway (*Carum carvi*) does well in Southern gardens, except in the hot, humid weather of Florida and the Gulf South. In these areas, try growing it as an annual, planting in early fall.

Elsewhere, this herb is a biennial. The first year, it grows as a bushy mound of aromatic foliage, about 8 inches high. The foliage is feathery like carrot foliage but a deeper, glossier green. In the South, the foliage remains through the winter. During the second year, after a winter, caraway produces 2- to 3-foot stalks with greenish white flowers that resemble Queen Anne's lace. By midsummer, these flowers develop into seeds. The plant dies after the seeds have ripened.

Plant in full sun. You can plant in early spring around the last frost date for a crop of seeds the second season (the plants will be in the garden almost 1½ years). Or, to lessen the time the plants are in the garden, plant in fall for a crop the following fall.

It is best to sow seeds where they are to grow, because caraway has a deep taproot and does not transplant well.

Sow seeds in shallow furrows and barely cover them with soil. When plants are 2 to 3 inches tall, thin to 6 to 12 inches apart.

You can harvest the foliage lightly through the season for use in salads; but be careful not to harvest too much, or you will weaken the plant and decrease your harvest of seeds. In late summer, the seeds will turn brown as they ripen; they are ready for harvest when most come loose with gentle pulling. Watch carefully because the seeds ripen quickly and may be eaten by birds or blown by the wind if you do not harvest in time.

To collect the seeds, cut the stalk about halfway down and suspend the flower head upside down in a paper bag. As the seeds ripen, they will drop readily. (Plants self-sow easily, so if you want caraway to reseed, leave one or two flowers in the garden.) Once the seeds are harvested, you can pull the roots; they are thick and sweet and may be used like carrots.

Before using seeds in cooking, you may want to pour boiling water over them to make sure there are no bugs. Do not do this with seeds to be planted, however, as it will kill the embryo. (*See page 214 for drying and storing.*)

AT A GLANCE

Light: Full sun
Propagation: Seeds
Spacing: 6-12 inches between plants
Part Used: Seeds, foliage, taproot
Type of Plant: Biennial

Seeds turn from green to tan to brown as they ripen. The seeds in the lower part of the photo are ready to be harvested. Notice how they have become shrunken and ridged.

CHEESE CARAWAY BREAD
    2 cups all-purpose flour
    1 tablespoon plus 1 teaspoon baking powder
    ½ teaspoon salt
    6 (¾-ounce) slices process pimiento cheese, shredded
  1½ teaspoons caraway seeds
    1 cup milk
    ¼ cup butter or margarine, melted
    2 eggs, beaten
       Caraway seeds

Combine first 5 ingredients; mix well. Combine milk, butter, and eggs, stirring well; add to flour mixture, stirring just until moistened. Spoon into a greased and floured 9- x 5- x 3-inch loafpan; sprinkle additional caraway seeds on top. Bake at 350° for 45 to 50 minutes or until a wooden pick inserted in center comes out clean. Yield: 1 loaf.

Preceding page. *Cold herb soups are an attractive way to stimulate appetites. Our selection includes: (from top) Cold Dill Soup (page 233), Savory Carrot Soup (page 255), and Burnet-Celery Soup (page 223).*

Turn homegrown herbs into a beautiful array of tangy vinegars or flavorful butters and sauces: (from left) Tarragon Vinegar (page 259), Mixed Herb Vinegar (page 251), Mint Sauce (page 245), Salsa Picante (page 231), Garlic Butter (page 237), and Dill Sauce (page 233).

Following page. This exciting pesto features the flavors of crushed garlic, parsley, basil, and tarragon (page 237).

Chives

Chives (*Allium sp.*) grow as tufted clumps of grasslike leaves that rise from a cluster of small bulbs. The snipped leaves are a popular addition to soups, salads, and vegetable dishes, providing both color and a mild onion or garlic flavor.

Plant chives in full sun and rich, well-drained soil. They will survive in partial shade but will not be as erect.

The easiest way to start chives is to purchase plants from a garden center or herb grower and set them out in the garden in early spring.

Chives can also be grown from seed, but will take a year to produce usable plants. Start seeds indoors 5 to 8 weeks before the last frost and set them out once the ground warms. Or sow them directly in the garden after the last frost.

Plant in a shallow furrow about ¼ inch deep or simply broadcast them on the soil and cover with sifted soil or vermiculite. Seeds will take 10 to 14 days to germinate. When plants are about 3 inches tall, thin them to 8 inches apart.

Once a planting is established, you can propagate chives by division in early spring. Simply dig up the clumps and divide them, leaving one to four bulbs in each new clump. Replant the clumps, setting them slightly deeper.

Chives need little care. If you harvest often, fertilize plants every 2 weeks with liquid 18-18-18 or 20-20-20, diluted according to label directions. Divide the clumps every 3 to 4 years, as the bulbs become too crowded.

Harvest chives as you need them. In the Gulf South, it is especially important to harvest often to encourage new growth. Rather than shearing the entire plant, select leaves from the outside of the clump and cut each one to about ½ inch above soil level. Cutting them higher will leave unsightly brown stubs. You can also grow chives indoors in a sunny window during the winter.

If you have more chives than you can use fresh, freeze or dry them for winter use. The blooms are often used as a garnish.

Selections

Common chives (*A. schoenoprasum*) have tubular leaves with a mild onion flavor. Plants grow up to 12 inches in height and in spring produce lavender flowers that can be used to make a pretty rose-colored vinegar. The leaves disappear at first frost and reappear in early spring. It will self-sow if allowed to go to seed.

Garlic chives (*A. tuberosum*) are also called Chinese chives. The leaves are flat and wider than those of common chives, and have a mild garlic flavor. They grow up to 15 inches tall, and in mild winters are evergreen. Garlic chives bloom in mid- to late summer with white starlike clusters and will reseed prolifically.

AT A GLANCE

Light: Full sun, but tolerates partial shade
Propagation: Seeds, divisions
Spacing: 8 inches between plants
Part Used: Leaves, flowers
Type of Plant: Perennial

TANGY CHIVE DIP

1 cup mayonnaise
3 tablespoons chopped fresh chives
2 tablespoons chili sauce
2 teaspoons tarragon vinegar
½ teaspoon minced fresh thyme or ⅛ teaspoon ground thyme
½ teaspoon curry powder
¼ teaspoon salt

Combine all ingredients, blending well. Chill several hours or overnight. Serve with raw vegetables. Yield: about 1 cup.

When you harvest chives, snip them off at soil level. Otherwise, you will leave an unattractive brown stub that slows new growth.

Coriander

Known for its fragrant seeds, which add flavor to candy and pastries, coriander (*Coriandrum sativum*) is easy to grow. And growing your own gives you a bonus of fresh foliage (called cilantro or Chinese parsley), a necessary ingredient in many Latin American, Spanish, and Oriental dishes.

Coriander is a hardy annual and will grow 2 to 3 feet tall. It has delicate lacy leaves and bears flat umbels of white or pinkish blossoms in midsummer. The flowers eventually turn into light-brown fruit with an edible inner seed. Although the fresh seeds and foliage have a pungent odor, the ripe seeds are very fragrant and become even more so as they dry.

Grow coriander in full sun and well-drained soil. Sow seeds either after danger of frost has passed in the spring or early in the fall. The seedlings are evergreen in winter over most of the South. In the Gulf South sow seeds only in the fall, as plants do not tolerate summer heat and humidity well. Because it has a delicate taproot, coriander is difficult to transplant, so it is best to sow the large seeds where they are to grow. Press them into the soil but do not bury.

Keep the seeds moist until germination, which may take up to two weeks. When the seedlings are 3 inches tall, thin them to 10 inches apart. Once plants bloom, foliage becomes scarce; so for a steady supply of fresh foliage, make successive sowings every 3 to 4 weeks through fall.

AT A GLANCE

Light: Full sun
Propagation: Seeds
Spacing: 10 inches between plants
Part Used: Seeds, leaves
Type of Plant: Annual
Serious Insects: Aphids, whiteflies

Coriander, also known as Chinese parsley, is grown primarily for its seeds. The finely textured foliage has a spicy flavor that is essential to many Latin American, Spanish, and Oriental dishes.

You can harvest the foliage continually in the cooler months of spring and fall, and through winter in the Gulf South. But be careful not to cut more than one-half of the leaves at one time, as heavy harvesting will weaken the plant.

When the seeds are ripe, the fruit clusters will turn a beige brown and look dry. Harvest the seed heads as soon as they ripen, or the weak stems will bend and the seeds will drop. (To let coriander self-sow for next year's crop, leave a few seed heads standing in the garden.) Clip the seed head a short way down the stem, and place it in a paper bag or basket. Put the bag in a well-ventilated place to dry. In five to six days, the round fruit husks should be dry and will split into two halves, allowing the edible inner seed to drop out.

• Coriander attains an agreeable taste and fragrance only after the seed has ripened.

• Add a dash of coriander to canned or fresh mushrooms when heating or sautéing them.

Flowers appear in midsummer, followed by fruit clusters containing the edible seeds.

SALSA PICANTE

    2 fresh jalapeño peppers
   12 sprigs fresh coriander, chopped or 1 tablespoon
        plus 1 teaspoon dried whole cilantro
    3 medium tomatoes, cored and cut into eighths
    1 bunch green onions, cut into 1-inch pieces
    1 small green tomato, cored and cut into eighths
    1 medium avocado, peeled and cut into chunks
  ¼ cup olive oil
    2 to 3 tablespoons lime juice
    1 teaspoon garlic powder
    1 teaspoon ground cumin
    1 teaspoon salt
  ¼ teaspoon sugar

Place peppers on a baking sheet; broil 3 to 4 inches from heat, turning often with tongs, until peppers are blistered on all sides. Immediately place peppers in a plastic bag; fasten securely, and let steam 10 to 15 minutes. Remove peel of each pepper.

Cut a small slit in side of each pepper, and rinse under cold water to remove seeds. (Wear rubber or plastic gloves when rinsing and cutting peppers if you have sensitive skin.) Remove stems from peppers; quarter each pepper, and set aside.

Combine peppers and remaining ingredients in container of electric blender or food processor. Process 10 to 15 seconds or until chopped to desired texture. Chill before serving. Serve as a dip or with salad or black beans. Yield: about 3 cups.

FRESH MUSHROOM SOUP

    1 pound fresh mushrooms
  ¼ cup plus 2 tablespoons butter or margarine
    2 cups minced onion
  ½ teaspoon sugar
    3 tablespoons minced fresh coriander or 1
        tablespoon dried whole cilantro
  ¼ cup all-purpose flour
 1¾ cups chicken broth
    1 cup water
    1 cup dry vermouth
  ½ teaspoon salt
  ¼ teaspoon pepper

Slice one-third of mushrooms, and finely chop remainder. Melt butter; add onion and sugar, sautéing until onion is tender. Add mushrooms and coriander; cook 5 minutes, stirring often. Stir in flour; cook 2 minutes, stirring constantly.

Gradually add chicken broth and water; cook over medium heat, stirring constantly, until mixture is thickened and bubbly. Stir in remaining ingredients. Bring soup to a boil, stirring constantly; reduce heat, and simmer, uncovered, 10 minutes. Yield: 8 cups.

Dill

Although dillseeds are a must for making cucumber pickles, the best reason for growing this herb may be its aromatic foliage. Also known as dillweed, the feathery leaves have a more delicate flavor than the seeds. They may be used to season meats, fish, butter, sauces, beans, cauliflower, and cabbage.

Dill (*Anethum graveolens*) is an annual that grows 2 to 3 feet tall with leaves branching from a single hollow stem. Yellow flowers borne in flat umbels bloom in spring and early summer.

Plant dill in full sun and well-drained soil in a spot where the stalks will be protected from strong winds. Sow seeds 2 to 4 weeks before the last expected frost; or to have ripe seeds on hand as pickling cucumbers reach harvesting size, you can delay planting until a week or two after you plant cucumbers. To have a plentiful supply of foliage, make successive sowings every 2 weeks until seeds stop germinating in the heat of summer. For a fall crop, sow again about 2 months before frost, when nights have cooled.

It is best to sow the seeds where they are to grow. Dill has a long, carrotlike root that makes transplanting difficult, and dill started from transplants tends to go to seed quickly without producing much foliage. If you must start with transplants, you can do so successfully before seedlings are 2 to 3 inches tall.

Plant the seeds in rows or broadcast them over the surface of the soil and cover with ¼ inch of soil. The seeds should germinate in 10 to 14 days. When the plants are 2 to 3 inches tall, thin to 6 to 12 inches apart.

Dill does not require much care, but you will need to water it when the weather is dry. When plants are about 18 inches tall, you may want to stake them to help keep them from falling over.

AT A GLANCE

Light: Full sun
Propagation: Seeds
Spacing: 6-12 inches between plants
Part Used: Seeds, leaves
Type of Plant: Annual
Serious Insects: Parsleyworms

Yellow flowers appear in early summer.

Foliage is most aromatic just as the flowers open, but it is also less plentiful at this point because the stalks elongate as flowers form.

You can harvest dillweed any time from seedling stage until plants bloom. Foliage is most aromatic just as the flowers begin to open. However, it may not be plentiful at this point, because plants begin stretching out, and foliage becomes sparse as the flowers form.

Harvest the seeds when they first turn brown, or they will soon drop off. Dill self-sows readily, so you may want to leave a few seed heads in the garden to begin your crop for next year. Cut the stalk and seed head, and hang it upside down in a paper bag in a dry, well-ventilated place. The seeds should dry and drop into the bag. After all the seeds have been collected, place them in a low temperature oven for a few minutes to make sure they are dry. Then store them in an airtight container.

Selection

Dill bouquet (*A. graveolens* Dill Bouquet) is shorter and more compact than common dill. It only reaches 2 feet in height and does not need staking. Foliage is also more plentiful.

COLD DILL SOUP

1 pint half-and-half
2 (8-ounce) cartons plain yogurt
2 cucumbers, peeled, seeded, and diced
3 tablespoons minced fresh dillweed or 1 tablespoon dried whole dillweed
2 tablespoons lemon juice
1 tablespoon chopped green onions
½ teaspoon salt
⅛ to ¼ teaspoon white pepper
   Sliced cucumber (optional)
   Sprigs of fresh dillweed (optional)

Combine first 8 ingredients, stirring well; chill thoroughly. Stir well; garnish with sliced cucumber and dill sprigs, if desired. Yield: 4 cups.

DILL SAUCE

2 tablespoons butter or margarine
2 tablespoons all-purpose flour
1 cup fish broth or chicken broth
1 egg yolk, beaten
¼ cup commercial sour cream
2 tablespoons minced fresh dillweed or 2 teaspoons dried whole dillweed
   Sprigs of fresh dillweed (optional)

Melt butter in a heavy saucepan over low heat; add flour, stirring until smooth. Cook 1 minute, stirring constantly. Gradually add fish stock; cook over medium heat, stirring constantly, until thickened and bubbly. Gradually stir about one-fourth of hot mixture into egg yolk; add to remaining hot mixture, stirring constantly. Cook 5 minutes, stirring constantly. Remove from heat; stir in sour cream and 2 tablespoons dillweed. Cook over low heat just until heated (do not boil). Garnish with sprigs of fresh dillweed, if desired. Serve sauce over fish or seafood. Yield: about 1¼ cups.

DILLED CARROTS

8 medium carrots, scraped and cut into thin strips
¼ cup butter or margarine
2 tablespoons minced fresh dillweed or 2 teaspoons dried whole dillweed
2 tablespoons lemon juice

Cook carrots in a small amount of boiling water 8 to 10 minutes or until crisp-tender; drain. Add butter, dillweed, and lemon juice. Stir until carrots are coated. Yield: 6 to 8 servings.

• Dill leaves may be used in butters, meats, fish, sandwiches, sauces, and chicken.

• Dill makes a good salt substitute for low-sodium diets.

Harvest the seeds when they turn brown; if you delay, they may drop off before you can collect them.

Fennel

Nothing goes to waste when you grow fennel. Besides the licorice-flavored foliage and seeds, you can eat the stems (like celery) and the sweet-tasting root. You can also savor small sections of the yellow flower cluster as an after-dinner mint or use it as a garnish.

Sweet fennel (*Foeniculum vulgare*), also known as wild fennel, is a hardy perennial that will stay green through the winter in the Middle and Lower South. Plants grow 3 to 5 feet tall with shiny green, hollow stems and glossy, yellow-green feathery foliage that looks a lot like dill. The flowers bloom in summer in large yellow umbels up to 6 inches across. The ribbed seeds are light tan.

Plant sweet fennel at the rear of your garden where it can grow to its full height and not shade other plants. It needs full sun or partial shade and well-drained soil.

Sow fennel where it is to grow in the garden. It does not transplant well unless you have small seedlings. Broadcast seeds or sow them ½ inch deep when danger of frost is past. The seeds will germinate in about 2 weeks. When plants are 2 to 3 inches tall, thin to 8 to 12 inches apart.

Fennel grows quickly, but in spite of its height, the plant rarely needs staking. It is fairly frost-tolerant and remains in edible condition for several months in cool weather.

You can harvest the foliage and stems of sweet fennel anytime. Harvest the seeds when the stalks are dry and the umbels have turned brown. Cut the seed heads and a short piece of stem and hang them upside down inside a paper bag. In 5 to 6 days, the seeds should dry and fall. If you leave some seed heads in the garden, sweet fennel will self-sow. Watch for the seedlings the following spring, and transplant them to the proper spacing before they get too tall.

AT A GLANCE

Light: Full sun to partial shade
Propagation: Seeds, root divisions
Spacing: Sweet fennel, 8-12 inches between plants; Florence fennel, 6-8 inches
Part Used: Seeds, stems, foliage, roots, flowers
Type of Plant: Perennial
Serious Insects: Aphids, parsleyworms

The flowers, which bloom in summer, can be used as refreshing after-dinner mints.

From a distance, sweet fennel resembles dill; but fennel is taller and remains green through the winter in the Middle and Lower South.

Selections

Bronze fennel (*F. vulgare* Baloquese), a selection of sweet fennel, has plumes of coppery leaves that are denser that the species. It is grown as an ornamental as well as an herb.

Florence fennel or Finocchio (*F. vulgare* Azoricum) is a dwarf selection grown for its swollen leaf bases, which overlap to form a false bulb that is eaten like a vegetable. It resembles celery, but the leaves are finer and more feathery. Florence fennel grows 1 to 2 feet tall and is hardy in all but the coldest regions of the South. Along the Gulf Coast and in Florida, however, it may not grow well because the cool season is so brief.

Florence fennel requires a richer soil and more moisture than other types of fennel. Plant as you would sweet fennel and thin to 6 to 8 inches apart. When the base is the size of an egg, some gardeners mound soil around it to blanch it, which makes it milder in flavor and more tender. Harvest the bulb when it reaches 2½ to 3 inches in diameter. You can eat it raw or cooked. The foliage is also used for flavoring in salads, dressings, fish, and soups. For seed production, which occurs the second summer, leave plants in the garden through winter.

Florence fennel should be harvested when the false bulb is 2½ to 3 inches in diameter. You can eat it like a vegetable, raw or cooked.

MAKE-AHEAD FENNEL PIZZA SNACKS

- 1 pound Italian sausage
- 1 pound hot bulk sausage
- 1 cup chopped onion
- ½ green pepper, chopped
- 1 tablespoon fennel seeds
- 2 teaspoons dried whole oregano
- 1 teaspoon garlic salt
- 1 pound process American cheese, cut into small cubes
- 1 pound mozzarella cheese, cut into small cubes
- 3 (8-ounce) loaves party rye bread

Remove casing from Italian sausage; crumble into a large skillet. Add hot sausage, onion, and green pepper; cook until meat is browned. Drain well on paper towels.

Return meat mixture to skillet, and add seasonings; heat gently over low heat. Stir in cheese until melted, and remove from heat.

Spread a scant tablespoon of meat mixture on each bread slice. Place slices in a single layer on large baking sheets; freeze. When slices are frozen, place in plastic bags and store in freezer until needed.

To serve, thaw and place on lightly greased baking sheets. Bake at 425° for 8 to 10 minutes. Yield: about 11 dozen.

FENNEL COOKIES

- ½ cup butter or margarine, softened
- 1 cup sugar
- 1 egg
- 1¾ cups all-purpose flour
- 1½ teaspoons baking powder
- ¼ teaspoon salt
- 1½ teaspoons ground fennel seeds

Cream butter; gradually add sugar, beating well. Add egg, beating well.

Combine flour, baking powder, salt, and fennel seeds; add to creamed mixture, mixing well. Chill 2 hours.

Shape dough into 1-inch balls. Place about 2 inches apart on lightly greased cookie sheets; flatten each slightly. Bake at 350° for 10 minutes. Yield: about 5½ dozen.

The distinctive, lingering smell and taste of garlic are so pungent that a little goes a long way; but you would not want to be without it. It is an essential ingredient in many types of cooking, and you can easily grow an abundant supply in your garden.

A hardy perennial, garlic (*Allium sativum*) is a relative of the onion. It has flat, straplike leaves that grow 1 to 3 feet tall. The bulb is made up of 8 to 12 small cloves, which are used both for cooking and for propagation. Each clove has a papery covering, and the entire bulb is enclosed within a white skin. Since cloves are so easy to plant, garlic is rarely propagated from seed.

Garlic

Plant in early spring, 6 weeks before the last frost, for harvests in fall. Or set cloves out in late summer to harvest the following year in spring or early summer. In the Gulf South, it is best to plant in October.

Plant in full sun and a rich, deep soil. Space cloves 4 to 6 inches apart, making sure the pointed end is up, and cover with 3 inches of soil. When the flower stalk appears in early to midsummer, clip it off to allow the plant to put its energy into producing the bulb.

If you plant in late summer or early fall, garlic will produce foliage through the winter unless the weather is unusually severe. The bulbs may multiply to form a large bulb and several small ones by harvesttime. You can replant these small bulbs for next season's harvests.

The leaves of garlic make a wonderful addition to salads, imparting a mild garlic flavor. You

AT A GLANCE

Light: Full sun
Propagation: Cloves (segments of a bulb)
Spacing: True garlic, 4-6 inches between plants; elephant garlic, 12 inches
Part Used: Bulbs, leaves
Type of Plant: Perennial

Garlic planted in late summer produces foliage through the winter unless the weather is unusually cold. When leaves turn yellow and wither, the bulbs are ready to be harvested.

can use the leaves until the bulbs are large enough to harvest. But be careful not to take too much foliage from any one plant, or it will be weakened.

When the foliage has yellowed and withered, the bulbs are ready for harvest. Dig them and dry in a well-ventilated place out of direct sun for several days. You can also braid the tops and hang them to dry. Store loose bulbs in net bags, or freeze cloves, peeled or unpeeled.

Giant garlic or elephant garlic (*A. scorodoprasum*) has a milder flavor than true garlic, but produces larger bulbs. Foliage grows up to 3 feet tall and produces cloves the size of small tulip bulbs, with 5 cloves to a bulb. Like true garlic, the cloves can be planted in early spring or late summer. Plant them 12 inches apart, with the pointed end up, and cover with 3 inches of soil. Clip flower stalks as they appear. Harvest giant garlic as you would true garlic. There are often small bulblets growing at the base of the bulb. You can separate these from the bulbs and plant them like cloves. However, they will take 2 to 3 years to reach full size.

GARLIC PESTO

- 5 ounces fresh spinach
- 6 cloves garlic, crushed
- 1 cup fresh parsley sprigs
- ⅔ cup grated Parmesan cheese
- ½ cup finely chopped walnuts
- 4 anchovy filets
- 3 tablespoons minced fresh tarragon or 1 tablespoon dried whole tarragon
- 1 tablespoon minced fresh basil or 1 teaspoon dried whole basil
- ½ teaspoon salt
- ½ teaspoon pepper
- ¾ cup olive oil
- 1 (16-ounce) package thin spaghetti
  Pimiento strips (optional)
  Fresh basil leaves (optional)

Remove stems from spinach. Wash leaves thoroughly in lukewarm water; tear into bite-size pieces.

Position knife blade in food processor bowl; add spinach and next 9 ingredients, and top with cover; process until smooth. With processor running, pour oil through food chute in a slow steady stream until combined.

Prepare spaghetti according to package directions; drain well. Toss spaghetti with garlic mixture. Garnish with pimiento and basil leaves, if desired. Yield: 8 to 10 servings.

GARLIC BUTTER

- ½ cup butter or margarine, softened
- 2 or 3 cloves garlic, minced
- 2 tablespoons chopped fresh chives
  Dash of salt

Cream butter until light and fluffy; blend in remaining ingredients. Chill several hours before serving. Yield: ½ cup.

GARLIC SALAD DRESSING

- 1 cup vegetable oil
- ¼ cup red wine vinegar
- 2 tablespoons sugar
- 1 cup finely chopped green onions
- ⅔ cup catsup
- ½ cup chili sauce
- 4 cloves garlic, crushed
- 1 teaspoon salt
- 1 teaspoon paprika
  Juice of 1 lemon

Combine oil, vinegar, and sugar; beat with wire whisk until blended. Add remaining ingredients; mix well. Chill. Yield: about 3½ cups.

When you plant garlic, break up the bulb into cloves and set the cloves 3 inches deep and 4 to 6 inches apart.

Grown for its hot-tasting roots, horseradish thrives throughout the South. And once your planting is started, you can keep it going with little trouble.

Horseradish (*Amoracia rusticana*) is a hardy perennial. However, because it can take over the garden if left in place year after year, many gardeners grow it as an annual, digging roots every year in late fall and planting new roots or cuttings each spring.

Horseradish

The first foliage to appear in spring is feathery, followed by long, dark-green leaves. Plants are coarse textured and large, reaching a height of 2 to 3 feet. The main root is long, thick, and cylindrical, with rough, cream-colored skin and white flesh. The pencillike secondary roots that branch from the main root send up new plants around the mother plant.

Plant horseradish in full sun and rich, moist soil prepared to a depth of 10 inches. Remove rocks and clods, as any obstructions to growth will cause roots to be irregularly shaped and therefore more difficult to use.

You can start horseradish from whole roots, root cuttings, or crown divisions. Root cuttings

are the best method once you have a crop established, because you can use the main root for culinary purposes and start a new crop from the cuttings.

To start your first planting, you will probably have to purchase whole roots or root pieces (cuttings) from a mail-order source. Set them out in spring 4 weeks before the last frost. Space them 12 to 18 inches apart and set whole roots so the top is at ground level. Be careful not to bury the crown. Place root cuttings horizontally in a trench 3 to 5 inches deep, angling them so that the top end is deeper than the bottom end. Make sure the larger end of all the pieces points in the same direction, so that plants will be evenly spaced. Cover with soil to ground level.

AT A GLANCE

Light: Full sun
Propagation: Whole roots, root cuttings, crown divisions
Spacing: 12-18 inches between plants
Part Used: Roots, leaves
Type of Plant: Perennial
Serious Insects: Japanese beetles, cabbageworms

When planting a whole root, set it so that the top with its young leaves is at ground level.

Grow horseradish for the fiery flavor of the roots but take advantage of its ornamental value, too. The coarse texture contrasts well with fine-textured flowers or foliage of other herbs.

You can harvest young leaves in summer to add to salads; but do not pick too many, or you will weaken the plants. Roots are ready for harvest in fall, after the first hard frost. The flavor of horseradish is best after several freezes. In areas where the soil does not freeze, you can continue harvesting through winter. When you dig, be sure to get the whole root. Any pieces that remain in the ground will grow into new plants, but the spacing may be haphazard, making less efficient use of garden space. Unharvested roots will grow thicker and larger during the next season. Any left in place after 3 years should be dug and discarded, because they will be tough and woody.

In the Upper South and mountainous areas of the Middle South, dig the roots in late fall and store them for winter use. Also make root cuttings at this time for starting next year's crop.

Plants reach a height of 2 to 3 feet, with long, dark-green leaves. Plant in full sun for best growth.

Cut off the secondary roots, making the cuttings as long as possible. To help distinguish top from bottom, cut the top of each side shoot flat and the bottom at a slant. Tie the root pieces in bundles, pack them in damp sand or sawdust, and store in a cool place. Or store in a plastic bag in your vegetable crisper. (Store roots for winter use the same way.)

In early spring, plant the root cuttings or whole roots. Or you can make crown divisions. Cut the main root lengthwise into strips, making sure that each has a piece of root and a piece of crown. Plant as you would whole roots.

MUSTARD AND HORSERADISH CREAM
About ¼ cup freshly grated horseradish
½ teaspoon Dijon mustard
½ cup whipping cream, whipped

Fold horseradish and mustard into whipped cream. Cover and chill 15 minutes. Serve as a sandwich spread. Yield: about 2½ cups.

HORSERADISH SPREAD
1¼ cups commercial sour cream
2 tablespoons freshly grated horseradish
2 teaspoons lemon juice
¼ teaspoon salt
⅛ teaspoon pepper

Combine all ingredients; stir well. Serve on roast beef or ham sandwiches. Yield: about 1¼ cups.

VEGETABLE HORSERADISH DIP
½ cup commercial sour cream
½ cup mayonnaise
1 tablespoon vinegar
1 tablespoon freshly grated horseradish
1 small clove garlic, crushed
1 teaspoon grated onion
1 teaspoon sugar
1 teaspoon curry powder

Combine all ingredients; mix well. Serve with assorted vegetables. Yield: 1 cup.

• Use horseradish in sauces, spreads, dips, dressings, salads, and beef or lamb dishes.

• Use fresh horseradish, grated into sour cream, for a pleasant change from mustard.

• Grated horseradish will keep its pungency if you mix it with white vinegar (2 parts horseradish to 1 part vinegar) and store it in an airtight container in the refrigerator.

The delightful lemony fragrance of lemon balm is reason enough to grow this herb. You can enjoy its strong fruity scent all summer in the garden, and use the leaves for teas or potpourri.

Lemon balm (*Melissa officinalis*) is perennial throughout the South. A thick, bushy plant that grows up to 2 feet tall, it dies back in autumn, but returns in early spring. It is a relative of mint and has the same square stems with opposite, paired leaves. Small, inconspicuous white flowers appear throughout the summer.

Lemon Balm

Plant lemon balm in full sun or partial shade and well-drained soil. The further south you live, the more shade it needs. You can start from seeds, cuttings, or crown divisions. Or purchase transplants from a garden center or herb grower.

It is best to sow seeds in fall, about 4 weeks before the first frost. Sow seeds ½ inch deep where they are to grow and keep the soil evenly moist. They will germinate in fall, go dormant in winter, and resume growth when the weather warms. In spring, thin plants to 10 to 12 inches apart. Once the plants are started, they grow quickly. Be sure to water during dry spells to keep the soil moist, or the plants will wilt.

AT A GLANCE

Light: Sun to partial shade; full shade in Florida and along Gulf Coast
Propagation: Seeds, stem cuttings, crown divisions
Spacing: 10-12 inches between plants
Part Used: Leaves
Type of Plant: Perennial
Serious Insects: Whiteflies
Comments: In all areas, golden lemon balm needs filtered shade.

The leaves are best used fresh, when their lemony fragrance is strongest; but you can also dry the foliage.

Lemon balm is thick and bushy, growing up to 2 feet tall.

You can divide established plants in spring or fall. Lift a clump and slice it apart with a knife or shovel, making sure that each slice includes a piece of the crown and root. You can also make stem cuttings in spring or summer.

Harvest leaves anytime to use them fresh. Bundles of fresh sprigs can be used to make a delightful lemony tea. You can also dry lemon balm, but leaves will not be as strongly scented as when fresh. The best time to harvest foliage for drying is just before the flowers begin to open. The essential oils will be most concentrated then. Harvest a few leaves at a time, or cut the entire plant to 2 inches above the ground. The plants will put out new growth for at least 2 more such harvests per season. Cutting back leggy plants helps keep them bushy. Rinse harvested plants in warm water and pat dry. Strip leaves from stems before drying. (*See page 214.*) You can also freeze leaves to use in tea.

If your lemon balm patch begins to grow out-of-bounds, divide clumps in early spring when new growth first appears.

Selections

Golden lemon balm (*Melissa officinalis* Variegata) is a more prostrate form of lemon balm, with golden variegated leaves and a lighter lemon scent. It is an evergreen perennial in mild winters in the Middle and Lower South. In full sun, golden lemon balm loses its variegated markings; some strains go completely green in the summer, even in shade, showing the variegation only in early spring or late fall.

SYLLABUB WITH LEMON BALM

2½ cups whipping cream
⅔ cup sweet white wine
3 tablespoons crushed fresh lemon balm
Grated rind of 1 lemon
Juice of 1 lemon
2 teaspoons sugar
Grated nutmeg

Beat together first 6 ingredients until thickened. Cover and chill 2 hours. Spoon into frosted glasses. Garnish with nutmeg. Yield: 5½ cups.

LEMON BALMADE

½ cup fresh lemon balm leaves, crushed
½ cup fresh mint leaves, crushed
½ cup honey
½ cup lemon juice, chilled
½ cup orange juice, chilled
4 quarts ginger ale, chilled

Combine all ingredients, except ginger ale; mix well. Cover and chill 1 hour; strain, discarding leaves. Stir in ginger ale. Yield: about 1 gallon.

LEMON BALM PUNCH

¼ cup sugar
¼ cup water
¾ cup fresh lemon balm leaves, finely chopped
½ cup fresh mint leaves, finely chopped
½ cup lemon juice
4 quarts ginger ale, chilled

Combine sugar and water in a small bowl; stir until sugar dissolves. Add lemon balm, mint, and lemon juice; stir gently. Cover and chill 8 hours or overnight.

Strain syrup mixture, discarding leaves, into a large pitcher or punch bowl; stir in ginger ale. Yield: 1 gallon.

• Steep lemon balm leaves in boiling water for a delicate, aromatic drink.

• Try using lemon balm in stuffings for lamb or pork, or to cover a chicken before roasting.

Marjoram

Marjoram is one of the most versatile of herbs. Its pleasant odor and warm aromatic taste add a delicious mellow flavor to all types of meats, egg dishes, soups, and vegetables. Sweet marjoram (*Origanum majorana*) is the most widely grown selection of marjoram. Another popular type is evergreen marjoram (*Origanum majoricum*).

Sweet Marjoram

Sweet marjoram is a tender perennial. Because the roots are susceptible to frost damage, it must be treated as an annual in the Middle and Upper South. In the Lower South, it will survive winter with a protective mulch. However, in the Gulf South, it may be killed by hot, humid summers.

Sweet marjoram is an upright bushy plant that grows to 12 inches in height. The flower buds, which appear in early summer, look like small knots along the stem, giving the plant its alternate name of "knotted marjoram." The open blooms range in color from white to lilac.

Plant sweet marjoram in well-drained soil and partial shade. You can propagate it from seeds or cuttings. The seeds germinate rapidly, but the seedlings are weak and subject to damping off. Sow them indoors in a sterile mix, and keep them shaded from direct sun until they are well started. Plant seedlings in the garden when they are 2 to 3 inches tall and the danger of frost is past. You can also start from cuttings, which root easily, or buy transplants.

AT A GLANCE

Light: Full sun to partial shade
Propagation: Seeds, cuttings, divisions
Spacing: 6-10 inches between plants
Part Used: Leaves
Type of Plant: Sweet marjoram, tender perennial; evergreen marjoram, perennial
Serious Insects: Whiteflies

Sweet marjoram is an upright bushy plant that grows as a perennial in the Lower South. Elsewhere, treat it like an annual.

You can begin harvesting sweet marjoram four to six weeks after transplanting it into the garden. Just pick fresh leaves as needed. For drying, harvest after the buds have formed but before they bloom. Cut no more than half of the leaves on the plant at one time. A second cutting can be made when flowers begin to form again later in the season. Marjoram retains its full flavor when dried. (*See page 214.*) Strip leaves from the stems after drying.

Evergreen Marjoram

This species takes sun or partial shade and prefers well-drained soil. It is an evergreen perennial in the Middle and Lower South and will keep its leaves through mild winters in the Upper South. You can propagate it by taking cuttings or divisions in early spring.

• Use marjoram lightly for a delicious, mellow flavor.

• Marjoram is particularly good with vegetables such as beans, peas, carrots, and spinach.

MARJORAM PATE

    4 slices bacon
    2 pounds ground pork
    ½ pound chicken livers, finely chopped
    1 cup finely chopped onion
    ⅓ cup shelled salted pistachios, coarsely chopped
    ¼ cup chopped fresh marjoram or 1½ tablepoons
         dried whole marjoram
    ¼ cup brandy
    1 egg
    1 clove garlic, crushed
    2 teaspoons salt
    ⅛ teaspoon pepper
         Pinch of ground allspice
    4 slices bacon

Arrange 4 slices bacon, evenly spaced, crosswise in a 9- x 5- x 3-inch loafpan, allowing ends to come up sides.

Combine remaining ingredients, except remaining bacon; mix well. Spoon into loafpan; place remaining bacon lengthwise across top.

Cover with aluminum foil; bake at 350° for 1 hour. Remove foil; bake 30 additional minutes. Cool 10 minutes. Pour off drippings. Cover and chill 8 hours or overnight. Unmold before serving. Slice thin; serve with assorted crackers. Yield: 1 loaf.

ZESTY MEAT LOAF

    1 tablespoon minced fresh marjoram or 1 teaspoon
         dried whole marjoram
    ¼ cup milk
    2 pounds ground beef
    2 cups soft breadcrumbs
    1 medium onion, chopped
    ¼ cup minced green pepper
    2 eggs, beaten
    3 tablespoons prepared horseradish
    1 teaspoon salt
    1 teaspoon dry mustard
    1 tablespoon Worcestershire sauce
    ½ cup catsup

Crush marjoram using the back of a wooden spoon; add milk. Let stand 10 minutes.

Combine marjoram mixture and remaining ingredients, except catsup, in a large mixing bowl; mix well. Place mixture in a 9- x 5- x 3-inch loafpan, and shape into a loaf; pour catsup over top. Bake at 375° for 1 hour and 15 minutes or until done. Yield: 8 servings.

Sweet marjoram is often called knotted marjoram because the flower buds look like small knots along the stem.

Herbs 243

Everyone recognizes the cool, refreshing scent of mint. You only have to brush against the leaves to release the delicious fragrance. Mint is a wonderful addition to everything from lamb to iced drinks, and it is one of the easiest herbs to grow. Your biggest problem may be choosing which of the many types to add to your garden.

Mint (*Mentha sp.*) is a perennial. Most types die back in winter, except pineapple mint, which is evergreen in the mild winters of the Lower South. All types have square stems with opposite-paired leaves.

Mint grows and spreads rapidly by means of stems that creep above and just below the surface of the soil. It will spread to form large patches, so choose a site where you can restrict its growth. You may even want to use an edging to keep plants from spreading, or plant mint in clay pots and sink the pots in the ground. Spearmint, peppermint, orange mint, and curly mint are the most rapid spreaders. Apple mint is much slower, with pineapple mint and Corsican mint the tamest.

Mint

Plant mint in an area where it will get plenty of moisture. It prefers full sun or partial shade and fertile soil.

You can propagate mint by several methods. Using seed is not recommended, because mint cross-pollinates so readily that it rarely comes true from seed. Instead, start with young plants that you buy at a nursery, root stem cuttings, or dig plants from a friend's patch. Mint propagates itself by runners. As these runners creep along and form a mat, they root and send up new plants. After the last spring frost, move a few of these new plants to your garden. Leave at least 1 foot between plants of the same type and 4 feet between different types.

Mint blooms in late spring or summer, with whorls of small flowers. To conserve the energy of the plant, cut the flowers before they open.

To keep the mint bed tidy and prevent its becoming overcrowded, clean it out in the spring. Dig around the edge of the bed and in between plants, thrusting a shovel or spade into the ground to cut the runners between plants. Also, remove and transplant any runners that have wandered out-of-bounds. Through the rest of the season, mint needs little special attention.

Eventually, the flavor and fragrance of a patch of mint will diminish and the patch may begin to die out. To keep yours going, lift and reset the plants in a new site every 3 or 4 years.

AT A GLANCE

Light: Full sun or partial shade
Propagation: Runners
Spacing: 1 foot between plants of the same type, 4 feet between different types
Part Used: Leaves
Type of Plant: Perennial
Serious Insects and Diseases: Whiteflies, blackflies, snails and slugs when plants are young; rust

To grow a border of mint this lush and healthy, be sure to supply plenty of moisture and cut the plants back just before they bloom.

Mint can be harvested anytime from early spring into late fall. The flavor in the leaves is most concentrated just before flowering, so you may want to make a big harvest then, cutting the entire plant to just above the first or second pair of leaves. The lower leaves are beginning to yellow around this time too, so cutting the plant back neatens the garden and produces bushier plants. You can usually make three such harvests per season.

Use mint fresh, dried, or frozen. (*See page 214.*)

Selections

Some of the most popular types include the following.

Peppermint (*M. x piperita*) is the source of true peppermint flavor. It has narrow, dark-green leaves with purple stems, and reaches a height of about 2 feet.

Orange mint or bergamot (*M. x piperita* Citrata) is one of the most fragrant of the mints, with a delightful citrusy aroma. It grows 1 to 2 feet tall with reddish green stems, purple-edged leaves, and purple flowers. It spreads rapidly.

Spearmint (*M. spicata*) is the mint used in spearmint flavors and mint sauces. It grows 2 to 2½ feet tall with reddish stems and heavily veined, finely toothed, pointed leaves and lavender flowers. Spearmint spreads rapidly and in very mild winters may be evergreen.

Apple mint (*M. suaveolens*) has rounded woolly leaves that give off a slight apple scent. It grows 2 to 3 feet tall, with upright, stiff stems and gray-white blossoms that shade to pink. It does better than any other mint under dry conditions and spreads only moderately.

Pineapple mint (*M. suaveolens* Variegata) has cream-and-green-splotched leaves with a pleasant, fruity aroma. It will reach 18 inches in height and needs partial shade to retain its coloration. In mild winters, it is evergreen but should be mulched for protection. Pineapple mint spreads slowly.

Corsican mint (*M. requienii*) has an intense crème de menthe fragrance. It spreads slowly, creeping along the ground, rarely over ½ inch tall. Its bright-green, round leaves are less than ¼ inch in diameter, and it bears tiny purple flowers. This mint needs partial shade and plenty of moisture. It is not very cold hardy and may need some protection in winter.

Curly mint (*M. aquatica* Crispa) has bright-green, crinkled leaves with a crisp spearmint flavor. It grows up to 2 feet and has a sprawling growth habit. Flowers are pale purple.

MINT SAUCE

½ cup vinegar
1 cup water
½ cup chopped fresh mint leaves, divided
½ cup water
¼ cup lemon juice
2½ tablespoons sugar
Dash of salt

Combine vinegar, 1 cup water, and ¼ cup mint in a small saucepan; bring to a boil. Reduce heat and simmer until liquid is reduced by half; strain. Add ½ cup water, lemon juice, sugar, and salt. Chill. To serve, stir in remaining ¼ cup mint and serve over fish or lamb. Yield: about 1½ cups.

MINT GLAZED CARROTS WITH PEAS

3 medium carrots, scraped and sliced
⅓ cup butter or margarine
⅓ cup sugar
1 tablespoon chopped fresh mint leaves
1 (10-ounce) package frozen English peas, thawed or 1 cup fresh English peas, cooked

Cook carrots in small amount of boiling water 5 to 8 minutes or until crisp-tender; drain. Add butter; cook over medium heat 5 minutes, stirring constantly. Add sugar and mint; cook, stirring often, until carrots are glazed. Stir in peas. Yield: 4 to 6 servings.

One way to contain mints that are rampant spreaders is to plant them in partially sunken containers. Even a flue liner can be used as a container.

Herbs 245

Oregano

What would spaghetti be without oregano? The pungent flavor of this classic seasoning is an essential ingredient in Italian dishes, as well as in French, Mexican, and other ethnic cuisine.

Because not all oreganos are good for cooking, you must be selective. Oregano can be grown from seeds, but plants often cross-pollinate and you cannot be sure that seedlings will be the flavor you want.

It is best to purchase plants or to divide established plants. You can also take stem cuttings in the spring or fall. And most types of oregano send out runners that will layer naturally to start new plants. You can separate these and transplant them.

Although oregano (*Origanum sp.*) is classified as a perennial, some types must be treated as annuals in the Upper South. Plant in well-drained soil with full sun to partial shade.

Cut oregano often to keep plants producing tender new growth. For a large harvest for drying, wait until just before plants bloom and cut the stems above the lowest set of leaves. New foliage will sprout and you can make another cutting in late summer. Do not harvest within a month before the first expected frost, however; the plants need time to reestablish themselves before cold weather. Strip leaves from stems after drying. (*See page 214.*)

There are several types of oregano; some are easily confused with marjoram unless you are familiar with their taste. Also note that some oreganos are evergreen in the South, while others are tender and will be killed by frost.

Selections

Greek oregano (*O. vulgare* Hirtum) is native to Greece, as its name indicates. It is a tender perennial; you will need to protect plants with mulch over the winter in the Lower South. In the Middle and Upper South, treat it as an annual. Greek oregano has a trailing habit, and is grown for its sharp, biting flavor. It grows up to 12 inches tall, with small, bright-green leaves and white flowers. If grown with other selections, it will be overrun by the coarser ones. To promote a bushier plant, you may want to cut it back to one-third its size in late spring.

Wild marjoram (*O. vulgare*) is a hardy perennial remaining evergreen through mild winters in the South. It is the most common oregano grown. Plants are bushy and shrublike, growing 1 to 3 feet tall. The dark-green leaves are broad, oval, and 1 inch long; plants bear lavender or pink flowers in clusters.

Oregano is the classic seasoning for Italian, French, and Mexican cooking. Grow it in full sun or partial shade.

AT A GLANCE

Light: Full sun to partial shade
Propagation: Cuttings, divisions, layering
Spacing: 16 inches between plants
Part Used: Leaves
Type of Plant: Perennial
Serious Insects: Whiteflies

You can start wild marjoram from stem cuttings or divisions, but the best method is cuttings. They root quickly and take less time to produce a sizeable plant than other methods. Once plants are established, they will self-sow if allowed. In spring, before new growth begins, cut out dead stems. Keep plants pinched back to encourage bushiness.

Golden creeping oregano (*O. vulgare* Golden Creeping) and erect golden oregano (*O. vulgare* Aureum) are forms of wild marjoram. While their yellow leaves are attractive, they are not good for culinary use.

Pot marjoram (*O. onites*) is not marjoram at all, but another selection of oregano. It has a sharp flavor that is stronger than other types.

Pot marjoram is a shrubby perennial, growing up to 2 feet tall with small gray-green leaves. It is best used fresh. In the Upper South, pot marjoram is tender and must be grown as an annual.

Most types of oregano have a trailing growth habit, and the runners easily take root to start new plants.

MARINATED OREGANO MUSHROOMS

2 pounds small fresh mushrooms
¾ cup cider vinegar
½ cup vegetable oil
3 tablespoons chopped fresh oregano or 1 tablespoon dried whole oregano
1½ tablespoons minced fresh thyme or two teaspoons dried whole thyme
1½ teaspoons minced fresh chervil or ½ teaspoon dried whole chervil
½ teaspoon peppercorns
1 clove garlic
1 bay leaf
Chopped fresh parsley

Clean mushrooms with damp paper towels. Combine mushrooms with next 8 ingredients; cover and chill. Drain well, and sprinkle with parsley. Yield: 8 to 10 servings.

ITALIAN EGGPLANT

2 small eggplants, peeled and cut into ½-inch slices
2 eggs, slightly beaten
1 cup fine, dry breadcrumbs
Vegetable oil
⅔ cup chopped onion
1 or 2 cloves garlic, minced
2 tablespoons olive oil
1 (29-ounce) can tomato sauce
1 tablespoon minced fresh basil or 1 teaspoon dried whole basil
1 tablespoon minced fresh oregano or 1 teaspoon dried whole oregano
¼ teaspoon coarsely ground black pepper
2 tablespoons grated Parmesan cheese
10 ounces sliced mozzarella cheese

Dip eggplant slices in egg and coat in breadcrumbs; fry in hot vegetable oil (350°) until golden brown. Drain on paper towels and set aside.

Sauté onion and garlic in olive oil until onion is tender. Stir in tomato sauce, basil, oregano, and pepper; simmer 5 minutes. Remove from heat.

Pour one-third of sauce into a lightly greased 13- x 9- x 2-inch baking dish. Arrange half of eggplant slices on top of sauce; sprinkle with Parmesan cheese. Top with half of mozzarella cheese; spoon one-third of sauce on top of mozzarella. Top with remaining eggplant, remaining mozzarella cheese, and remaining sauce. Bake at 350° for 30 minutes. Yield: 8 to 10 servings.

• Use oregano with Italian dishes, meat, cheese, fish, eggs, fresh and cooked tomatoes, zucchini, snap beans, and in marinades.

• Sprinkle oregano lightly over tossed salad before adding the dressing.

Parsley

Many people think of parsley as an attractive garnish that is simply discarded after the meal. But parsley has a distinctive, mild peppery taste that enhances a variety of dishes. And the fresh leaves and stems can be eaten as a natural breath freshener. (In fact, most of the flavor is in the stems.)

Parsley (*Petroselinum crispum*) is a biennial, germinating and growing the first year and then blooming, setting seed, and dying the second year. In the Middle and Lower South, it stays green through the winter, but in the Upper South, parsley dies back. In all regions, it is best to plant a new crop of parsley each year so you will have a constant supply.

Depending on the selection, plants have curly or flat leaves and grow 1 to 2 feet in height. Borne in tall umbels, the flowers are inconspicuous, but if allowed, they may set seed and self-sow.

Plant in sun or partial shade in a moist, well-drained soil. You can start parsley from purchased transplants or grow your own from seed. Parsley seeds are slow to germinate; soaking them in water for 24 hours before planting helps speed the process, but even after soaking, the seeds will take several weeks to sprout. Start seeds indoors 4 to 6 weeks before the last frost and set them out 2 weeks after the last frost. Be sure to set out while the seedlings are young, because plants develop a long taproot that makes later transplanting difficult.

In the Gulf South, plant in fall instead of spring; summer rains followed by high temperatures can kill parsley. Never let parsley get so dry that it wilts. This causes the edges to turn yellow.

Parsley makes a good border plant in the garden. Because it is a biennial, you will need to start a new crop every year to have a continuous supply.

AT A GLANCE

Light: Full sun to partial shade
Propagation: Seeds, transplants
Spacing: 6-8 inches between plants
Part Used: Leaves, tender stems
Type of Plant: Biennial
Serious Insects: Parsleyworms, whiteflies
Comments: In the Gulf South, sow seeds in early fall for best results.

Harvest the fresh leaves and stems as you need them. Snip the leaf stalks from the outside edge of the crown, cutting at the base, not more than 1 inch above the soil. This low clipping encourages bushier plants. The flower stalk can be eaten like celery. If you keep the flower stalks cut, the plants may last several years.

To store parsley for winter use in the Upper South, freeze sprigs or dry them in a microwave.

Selections

Curly parsley (*P. crispum* var. Crispum) is commonly used for garnishing and seasoning. It has bright-green, tightly curled leaves and grows 10 to 12 inches tall. Selections include Extra Curled Dwarf and Evergreen (green through mild winters, even in the Upper South).

Italian parsley (*P. crispum* var. Neapolitan) is used primarily for seasoning. It has flat leaves and will grow up to 2 feet. It dries more easily than the curly-leaved selections.

Hamburg parsley (*P. crispum* var. tuberosum) is less common and is grown for its edible root.

Remember that the stems are as flavorful as the leaves. Eaten fresh, parsley acts as a natural breath freshener.

TABOULI

2 cups uncooked bulgur wheat
1½ cups hot water
2 medium tomatoes, peeled and chopped
1 medium onion, minced
1 cup chopped fresh parsley
3 tablespoons chopped fresh coriander or cilantro leaves
2 to 3 tablespoons chopped fresh mint leaves
1 clove garlic, crushed
2 tablespoons olive oil
1 teaspoon salt
½ teaspoon pepper

Combine bulgur and 1½ cups hot water; stir well and let stand 30 minutes. Add remaining ingredients; cover and chill several hours or overnight. Yield: 8 to 10 servings.

SWISS OVEN OMELET

6 slices bacon
⅓ cup finely chopped onion
8 eggs, beaten
1 cup milk
1 teaspoon salt
¼ teaspoon pepper
2 tablespoons chopped fresh parsley
2 cups (8 ounces) shredded Swiss cheese

Cook bacon until transparent; remove bacon, reserving 1 tablespoon drippings in skillet; drain bacon on paper towels. Sauté onion in drippings until tender. Remove onion with a slotted spoon and set aside.

Combine eggs, milk, salt, and pepper; beat with a wire whisk. Stir in onion and parsley. Pour into a lightly greased 1½-quart baking dish; top with cheese and bacon. Bake at 350° for 30 to 35 minutes; serve immediately. Yield: 4 to 6 servings.

Two popular types of parsley are Italian (left) and curly (right). Italian is most often used for seasoning; it dries more easily than the curly-leaved type.

Rub the leaves of rosemary, and the air will be filled with the familiar piney fragrance for which the herb is famous. The strong flavor combines well with other herbs and if used sparingly, it is a light accent for soups, poultry, stews, and sauces.

Rosemary (*Rosmarinus officinalis*) is slow-growing and bushy, reaching 3 to 4 feet in height after several years of growth. The stems, which become woody with age, are covered with green needlelike foliage. The leaves have a grayish cast because of 2 white bands on the underside. Flower color and blooming time depend on the selection.

This evergreen perennial thrives without protection in the Lower South. In the Upper South, grow it in a large pot that you can bring indoors in the winter. (*See below.*) In the Middle South, it may be damaged by severe winters, so plant it

Rosemary

beside a south-facing masonry wall. This will absorb the sun's warmth and radiate the heat at night; and it will shield the plant from north winds. In all regions, winter winds can be damaging. If you live in a windy location, choose a protected spot for your rosemary.

Rosemary requires moist, well-drained soil. It cannot survive drought but is susceptible to root rot if kept too wet. Plants prefer full sun but tolerate partial shade.

Rosemary grows well in containers. During the summer, plunge the container into the ground. When the weather begins to turn cold, lift the pot and move it to a protected location or bring it indoors and put it in a cool spot with bright sunlight. Mist the foliage regularly.

To start rosemary, purchase small plants from a nursery, or obtain stem cuttings from a gardening friend. Starting from seed is not practical for home gardeners. Seeds are slow to germinate and the germination rate is poor. It takes 3 years to produce a good-sized plant from seed.

Take stem cuttings in spring. (*See page 210.*) Once you have a planting started, layering is an almost foolproof method of obtaining new plants. (*See page 211.*)

AT A GLANCE

Light: Full sun to partial shade
Propagation: Stem cuttings, layering
Spacing: 2-3 feet between plants
Part Used: Leaves
Type of Plant: Tender perennial
Serious Diseases: Powdery mildew

The key to growing rosemary is a well-drained soil that stays evenly moist. Plants do not tolerate drought nor soggy soil.

Rosemary grows well in containers. In the Upper South, you will need to bring it indoors in winter.

For fresh use, cut stems anytime. If you want to dry the leaves, harvest in early spring just before the plant blooms. The flavor will be stronger then, and it is the best time to prune plants. Dry stems on a rack or bunch together several sprigs and hang them to dry. After they are dry, strip the leaves from the stem.

Selections

Many selections of rosemary are available. Most have a similar erect growth habit. The creeping rosemaries are an exception. These selections rarely grow taller than 1 to 2 feet, with shorter, narrower leaves. They need the same care as the common type but are not as cold hardy. In fact, the prostrate types should be grown in containers or hanging baskets that can be moved to a protected location. Only in the Gulf South and warmer regions of the Lower South can they grow well in the ground.

Selections of rosemary also vary in flavor. Read catalog descriptions carefully. For culinary use, avoid the strongly pine-scented selections.

While most types have pale-lavender flowers, selections of rosemary such as Beneden Blue, Collingwood Ingram, Logee's Blue, and Tuscan Blue have blue blooms that are quite showy. There are also types with pink flowers and white flowers.

Unlike most herbs, rosemary has a stronger flavor when fresh than when dried. Cut sprigs anytime for fresh use.

MIXED HERB VINEGAR

½ cup chopped fresh rosemary
½ cup chopped fresh thyme
4 shallots, thinly sliced
1 sprig fresh parsley, chopped
12 peppercorns
3¾ cups white vinegar (5% acidity)
   Sprigs of fresh rosemary and thyme (optional)

Place first 5 ingredients in a wide-mouth glass jar. Place vinegar in a medium saucepan; bring to a boil. Pour vinegar over herbs; cover with metal lids and screw bands tight. Let stand at room temperature for 2 weeks.

Strain vinegar into decorative jars, discarding herb residue; add additional sprigs of fresh rosemary and thyme, if desired. Seal jars with a cork or other airtight lid. Yield: 4 cups.

ROSEMARY-LEMON COOKIES

1 cup all-purpose flour
½ cup butter or margarine
½ cup sugar
1 egg yolk, beaten
½ teaspoon vanilla extract
2 tablespoons minced fresh rosemary
1¾ teaspoons grated lemon rind
   Powdered sugar

Combine flour and butter in a bowl; cut in butter with pastry blender until mixture resembles coarse meal. Add sugar, mixing well. Add egg yolk, vanilla, rosemary, and lemon rind. Blend well.

Roll dough to ⅛-inch thickness between sheets of waxed paper. Sprinkle one side of cookie dough with powdered sugar. Cut dough with a 2-inch cookie cutter; place on ungreased cookie sheets with sugar side up. Bake at 350° for 10 minutes. Yield: 3 dozen.

ROSEMARY CHICKEN

8 boneless chicken breast halves
¼ cup minced onion
½ teaspoon salt
¼ teaspoon minced fresh rosemary or ½ teaspoon dried whole rosemary
⅛ teaspoon pepper
1 tablespoon all-purpose flour or cornstarch
2 cups orange juice
   Hot cooked medium egg noodles

Place chicken in 12- x 8- x 2-inch baking dish. Sprinkle with onion, salt, rosemary, and pepper. Combine flour and orange juice; mix well and pour over chicken. Bake at 350° for 45 minutes to 1 hour, basting occasionally with pan juices. Arrange chicken over noodles; pour pan juices over chicken. Yield: 8 servings.

Sage

Holiday turkey just does not taste right without a pinch of sage in the stuffing. It is sage that gives the dressing its characteristic flavor. The strong, aromatic smell and sharp taste can easily overwhelm other flavors, so use it sparingly. Sage is easy to grow, and the gray green or variegated foliage adds color to the garden.

Garden sage (*Salvia officinalis*) is the most commonly grown selection. A small, sprawling shrub, it grows 2 to 3 feet tall, with pebbled, gray green leaves. Garden sage is a hardy perennial, and the leaves linger on the stems through the winter. In late spring, spikes of pinkish purple flowers appear. Garden sage usually does not survive the hot, humid summers of the Lower South. In this region, dwarf sage and other selections will be more reliable.

Plant sage in well-drained, sandy soil and full sun. You can propagate it by seeds or cuttings. Sow seeds in spring or early fall. For a spring planting, start them indoors 6 to 8 weeks before the last frost and set out transplants when the ground is warm. Or sow them directly in the garden after danger of frost is past, planting them about ¼ inch deep. Seedlings should appear in 2 to 3 weeks. When they are about 2 inches tall, thin to 18 to 24 inches apart. You can also root stem cuttings of sage in fall or spring, or layer side branches.

The foliage of sage looks lifeless through winter and into spring, so each year in early spring, prune plants back, cutting out the oldest growth. This helps stimulate new growth.

Sage will also grow well in 8-inch pots. Dig small plants from the garden or sow seeds in a container and place the pots in full sun. Make sure the soil is well drained.

You can begin harvesting sage the first year, but harvest only lightly. After the first year, harvest as needed; frequent harvesting helps keep the plant shapely. Pinch a leaf at a time, or if you need more sage, cut an entire stem. Allow 2 months between the last big harvest and the first frost.

You can use sage fresh, dried, or frozen. To dry sage, hang stems in bunches; when leaves are dry, strip them from the stem and store. To grind the dried leaves, rub them between your palms; this produces the fluffy, cottony material that is marketed as rubbed sage.

Selections

Tricolor sage (*S. officinalis* Tricolor) grows up to 15 inches and has gray leaves streaked with purple and white. It has the same flavor as garden sage, but is less cold hardy.

AT A GLANCE

Light: Full sun
Propagation: Seeds, cuttings
Spacing: 18-24 inches between plants
Part Used: Leaves
Type of Plant: Perennial
Serious Diseases: Mildew
Comments: Pineapple sage is not hardy except in the Gulf South, where it should be cut to the ground in fall and mulched. Elsewhere plant it as a summer annual.

Harvest sage lightly the first year, while it is becoming established. After that, harvest leaves as needed.

Purple sage (*S. officinalis* Purpurea) grows up to 15 inches with purplish leaves. It has the same flavor as garden sage but is slightly hardier.

Dwarf sage (*S. officinalis* Compacta) grows up to 8 inches in height and is a miniature of garden sage, with the same gray green color and traditional flavor. It is often used in confined areas and as a winter houseplant. Dwarf sage performs better in Southern gardens and is more attractive year-round than garden sage.

Golden sage (*S. officinalis* Aurea) grows up to 15 inches with yellow-edged leaves.

Pineapple sage (*S. elegans*) grows 3 to 5 feet tall and is known for its delicious pineapple scent and the bright-red flowers that appear in late summer or early fall. The plant grows as an upright shrub with rough, pointed dark-green leaves. Unlike garden sage, it is a tender perennial. Propagate pineapple sage from cuttings or divisions. In the Middle and Upper South, take cuttings each fall to root indoors and overwinter for planting outdoors next spring. In the Gulf South, cut plants back to the ground in fall and mulch over the winter. It will do well in any garden soil and prefers full sun to partial shade. Pineapple sage is best used fresh.

SAGED SAUSAGE BALLS

1 pound mild bulk pork sausage
2 cups biscuit mix
2 cups (8 ounces) shredded mild Cheddar cheese
1 tablespoon chopped fresh sage or 1 teaspoon rubbed sage
2 dashes hot sauce

Combine all ingredients, mixing well (mixture will be stiff). Shape into 1-inch balls; place on ungreased baking sheets. Bake at 400° for 15 minutes or until lightly browned. Yield: about 4½ dozen.

SAGE BUTTERMILK CORN MUFFINS

1½ cups all-purpose flour
1½ cups yellow cornmeal
1 tablespoon baking powder
1½ teaspoons baking soda
1½ teaspoons salt
1½ cups buttermilk
3 eggs, beaten
¼ cup plus 2 tablespoons butter or margarine, melted
3 tablespoons minced fresh sage or 1 tablespoon rubbed sage

Combine first 5 ingredients in a large bowl; make a well in center of mixture. Combine buttermilk, eggs, butter, and sage; add to dry ingredients, stirring just until moistened. Spoon into lightly greased muffin pans, filling two-thirds full. Bake at 425° for 15 to 20 minutes. Yield: 1½ dozen.

BAKED STUFFED SQUASH BOATS

6 medium-size yellow squash
1 cup fine, dry breadcrumbs
1 cup cornbread crumbs
½ cup minced onion
1 cup milk
1 egg, beaten
2 to 3 tablespoons minced fresh sage or 2 teaspoons rubbed sage
½ teaspoon salt
¼ cup vegetable oil

Wash squash thoroughly; cover with salted water and bring to a boil. Reduce heat, cover, and simmer 10 minutes or until tender but still firm. Drain and cool slightly. Trim off stems. Cut squash in half lengthwise; remove and reserve pulp, leaving a firm shell. Place squash shells in a 13- x 9- x 2-inch baking dish.

Combine squash pulp and next 7 ingredients, mixing well. Spoon sage mixture into squash shells; drizzle oil over stuffed squash. Cover and bake at 350° for 15 minutes; remove cover, and bake 15 additional minutes. Yield: 12 servings.

You can use the foliage fresh or dried. Or store it in the freezer for winter use.

The name savory automatically conjures up a description of good things to eat. Its sharp, spicy taste and strong, pleasant fragrance make it a favorite in the kitchen. A versatile herb in cooking, it is used in sauces, vinegars, meat stuffings, stews, soups, and vegetables. Often called the "green bean herb," it is a must with snap beans.

Savory

There are two types of savory: summer savory (*Satureja hortensis*) and winter savory (*S. montana*). The two taste much the same, but have different growth habits and uses. Summer savory, which is an annual, is the preferred herb because of its mild, delicate flavor. It is not available year-round, however, and does not retain its flavor well when dried. In the Gulf South, it may go to seed very quickly, providing only a short harvest period. Winter savory is a perennial and has a much stronger, pungent flavor. In the Lower South and during mild winters in the Middle South, winter savory is evergreen and so is available for harvesting year-round. The flavor of soft, new growth is very good. In addition, winter savory retains its flavor well when dried.

Summer Savory

Summer savory grows quickly to reach a height of 18 inches. It has narrow, ½-inch-long leaves that grow in pairs on short, branching stems. The plant tends to be top-heavy when it is mature. In summer, small, pinkish white flowers appear.

Plant summer savory in full sun to partial shade and a well-drained soil. It needs a lot of moisture. Seedlings transplant well, so you can start them indoors 2 weeks before the last expected frost and set them out when plants are 4 weeks old. Or sow seeds outdoors after frost, planting them only ⅛ inch deep. When seedlings are 2 to 3 inches tall, thin to 10 to 12 inches apart. To have cuttings for the kitchen all summer, make several successive sowings 3 weeks apart. To provide some support for the weak stems, set forked branches next to the plants after thinning. Or plant in 3 rows spaced 2 feet apart. Adjacent plants will hold each other up.

You can begin harvesting when the plant is only 6 inches tall. Since summer savory grows so quickly, you can frequently pinch the plant back. This gives you continuous harvests and also encourages the plant to sprout new leaves and remain bushy.

Winter Savory

Winter savory has shiny, dark-green, pointed leaves and a low, sprawling growth habit, reaching only 12 inches in height. Plants bloom about a month earlier than summer savory. In fall, the plant turns a reddish color.

AT A GLANCE

Light: Full sun to partial shade
Propagation: Seeds, stem cuttings; also root divisions and layering for winter savory
Spacing: 10-12 inches between plants
Part Used: Leaves
Type of Plant: Summer savory, annual; winter savory, perennial
Comments: Winter savory declines after several years, so plan to replace plants every 2 to 3 years.

Winter savory has a low, sprawling growth habit and is evergreen in the Lower South.

Plant in full sun in the Gulf South. Elsewhere, plant in full sun to partial shade. If the soil is too rich, plants will be too succulent and will not survive the winter. A soil that is too wet promotes root rot.

Propagate winter savory from seeds, cuttings, divisions, or by layering. Seeds take 2 to 3 weeks to germinate and plants take 2 years to reach flowering size. Sow seeds outdoors about 4 weeks before the first fall frost, barely covering them with soil. Or start them indoors 6 to 8 weeks before the last frost to set out after the last frost. Space plants 10 to 12 inches apart.

Winter savory can also be propagated by cuttings from side shoots, dividing clumps in fall or early spring, or layering. (*See page 210.*) Plants need little care, except pruning of woody growth in spring to keep plants compact and neat looking. Plants will begin to decline after several years, so plan to replace them every 2 to 3 years.

Harvest sprigs of winter savory whenever you need them. For major harvests, cut the plant back in midsummer and early fall. Do not cut winter savory heavily as cold weather approaches, however.

Winter savory retains much of its flavor when dried. Simply hang the branches until crisp and then strip the leaves from the stems.

Dwarf winter savory (*S. montana* Pygmaea) grows only 4 inches tall and is good for pots.

SAVORY CARROT SOUP

1 medium onion, chopped
2 tablespoons butter or margarine, melted
4 carrots, scraped and coarsely chopped
4 cups chicken broth
1 (2- x 1-inch) strip lemon rind
1 tablespoon minced fresh savory or 1 teaspoon
    dried whole savory
2 teaspoons sugar
½ to 1 teaspoon curry powder
¼ teaspoon salt
¼ teaspoon pepper
3 tablespoons dry sherry
    Thinly sliced carrot strips (optional)

Sauté onion in butter in a large skillet until tender. Add next 8 ingredients. Reduce heat, cover, and simmer 20 minutes or until carrots are tender.

Pour half of mixture into container of electric blender; process until smooth. Pour into a bowl or pitcher; repeat with remaining mixture. Stir in sherry. Cover and chill. Garnish with carrot strips, if desired. Yield: about 5 cups.

SAVORY BEANS AND MUSHROOMS

1½ pounds fresh green beans
3 tablespoons butter or margarine
½ pound fresh mushrooms, sliced
1 tablespoon chopped green onions
⅓ cup vegetable oil
2 tablespoons chopped fresh savory or 2 teaspoons
    dried whole savory
1 tablespoon vinegar
1 tablespoon lemon juice
1 tablespoon chopped fresh parsley
1 teaspoon sugar
1 teaspoon salt
⅛ teaspoon pepper
4 slices bacon, cooked and crumbled

Remove strings from beans; cut beans into 1½-inch pieces. Wash thoroughly. Cover and cook in 1-inch boiling water for 8 to 10 minutes. Reduce heat, and simmer 3 to 5 minutes. Drain.

Melt butter in a large skillet; add mushrooms and onions. Sauté 5 minutes; stir in beans.

Combine next 8 ingredients in a small saucepan; mix well. Bring to a boil. Pour over bean mixture; stir well. Place in serving dish. Sprinkle bacon over top. Yield: 6 servings.

Harvest savory by pinching off sprigs as needed. This encourages plants to sprout new leaves and remain bushy. But do not harvest winter savory heavily as cold weather approaches.

Prized in French cooking, sorrel's sour, citruslike flavor is a tangy addition to soups, sauces, and salads. French sorrel (*Rumex scutatus*) is the preferred selection because its leaves are broader, fleshier, and have a finer flavor than other selections.

The 8-inch-long, lance-shaped leaves of French sorrel grow from the base of the plant and will reach 2 feet in height. A hardy perennial, sorrel usually dies back in winter and returns in spring.

Plant in well-drained soil. It will take sun, but if grown in partial shade the leaves are often more tender.

French sorrel can be started easily from seed sowed directly in the garden. Plant in the fall, 4 weeks before the first frost; or sow seed in

Sorrel

spring, several weeks before the last expected frost. Cover seeds with ½ inch of soil. When seedlings are 1 to 2 inches tall, thin to 12 inches apart. You can also start French sorrel from crown divisions made in spring or fall.

French sorrel needs little care. Hot weather causes it to bloom in spring, so cut back the leaves and flower stalks to the ground and fertilize with liquid 20-20-20 diluted at half the rate recommended in the label directions. The roots will send up tender new leaves. Keeping flower stalks removed helps direct energy into the production of foliage. Also, if sorrel is allowed to set seed, it will self-sow and the seedlings can be difficult to eliminate from the garden.

Harvest whole leaves as you need them. For salads, young leaves are best. For cooking, cut or pinch off the outer leaves of the plant, leaving a rosette of young growth in the center. After a summer harvest, you may cut the plant to the ground to encourage new growth for a fall crop.

AT A GLANCE

Light: Full sun to partial shade
Propagation: Seeds, crown divisions
Spacing: 2 feet between plants
Part Used: Leaves
Type of Plant: Perennial

Plant sorrel in well-drained soil and full sun or partial shade.

Sorrel leaves wilt quickly after harvest, so do not cut leaves until you are ready to use them. Remove the tough midrib and stem before adding the leaves to dishes. Sorrel is best used fresh, but can be frozen. Drying does not preserve the flavor well.

Selections

There are a number of selections of wild sorrel, but broad-leaved garden sorrel (*R. acetosa*) is the only other type commonly used in cooking. Although its flavor is not as good, it is often substituted for French sorrel if that selection is not available. Broad-leaved garden sorrel grows up to 3 feet with thin, oblong, lancelike leaves. Although almost tasteless in early spring, it takes on the characteristic sour, acid taste later in the season. It is widely adaptable and will thrive in ordinary or even poor soil, but it requires plenty of moisture. You may want to dig up garden sorrel every 4 to 5 years and replant. It needs much the same care as French sorrel and can also be propagated by seeds and divisions.

Harvest whole leaves as you need them. Be sure to remove the tough midrib before using.

FRENCH SORREL SOUP

7 cups water, divided
2 medium carrots, scraped and diced
2 stalks celery, chopped
¾ cup chopped cucumber
1 medium onion, chopped
2 large cabbage leaves, chopped
½ teaspoon minced fresh thyme or ⅛ teaspoon dried whole thyme
5 vegetable-flavored bouillon cubes
¼ cup chopped fresh parsley or 1½ tablespoons dried parsley flakes
6 large sorrel leaves and stems
¼ cup water
1 tablespoon lemon juice
Whipped cream or commercial sour cream

Combine 3 cups water with next 8 ingredients in a pressure cooker; cover and cook 10 minutes at 15 pounds of pressure. Remove from heat. Stir in 4 cups water and set aside.

Combine sorrel with ¼ cup water in a small saucepan; bring to a boil. Reduce heat, and simmer 5 minutes; drain well.

Stir sorrel mixture into vegetable mixture. Pour into blender; process until smooth. Strain well; stir in lemon juice.

Chill soup overnight; serve hot or cold. For hot soup, place over medium heat and cook just until thoroughly heated. Serve with a dollop of whipped cream or sour cream. Yield: 7 cups.

SORREL-POTATO MARINADE

1 head leaf lettuce
½ pound new potatoes
¼ cup olive oil, divided
4 hard-cooked eggs, sliced
¼ cup shredded fresh sorrel
½ teaspoon salt
½ teaspoon coarsely ground black pepper
Pinch of sugar
½ teaspoon Dijon mustard
1 tablespoon white wine vinegar

Wash and dry lettuce. Line a large salad bowl with 4 or 5 lettuce leaves. Tear remaining lettuce into bite-size pieces and place in bowl. Wash potatoes; cook, covered, in boiling water 25 minutes or until tender. Peel potatoes; slice into thick slices. Arrange potato slices over lettuce. Pour 2 tablespoons olive oil over potatoes. Arrange egg slices around potatoes. Sprinkle sorrel over salad. Combine salt, pepper, sugar, mustard, vinegar, and remaining 2 tablespoons oil in a small jar; cover tightly and shake vigorously. Pour over salad just before serving. Yield: 8 to 10 servings.

French tarragon is an herb for the gourmet. Its unique, aniselike flavor is an aromatic addition to vinegars, butters, and mustards. Widely used with poultry, fish, carrots, and in salads, it has a rich, cool flavor that lingers on the tongue.

The flavorful tarragon is French tarragon (*Artemisia dracunculus* Sativa). It is a hardy perennial that dies back for only a couple of months in midwinter. It grows about 2 feet tall with an erect shrubby habit, but has a tendency to sprawl if left untrimmed. The leaves are up to 3 inches long, narrow, and dark green; plants rarely flower.

Tarragon grows best in the Upper and Middle South where you may need to cover it with a protective mulch in winter. In the Lower South, tarragon may not do well in the garden because winters are too mild for the plant to go dormant; nor do plants tolerate summer heat well.

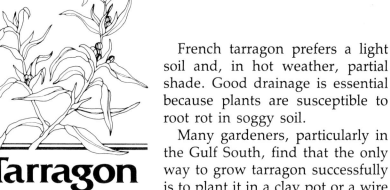

Tarragon

French tarragon prefers a light soil and, in hot weather, partial shade. Good drainage is essential because plants are susceptible to root rot in soggy soil.

Many gardeners, particularly in the Gulf South, find that the only way to grow tarragon successfully is to plant it in a clay pot or a wire basket lined with sphagnum peat moss. This allows the good drainage tarragon needs. In winter, move plants to a cold frame or sunny window. During summer, give them full to partial sun and protect them from receiving too much moisture in rainy weather.

French tarragon does not set seed so you will need to buy a small plant or obtain a division or cutting from a friend to start it. About every 3 years, divide clumps in early spring and replant the divisions, spacing them 18 inches apart.

AT A GLANCE

Light: Full sun to partial shade
Propagation: Cuttings, divisions
Spacing: 18 inches between plants
Part Used: Leaves
Type of Plant: Perennial
Serious Insects: Sow bugs, mealy bugs, whiteflies

Snip sprigs of tarragon as needed, beginning in spring. When the lower leaves turn yellow, cut the plant back to 3 inches above the ground to encourage new growth.

French tarragon does not set seed, so you will have to start from divisions, rooted cuttings, or purchased plants.

Take cuttings in midsummer. They will root in about 2 months and should be kept in a cold frame or greenhouse through the first winter.

You can snip fresh sprigs of tarragon whenever you need them, taking the first cuttings in spring. In spring and again in fall before frost, you can harvest the entire plant by cutting it to 3 inches above the ground. To dry French tarragon, strip the leaves from the stems and dry in a warm place. (*See page 214*).

Selections

Russian tarragon (*A. dracunculus* Inodora or *A. redowski*), sometimes substituted for French tarragon in catalogs, is not recommended. Its leaves have no flavor and although it is easy to grow and produces many seeds, it has none of the good qualities of French tarragon.

Russian tarragon looks very much like French tarragon, but its leaves have no flavor.

TARRAGON VINEGAR

```
1 cup chopped fresh tarragon
3¾ cups white vinegar (5% acidity)
   Fresh tarragon sprigs (optional)
```

Place chopped tarragon in wide-mouth glass jars. Place vinegar in a medium saucepan; bring to a boil. Pour vinegar over chopped tarragon; cover with metal lids and screw bands tight. Let stand at room temperature for 2 weeks.

Strain vinegar into decorative jars, discarding herb residue; add additional sprigs of fresh tarragon, if desired. Seal jars with a cork or other airtight lid. Yield: 4 cups.

GREEN MAYONNAISE

```
1½ cups mayonnaise
  2 tablespoons finely chopped fresh parsley
  1 tablespoon finely chopped fresh chives
  1 tablespoon finely chopped fresh tarragon or 1
    teaspoon dried whole tarragon
  1 teaspoon finely chopped fresh dillweed or ¼
    teaspoon dried whole dillweed
```

Combine all ingredients, stirring well; cover and chill 8 hours or overnight. Yield: 1½ cups.

TARRAGON CHICKEN

```
8 boneless chicken breast halves, skinned
  Salt and pepper to taste
1 to 2 tablespoons butter or margarine
2 green onions, chopped
1 cup white wine
1 cup whipping cream
2 tablespoons chopped fresh tarragon
1 tablespoon chopped fresh parsley
  Hot cooked noodles
```

Sprinkle chicken with salt and pepper. Melt butter in a large skillet. Brown chicken on both sides in butter; remove from skillet and place in a 10- x 6- x 2-inch baking dish. Cover and bake at 400° for 10 minutes.

Add onions to skillet and sauté until tender. Stir in wine; bring to a boil. Reduce heat, and simmer until liquid is reduced by half. Add next 3 ingredients, and cook just until thoroughly heated (do not boil).

Place chicken on bed of noodles. Pour sauce over chicken. Yield: 8 servings.

• Sprinkle tarragon over chicken, or stir it into Béarnaise sauce, omelets, or mushroom dishes.

• Because tarragon becomes bitter when cooked too long, add it near the end of cooking time.

Herbs 259

Thyme is a must for the herb garden. Besides having a warm, pungent flavor, it is one of the more ornamental herbs. The upright types grow into small, finely textured shrubs, while the creeping ones form a leafy carpet with a variety of flower and foliage colors. In early spring, the flowers open, sprinkling the evergreen foliage with white, pink, lavender, or rose. The foliage varies in color from dark green to gray to yellow. On some types, the tiny leaves are edged in yellow or white.

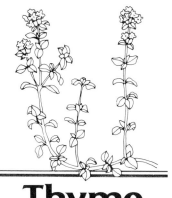

Thyme

Thyme (*Thymus sp.*) does best in an area with full sun to partial shade and well-drained soil. It can adapt to less than ideal conditions, but do not plant in soggy soil or deep shade.

You can propagate thyme by stem cuttings, divisions, or layering. Starting with seeds may demand some patience: Seeds of most selections do not germinate easily and because they are so tiny, they are difficult to handle. Sow them

indoors about 4 to 6 weeks before the last frost, then set out plants after danger of frost is past. Or you can sow seeds outdoors directly in the garden after the last frost. Distribute seeds evenly and pat them into the soil so they are barely cov- barely covered. The seeds should germinate in about 2 weeks. Thin to 12 inches apart.

For more reliable results, start with cuttings, purchased transplants, or divisions. You can make cuttings or divisions in fall or early spring. Some selections can also be propagated by layering. (*See Selections below.*)

Thyme needs little care except for a spring pruning. Prune upright selections to keep them shapely. Creeping types often become ragged in winter, so cut them back to the ground.

Harvest leaves of thyme as you need them. The flavor is most concentrated just before plants bloom. Thyme usually stays green through the winter so you do not have to dry or freeze it. But if you wish, you can hang stems and dry them, then strip leaves from the stems for storage.

Selections

Garden thyme (*T. vulgaris*) is also known as common, English, or French thyme. A hardy

---

AT A GLANCE

Light: Full sun to partial shade
Propagation: Seeds (not reliable for some selections), cuttings, divisions, layering
Spacing: 12 inches between plants
Part Used: Leaves
Type of Plant: Perennial

Upright types of thyme grow into small, finely textured shrubs. Prune them in spring to keep them neat and well shaped.

The flowers, which bloom in early spring, may be white, pink, lavender, or rose, depending on the selection. After the plants bloom, the flavor of the foliage will be less concentrated than just prior to blooming.

perennial, its flavor is pungent and strong, and it is the kind most often used as a seasoning. It can be started from seed more easily than other types. Plants grow upright and range in height from 8 to 12 inches depending on the selection. You will need to trim plants to keep them neat and to prevent them from getting too woody. Two popular selections are English, which has dark-green oval leaves, and French, which has narrow grayish leaves.

Mother-of-thyme (*T. praecox* Arcticus) or creeping thyme is a prostrate selection that grows only 3 to 5 inches tall. It has small oval leaves and bears purple flowers in early summer. Its seed does not germinate well, so it is best to start from divisions. Often the plants spread by themselves as the creeping stems put down roots. Cut this selection to the ground in spring to get rid of the ragged growth left from winter. It is not reliably hardy in the Upper South due to severe winters. There are a number of different selections with different flower and leaf colors.

Lemon thyme (*T. serpyllum*) is known for its distinct lemon scent and taste. Sometimes listed in catalogs as *T. x citriodorus*, it is a hardy perennial that grows 4 to 12 inches tall. Leaves may be green or edged in yellow, depending on the selection. It spreads rapidly, and bears pinkish flowers in summer.

To remove the leaves for fresh use, hold the top of each stem securely, and strip the leaves from it with your other hand.

Caraway thyme (*T. herba-barona*) has a mild caraway flavor. It is a hardy perennial that grows 2 to 5 inches tall, with narrow green leaves and rose-purple flowers that bloom in early summer. It has a neat growth habit and needs only minimal pruning; however, it spreads rapidly.

THYME POTATOES

- 6 medium potatoes, peeled and thinly sliced
- 3 tablespoons chopped fresh thyme or 1 tablespoon dried whole thyme
- ½ teaspoon salt
- ⅛ teaspoon pepper
- ¼ cup butter or margarine
- ¾ cup beef broth

Place half of potatoes in a lightly greased 9-inch square baking dish. Sprinkle with half each of thyme, salt, and pepper; dot with half of butter. Repeat layers. Pour broth over top; cover and bake at 350° for 45 minutes or until potatoes are tender. Yield: 6 servings.

THYME RICE

- 2 cups water
- 1 cup uncooked regular rice
- 2 teaspoons butter or margarine
- 1½ teaspoons beef-flavored bouillon granules
- 1 teaspoon Worcestershire sauce
- 1 teaspoon chopped fresh chives
- 1 to 1½ teaspoons chopped fresh thyme or ½ teaspoon dried whole thyme
- ½ teaspoon crushed garlic

Combine all ingredients in a heavy saucepan; bring to a boil. Stir well; reduce heat, cover, and simmer 20 minutes or until rice is done. Yield: 4 servings.

LEMON THYME COOKIES

- 1 cup butter
- 1½ cups sugar
- 2 eggs
- 2½ cups all-purpose flour
- 2 teaspoons cream of tartar
- ½ teaspoon salt
- ½ cup chopped fresh lemon thyme or 3 tablespoons dried whole lemon thyme

Cream butter; gradually add sugar, beating until light and fluffy. Add eggs, one at a time, beating well after each addition.

Combine flour, cream of tartar, and salt; add to creamed mixture. Blend in lemon thyme.

Shape dough into two oblong rolls. Wrap rolls in waxed paper, and chill overnight.

Unwrap rolls, and slice into ¼-inch slices; place on lightly greased baking sheets. Bake at 350° for 10 minutes. Yield: about 6 dozen.

HERB CHART

Herb	Description	Culture
Basil (*Ocimum basilicum*)	Tender annual. Clovelike fragrance & cool taste. Size varies with selection.	Full sun (Dark Opal needs partial shade). Medium-rich, light, well-drained soil. Sow seed. Likes hot, humid weather.
Bay (*Laurus nobilis*)	Tender perennial evergreen. Aromatic, with hint of balsam and honey. Shrublike tree 4-10' tall.	Full or filtered sun. Average to rich, well-drained soil. Best to buy a young plant. Grow in a container except in Gulf South, where it can grow in ground.
Burnet (*Poterium sanguisorba*)	Perennial evergreen. Mild cucumber taste. Grows as rosette 1-2' tall.	Filtered sun. Average, well-drained soil. Sow seed in spring or fall, or let self-sow. Does best if mulched year-round and given some shade in summer.
Caraway (*Carum carvi*)	Biennial. Licorice-like taste. Flower stalks 2-3' tall.	Full sun. Average, well-drained soil. Sow seed in spring or fall, or let self-sow.
Chives (*Allium schoenoprasum*) or garlic chives (*A. tuberosum*)	Perennial; garlic chives are evergreen in mild winters. Mild onion or garlic flavor. Clumps of grasslike leaves 1' tall.	Full sun, but will tolerate partial shade. Rich, well-drained soil. Sow seed, or divide clumps.
Coriander (*Coriandrum sativum*)	Annual. Fragrant seeds. Lacy leaves on stems 2-3' tall.	Full sun. Medium-rich, well-drained soil. Sow seed in spring or fall, or let self-sow. Delicate taproot.
Dill (*Anethum graveolens*)	Annual. Strong, pungent flavor. Leaves branch from single hollow stem 2-3' tall.	Full sun. Medium-rich, well-drained soil. Sow seed before last spring frost. Make successive sowings for foliage supply. Taproot difficult to transplant.
Sweet Fennel (*Foeniculum vulgare*)	Perennial; evergreen in Lower and Middle South. Feathery foliage on stems 3-5' tall.	Full sun or partial shade. Medium-rich, well-drained soil. Sow seed after last spring frost, or let self-sow.
Garlic (*Allium sativum*) or elephant garlic (*A. scorodoprasum*)	Hardy perennial. Pungent taste and smell. Elephant garlic has milder flavor, larger cloves, straplike foliage 3' tall.	Full sun. Rich deep soil. Plant cloves in late summer or spring.
Horseradish (*Amoracia rusticana*)	Hardy perennial; often grown as an annual. Roots are hot-tasting. Coarse-textured with large, dark-green leaves 2-3' tall.	Full sun. Rich moist soil. Plant whole roots, root cuttings, or crown divisions.
Lemon Balm (*Melissa officinalis*)	Hardy perennial. Delightful lemony fragrance and taste. Thick bushy plant 2' tall.	Full sun or filtered shade. Well-drained soil. Sow seed, divide, or root stem cuttings.
Evergreen Marjoram (*Origanum majoricum*)	Perennial evergreen in Middle & Lower South, and in mild winters in Upper South.	Full sun or partial shade. Well-drained soil. Root cuttings, or make divisions in early spring.
Sweet Marjoram (*Origanum majorana*)	Tender perennial; treat as annual in Middle & Upper South. Bushy plant 1' tall.	Partial shade. Well-drained soil. Sow seed indoors to plant out after frost, or root cuttings.
Mint (*Mentha sp.*)	Perennial; some are evergreen. Cool refreshing scent and taste. Grows quickly and will spread. Height and growth habit depend on selection.	Partial shade (full sun if kept moist). Moderately rich soil. Root stem cuttings, or layer runners. Spade around plant in spring to keep bed from being overcrowded. Renew beds every 3-4 years.
Oregano (*Origanum sp.*)	Perennial; some are evergreen. Pungent flavor. Height and growth habit depend on selection.	Full or partial sun. Well-drained soil. Sow seed in spring, divide plants, or root stem cuttings. Some selections layer naturally.
Parsley (*Petroselinum crispum*)	Biennial evergreen in Middle & Lower South; treat as annual in Upper South. Distinctive, mild peppery taste. Curly or flat leaves (depending on selection) on stalks 1-2' tall.	Partial shade. Medium-rich, moist, well-drained soil. Start from transplants, or sow seed in spring or early fall. Taproot makes transplanting difficult.
Rosemary (*Rosemarinus officinalis*)	Tender perennial evergreen. Strong piney fragrance and flavor. Erect shrub 3-4' tall.	Full sun or partial shade. Well-drained soil. Purchase small plants, or root stem cuttings, or layer. Thrives outdoors in Middle & Lower South; put in container in Upper South and bring indoors in winter.
Sage (*Salvia officinalis*)	Hardy perennial. Sharp taste, aromatic smell. Small, sprawling shrub 2-3' tall.	Full sun. Sandy, well-drained soil. Sow seed in spring or early fall. Root stem cuttings, or divide. Sensitive to overwatering.
Pineapple Sage (*S. elegans*)	Tender perennial. Pineapple scent. Bright red flowers in summer. Shrub 2-3' tall.	Full sun or partial shade. Any garden soil. Root stem cuttings, or divide. Take cuttings indoors to overwinter.
Summer Savory (*Satureja hortensis*)	Annual. Sharp, spicy flavor. Top-heavy shrub 18" tall.	Full sun or partial shade. Medium-rich, well-drained soil. Needs a lot of moisture. Sow seed, or root stem cuttings. Make successive sowings.
Winter Savory (*S. montana*)	Hardy perennial. Sharp, spicy flavor, stronger and more pungent than summer savory.	Full sun or partial shade. Well-drained soil. Sow seed, root stem cuttings, divide, or layer. Replace plants every 2-3 years.
Sorrel (*Rumex scutatus*)	Hardy perennial; evergreen in mild winters. Sour, citruslike flavor. Large, shield-shaped leaves. Height 2' tall.	Full sun or partial shade. Well-drained soil. Sow seed in spring or fall, or divide roots. Replace older plants every 3-4 years.
French Tarragon (*Artemisia dracunculus* Sativa)	Hardy perennial. Aniselike flavor. Erect, shrubby growth habit 2' in height.	Partial shade. Rich, light soil. Root stem cuttings, or divide roots.
Thyme (*Thymus sp.*)	Hardy perennial; most are evergreen. Many different growth habits.	Partial shade. Well-drained soil. Sow seed (not reliable for some selections). Root stem cuttings, divide roots, or layer. Prune occasionally.

HERB CHART

Harvest	Uses
Pick leaves as needed for fresh use; harvest before bloom for drying. Clip back to ⅓ original size.	Use fresh or dried; in vinegars, on salads and tomatoes, in egg dishes.
Pick leaves year-round.	Use fresh or dried; in soups, sauces; with beef, lamb, and fish.
Pick leaves year-round.	Use fresh; in salads, cool drinks, or as a garnish.
Harvest ripened seeds in fall; foliage lightly when needed.	Use seeds in rye bread, cakes, and cabbage dishes. Add foliage to salads. Thick roots are sweet and can be eaten like carrots.
Pick side spears as needed. Cut each one to about ½" aboveground.	Use fresh, dried, or frozen. Blooms can be used as a garnish. Sprinkle over salads, cold soups; add to cheese and egg dishes, vegetables.
Harvest seeds when ripe; foliage in cooler months.	Use seeds in candy, pastries, coffee. Use foliage in many South American, Spanish, and Oriental dishes.
Pick foliage anytime from seedling stage until plants bloom; seeds when ripe and brown.	Use seeds in pickling recipes. Use foliage as a garnish for fish or cold soups; chop and add to salads.
Harvest foliage and stems anytime; seeds when stalks dry and umbels turn brown.	Use seeds in breads, pastries, candies, drinks. Use fresh leaves with fish; in sauces, salads. Prepare roots like a vegetable. Eat flowers as an after-dinner mint.
Harvest leaves sparingly until they begin to yellow and die as bulbs mature.	Use leaves in salads; cloves to flavor meats, soups, salads, pickles, and vinegars.
Harvest young leaves in summer; roots in fall after the first hard frost.	Use roots in sauces, spreads; with beef or lamb. Use young leaves in salads. Cooking removes pungency.
Harvest leaves anytime for fresh use; pick just before flowering for drying.	Use leaves in teas or potpourris and stuffings for lamb or pork.
Pick leaves as needed.	Use fresh or dried leaves in meat and egg dishes, soups, vegetables.
Pick leaves as needed for fresh use; cut after buds form but before blooming for drying.	Use fresh or dried leaves in meat and egg dishes, soups, vegetables.
Harvest from early spring into late fall as needed for fresh use; harvest just before flowering for drying, cutting entire plant to just above the 1st or 2nd set of leaves.	Use leaves dried, fresh, or frozen. Add to lamb, peas, carrot peas, and fruit.
Pick leaves as needed for fresh use; harvest just before flowering for drying, cutting stems above 1st set of leaves. Make another harvest in late summer.	Use fresh, dried, or frozen; with meat, cheese, fish, eggs, tomatoes, and snap beans.
Harvest leaves and tender stems as needed for fresh use. Snip leaf stalks off at base.	Use fresh or dried; in herb sauces, butters, scrambled eggs, canned soups, or as a garnish.
Begin harvesting leaves after 2nd year. Harvest anytime for fresh use; harvest just before flowering for drying.	Use leaves fresh or dried; with lamb, chicken, and on French bread.
Harvest only lightly the 1st year. Pluck whole leaf or entire stem as needed for fresh use; harvest just before flowering for drying.	Use leaves fresh, dried, or frozen. Add to stuffings, salads, and pork, poultry, cheese, and tomato dishes.
Pick leaves as needed.	Best used fresh.
Begin harvesting when plant is 6" tall. In early harvests pinch tips of stems as needed.	Best used fresh. Add to vegetables, especially snap beans; also to soups, stews, and salads.
Pick fresh sprigs as needed; harvest just before flowering for drying.	Use fresh or dried; same as summer savory.
Harvest whole leaves as needed for fresh use. Pick outer leaves and leave a rosette of young growth.	Use fresh or frozen. Use quickly after harvest or they wilt. Use in cream soups; with omelets and vegetables; a few fresh leaves in salads.
Cut sprigs as needed for fresh use. When lower leaves begin to yellow, make a big harvest, cutting entire plant to 3" above ground.	Use leaves fresh or dried. Add to vinegars, butters, sauces; in chicken, egg, and mushroom dishes.
Harvest leaves as needed for fresh use. In fall and winter, cut only upper ⅓ of plant.	Use leaves fresh, dried, frozen. Use with tomatoes, vinegars, beans, peas, spinach, and squash.

Mail-Order Sources

Vegetables

There are many mail-order seed companies. The list below includes those that offer selections adapted to the South. The selections recommended in the *Vegetables* section can be ordered from one or more of these companies.

W. Atlee Burpee Company
300 Park Avenue
Warminster, PA 18974

Joseph Harris Company, Inc.
Moreton Farm
3670 Buffalo Road
Rochester, NY 14624

Hastings
Seedsman to the South
P.O. Box 4274
Atlanta, GA 30302

Kilgore Seed Company
1400 West First Street
Sanford, FL 32771

Meyer Seeds
600 South Caroline Street
Baltimore, MD 21231

George W. Park Seed Company, Inc.
South Carolina Highway 254 North
Greenwood, SC 29647

Southland Garden Seed Company
P.O. Box 91076
Houston, TX 77291

George Tait & Sons
P.O. Box 2873
Norfolk, VA 23501

Otis Twilley Seed Company
P.O. Box 65
Trevose, PA 19047

Willhite Melon Seed Farms
P.O. Box 23
Poolville, TX 76076

Wyatt-Quarles Seed Company
Box 2131
Raleigh, NC 27602

Herbs

Carroll Gardens
P.O. Box 310
444 East Main Street
Westminster, MD 21157

Fox Hill Farm
Box 7
Parma, MI 49269

*indicates a nominal charge for the catalog.

Hastings
Seedsman to the South
P.O. Box 4274
Atlanta, GA 30302

The Herb Cottage*
Washington Cathedral
Mount St. Alban
Washington, DC 20016

Hilltop Herb Farm*
P.O. Box 1734
Cleveland, TX 77327

Nichols Garden Nursery
1190 North Pacific Highway
Albany, OR 97321

George W. Park Seed Company, Inc.
South Carolina Highway 254 North
Greenwood, SC 29647

The Sandy Mush Herb Nursery*
Route 2, Surrett Cove Road
Leicester, NC 28748

Wayside Gardens
P.O. Box 31
Hodges, SC 29647

Tools & Equipment

Smith & Hawken Tool Company
68 Homer
Palo Alto, CA 94301
(a source for weldless forks)

George W. Park Seed Company, Inc.
South Carolina Highway 254 North
Greenwood, SC 29647

W. Altee Burpee Company
300 Park Avenue
Warminster, PA 18974

Dalen Products
11110 Gilbert Drive
Knoxville, TN 37922
(manufacturer of cold frame, ventilator)

Bramen Company, Inc.
P.O. Box 70
Salem, MA 01970
(automatic ventilator for cold frame)

A. M. Leonard Equipment & Supplies
6665 Spiker Road
Piqua, OH 45356

Index

Recipe Index